D0308828

FORMULA ONE: MADE IN BRITAIN

The British Influence
in Formula One

FORMULA ONE: MADE IN BRITAIN

The British Influence in Formula One

Clive Couldwell

To my parents, Sheila and Len,
without whom this book wouldn't have been possible

First published in Great Britain in 2003 by
Virgin Books
Thames Wharf Studios
Rainville Road
London W6 9HA

A catalogue record for the book is available from the British
Library.

ISBN 1 85227 063 2

Typeset by TW Typesetting, Plymouth, Devon

Printed and bound in Great Britain by CPD Wales

CONTENTS

ACKNOWLEDGEMENTS

The fact that this very personal account of the British Formula One industry – its technologies and business – has been written at all is a miracle. Everyone on the circuit thought I was mad to try to write such a tome while so many changes were taking place within Formula One, both on the track and, more especially, off it. I'm therefore grateful to a number of people and organisations who gave up their precious time to talk to me and set up interviews when, quite frankly, their attention was obviously needed on more urgent matters. A selection of the well known and not so well known gave me their views and contributed their thoughts and ideas during a very hectic season in 2002, and into 2003. Some are quoted in the book, others aren't, but their words helped shape my thoughts nevertheless. I list them here in no particular order, and I'm extremely grateful to all of them for putting up with me: Sir Jackie Stewart, John Barnard, Damon Hill, Martin Whitmarsh, Clare Robertson, Pat Symonds, Mark Gallagher, Helen Temple, Tony Purnell, Nav Sidhu, Jane Stewart, David Richards, Hugh Chambers, Tracy Novak, Tony Jardine, Kenny Roberts, Jim Wright, Matthew Argenti, Chris Aylett and Pim van Baarsen at the Motor Industry Association (MIA) for their industry and case study insights, Dr Mark Jenkins, Clive Temple, Jeffrey Alcock, Steve Davies, Andy Smith and Clive Longbottom.

I also consulted a great many books, magazines and websites, most notably Beverly Aston and Mark Williams' *Playing to Win*, Russell Hotten's *Winning: The Business of Formula One*, Tim Collings' *The Piranha Club* and *Eddie Jordan: The Biography*; *F1 Racing* and *Formula 1* magazine; *Autosport*; AtlasF1.com, GrandPrix.com (formerly InsideF1.com), the prancinghorse.co.uk, itv-f1.com, speedtv.com, formulaschools.com, gpracing.net192.com, allf1.info, jaguar-racing.com, johnnyherbert.co.uk, piresearch.com, cosworth-racing.co.uk, bmw.williamsf1.com, f1jordan.com, mclaren.net, mercedes-ilmor.com and renaultf1.com.

Special thanks go to Jonathan Taylor at Virgin Books for his faith and support, and to Daniel Balado for his editorial work on my copy.

I don't think I've forgotten anyone, but if I have, I apologise.

Clive Couldwell
Southborough
April 2003

PREFACE

Formula One: Made in Britain is all about excellence and innovation, about striving to be the best. British manufacturing may no longer be what it once was, but the world of Formula One motor racing grows ever more dynamic, spectacular and exciting, and it's a sport that is economically and culturally rooted in Britain, which has been its technical centre of excellence for more than fifty years. 'We lead the world in this hi-tech industry,' said former F1 world champion Sir Jackie Stewart. 'Mercedes builds its engines in Northampton. The British-built Cosworth engine wins more races than anybody. If you are a top-line designer, you come here. If you want to build a race car, you come here.'

Four-times drivers' champion Alain Prost vowed never to work in his homeland again after the failure of his team in 2001. Eddie Jordan, who runs his operation next door to the Silverstone circuit, had suggested before Prost's troubles began that he move to Britain. 'I remember talking to him before the problems and saying wouldn't he be far better off coming to the UK,' Jordan recalled. 'It's far more reasonable in terms of suppliers, people understand motor racing here, and it's cheaper to be able to get things manufactured . . . People here have a much more entrepreneurial idea about their business than in, say, Germany or France . . . I think that is one of the greatest attributes that Britain has, and why Britain is such an outstanding place from which to run a Formula One team.'

For, as Prost found out, Formula One is not just about racing, it's also about managing a fast-moving business. All the problems you'd experience in a larger company are compacted within a Formula One team, and many bricks-and-mortar operations could learn a lot from how Formula One teams run their businesses, from the processes of product research, development and manufacturing through to marketing. But not many small- to medium-sized businesses are forced to act out their highs and lows on the global stage; nor are their operations scrutinised so intensely.

Watched by nearly 360 million people every two weeks for nine months of the year, the Formula One circuit is almost obscenely competitive and private – obsessively so in some cases. Yet the teams' products are hardly ever out of the spotlight. The movements of their staff, especially those in the front rank, are monitored and analysed in enormous detail, and their customers – the sponsors and fans – demand at times impossible levels of perfection, or at the very least improved performance. Above all, they want to be entertained.

In the face of such pressures, it seems remarkable that those small businesses that line up their cars on the grid during the Grand Prix season have made it there at all. The fact that they have is down to their having matured into finely tuned, energetic centres of commercial and engineering excellence. Throughout each developmental, manufacturing and testing cycle, the teams – motivated and professional staff who respond positively to the strong leadership of their charismatic principals – have been paddling like hell below the water line to keep a variety of projects on track. As a result, they get their products to market on time. It's no surprise, therefore, that business tends to admire Formula One. 'We all know how difficult organising management diaries for a meet is,' commented a former Jaguar executive. 'It's amazing, though, how those same diaries free up when you say you're holding it at a Formula One factory.'

The information technology (IT) industry has an especially close relationship with Formula One because of the link with technology and pioneering excellence. Take Hewlett-Packard, for example, which also requires rapid, high-quality product development. The average time it takes to progress a Formula One car from design to testing is four to six months; product cycles in the IT provider business operate on similar timescales – between six and nine months. Formula One teams are also customers with big needs. When it comes to design and materials they are forever working at the cutting edge, always on the lookout for new technologies; they can therefore act as an intelligent user to give the provider company feedback on product performance. At times, a team's service level requirements are also very high, so the IT company sees its client as someone who can help push it to get things done.

Businesses also get involved with Formula One in order to demonstrate to the world that they are big players doing well enough to afford the sizeable price tag. 'They want and need exposure for their brands globally,' said Matthew Argenti, head of international sales at sports marketing company Fast Track. 'There are no other sports that deliver this kind of branding sixteen times a year, attracting the kinds of audiences they do, and delivering a consistent message to over a hundred countries.'

Recently, however, it hasn't been plain sailing for Formula One businesses. Two of the teams that started the 2001 season – Prost and Arrows – have disappeared, and four of the ten teams contesting the 2003 season – Jaguar, BAR, Jordan and Minardi – have made redundancies. Of the eighteen teams who were in Formula One when McLaren was dominating the championship back in 1988, thirteen have gone bust. Formula One is both a rewarding and an unforgiving arena.

INTRODUCTION

In over fifty years of competition, British Formula One has seen it all – speed and spectacle, charisma and competition, domination and disaster. It has blossomed into one of the world's most glamorous and most professional sports, inspiring intrigue and passion with its mix of cutting-edge technology and high drama.

We should perhaps be thanking for all of this those Second World War military planners who decided to build huge airfields all over the country. The importance these strips of concrete and outbuildings played in helping Britain to become the centre of the modern motorsport industry cannot be underestimated. When the war ended, and the fleets of Allied bombers were grounded, these redundant airfields became ideal racing circuits for motorsport enthusiasts. Silverstone, the Northamptonshire track that sits at the hub of Britain's motor racing industry, started life as a base for American B-52 bombers. It holds a unique place in the history of Formula One, having staged the very first round of the official World Championship back in 1950, though it had actually hosted its first British Grand Prix two years earlier in 1948, the airfield's perimeter roads and runways roped in as part of the circuit. By the time the circuit joined the championship it just used the perimeter roads. Silverstone has been altered numerous times since, but has always remained one of the fastest and most exciting race tracks on the calendar.

Freddie March, the present Earl of March's grandfather, was a great motor racing enthusiast and one of the Brooklands personalities who raced successfully in the 1930s. After the war he converted another RAF airfield – known as RAF West Hampnett, which had been built on part of his estate – to a motor racing track, and for sixteen years Goodwood race track in Sussex was a major venue for all levels of motor racing. Other ex-airfields used as circuits include Castle Coombe (Wiltshire),

Croft Autodrome (Darlington), Llandow (south Glamorgan), Rufforth (Yorkshire), Snetterton (Norfolk), Thruxton and Eastney (Hampshire), Stapleford (Essex), Staverton and Fairford (Gloucestershire), Brough (Yorkshire) and Greenham Common (Berkshire). These and a host of other defunct sites around the country became thriving centres for club racing and the associated engineering firms that kept the cars in working order. The circuits became a melting pot of drivers, technicians and businessmen, all of whom had their own ideas about how to improve the cars and expand the sport. This in turn created a culture of invention and private entrepreneurship that used basic car components to create highly agile and fast racing cars.

This cross-fertilisation gave motorsport in Britain the start it needed to challenge the dominant racing teams in mainland Europe. The structure of the 'businesses' that grew up in club racing was unusual, probably unique to Britain. They'd created their own network: outfits built their cars by sourcing the most desirable engines, brakes, suspensions and transmissions from wherever they could, and in the period just after the war British club constructors had a number of proprietary engines to choose from, such as Coventry Climax, Bristol, Ford, ERA, MG-Morris and Lea Francis. This 'network' characteristic of the British constructors of the 1950s and 1960s, so different (apart from Vanwall and BRM) from the more established European Grand Prix teams of the time, irritated the founder and boss of Ferrari, Enzo Ferrari, so much that he described them pejoratively as *garagistes*. The well-financed and fully integrated organisations of Ferrari, Lancia, Alfa Romeo, Maserati, Lancia and Daimler Benz subsidised their Grand Prix activity by manufacturing exclusive sports cars for the super rich. But Alfa Romeo and Lancia had to withdraw from the sport in 1952 because of financial difficulties, so you could say that the networked *garagistes* had the last laugh. Smaller organisations could indeed produce competitive cars for much less money, and with far fewer people.

The process of running club races on smooth airfield runways also created a new and quite different approach to the design and construction of single-seat racing cars – and this, too, was probably unique to Britain. When you had found one, you tended to develop your car around a reliable engine and make it as competitive as possible by tweaking the weight and size of every other component on the car, such as its chassis, suspension, transmission, brakes and wheels. If you were racing on a smooth surface, you could, for example, win a race with an ultra-light car and by taking advantage of independent rear suspension, even though your engine might be underpowered. This kind of activity didn't exist in Europe, where racing was conducted on bumpy roads. France, Italy and Germany didn't have our concrete airfields to race on, so the teams there had to make their cars of more rugged stuff to withstand the stresses indifferent surfaces exerted upon them. For them, racing-car design and construction was all about engine power: the more you had, the more likely you were to outperform your competitors.

Still, the success of British club racing and its participants can be put down to an important rule change in Formula One which fundamentally biased the design of Grand Prix cars towards their particularly distinctive engineering capabilities. During the post-war years, engine size was reduced, but a rule change in 1958 made mandatory the use of aviation fuel and reduced the length of a race from 500 to 300 kilometres. A shorter race distance meant that you didn't have to refuel and change tyres, and consumption with aviation fuel was better than with alcohol fuels, so you could get away with a smaller tank. With a lighter load you could use smaller wheels and tyres, as well as lighter chassis components and downsized brakes. 'By scaling up light cars,' Beverly Aston observed in *Playing to Win: The Success of UK Motorsport Engineering*, 'the UK club constructors were competitive in F1 despite an underpowered engine, because minimal size and weight had been central to their design. As Grand Prix racing had historically been a heavyweight game, focused on engine power, it was difficult for the established organisations to adjust quickly. Moreover, they were not ideally structured for change.'

Because their organisations were fully integrated, continental outfits were less able to exploit expertise and technology, and to subcontract development from outside, than the much smaller British club constructors, even though they shared the same objective – faster lap times. It was only a matter of time before British constructors began to outperform their European counterparts because they were developing a superior understanding of roadholding. 'The traditional incumbents understood engine power, but they did not understand how to hold it down on the road – hence the racing authority's gradual reduction in engine capacity after 1946,' wrote Aston. 'The roadholding of any car has a definite limit. By starting with the power output of the engine, then building a car around it commensurate with that power output, the outcome is a heavy vehicle with limited race-performance potential because the roadholding is ultimately fixed, or relatively unadjustable. The heavier the car, the more difficult it is to control at the limit of adhesion, or to slow it down from high speed, as extra weight increases its kinetic energy; in the event of impact, the extra inertia results in more damage to everything and everybody concerned. However, as Lotus's Colin Chapman was to point out, if the starting point is the car rather than the engine, the point at which all "grip" is lost can be deferred by design that is aimed at keeping as much rubber on the road as possible. The limit of adhesion is extended by independent suspension to all four wheels, which helps to distribute the weight equally, and by designing a car that is not only light and structurally efficient but also "wind-cheating" (aerodynamic).'

In 1958, the small, rear-engined Cooper-Climax – a fundamental shift in the way Formula One cars were designed – tipped the balance of power away from northern Italy; and the 1959 and 1960 World Championships were dominated by the British Cooper team and Australian Jack Brabham. The frailties of the new cars hit hard, though, and Brabham had to push his machine over the finishing line in the US to take the 1959 title. Still, a revolution had begun.

Rear-engined cars were soon accepted in Formula One, and one partnership rose above all others: the innovative design genius of Colin Chapman paired with the pure driving talent of Jim Clark. Although Ferrari claimed two drivers' titles during the 1960s, the decade was really about the British manufacturers and drivers. There were successes for Clark (1963 and 1965), Graham Hill (1962 and 1968), John Surtees (1964) – the only man to win World Championships in motor racing and motorcycling – and Jackie Stewart (1969), each of them adding his name to a growing list of home-grown champions, but it was Chapman's Lotus team which pioneered technological innovations that shaped the face of modern Formula One. The team spearheaded the aerodynamic revolution of the 1960s, conducting a number of early experiments into the now fundamental concept of downforce, and in 1967 introduced the Ford Double Four Valve (DFV) engine, a powerplant that dominated Formula One throughout the 1970s until Renault, having introduced the turbocharged engine to the world in 1977, won their first race in 1979.

The 1960s were also the decade when Formula One lost its innocence. The death of undisputed champion driver Clark in 1968 rocked the sport to its foundations. However, that same year another Lotus innovation heralded another facet of modern Grand Prix racing's make-up – sponsorship. The colours of Gold Leaf cigarettes appeared on Chapman's cars during that 1968 season, and from then on Formula One began its growth into the global business it is today.

The 1970s began with the crowning of the sport's only posthumous world champion, the Austrian Jochen Rindt. His fatal accident at Monza hastened the technology of the sport turning in a new direction, towards safety, a process that had been initiated several years earlier by the sterling efforts of Jackie Stewart, the dominant driver of the day. Comprising driving improvements in all areas, from cars to circuits to equipment, Stewart's legacy to the sport is immense, extending beyond his three World Championships to a new appreciation of driver and spectator safety, not to mention a higher level of professionalism.

Then flamboyant characters such as British playboy James Hunt introduced another ingredient into the mix by ensuring that the world's media spotlight began to be thrown on the personalities of the sport as much as on the racing itself. The global profile of the Grand Prix circus began to grow as drivers from Brazil, Austria, South Africa and the US were crowned as world champions during the decade. At the same time, Bernie Ecclestone, the Brabham team owner, was raising his profile by establishing the Formula One Constructors Association (FOCA) in response to the perceived bias of the governing body, FISA (Fédération Internationale du Sport Automobile). This also reinforced the multinational nature of the sport. The conflict between FISA and FOCA raged through the late 1970s and came to a head in the early 1980s. The teams split into two camps over the issue of innovative technology being used by the smaller British constructors to counter the turbo revolution initiated by Renault. After a dramatic strike by the British teams, the dispute was eventually resolved, with one firm conclusion: Ecclestone's power and prominence had been reinforced.

The 1980s produced an unprecedented collection of great champions, the Brazilians Nelson Piquet and Ayrton Senna, Frenchman Alain Prost and Briton Nigel Mansell all fighting dramatic battles on the track and at the same time stoking intense rivalries. As the decade unfolded, the rewards went to the highly organised and financially strong teams such as McLaren and Williams. During the decade, McLaren took five drivers' championships and four constructors' titles. With Prost and Senna at the wheel, and powered by Honda engines, the team produced some of the most spectacular and hard-fought racing in the history of the sport. In 1988, the year of Senna's first title, McLaren triumphed in an astonishing fifteen out of the sixteen races. Yet, in the face of this machine-like domination, the human touch remained: Ferrari took the only non-McLaren victory, in front of the *tifosi* at their beloved Monza, just weeks after the death of founder Enzo Ferrari.

As the 1990s unfolded, technology progressed rapidly. By 1993, the year of Prost's final World Championship, his Williams-Renault was the most advanced racing car ever made, featuring antilock brakes, traction control and electronically controlled active suspension. However, in the late spring of 1994, during the weekend of the San Marino Grand Prix, Formula One was stunned into making fundamental changes that would reinforce the work Stewart had started a quarter of a century earlier. The deaths of Ayrton Senna and Roland Ratzenberger ushered in a year-by-year programme of safety improvements at the expense of technological wizardry. The sport had not witnessed a death since Elio de Angelis was killed while testing in 1986, and it was determined that the risks should be reduced as far as possible.

With Senna gone, a new star rose to fill his place. Michael Schumacher had been plucked from sports car racing in 1991, and he won titles for the charismatic and audacious Benetton team in 1994 and 1995. Intense battles between the new champion and his rivals followed, and Schumacher's 1996 move to Ferrari at last brought back the World Championship to Italy in 2000, ending 21 years of underachievement by the legendary team.

The sport's popularity exploded throughout these years. A new state-of-the-art facility was constructed in Malaysia, and there was a breakthrough in the US. China will be next. The colourful image of the Benetton team opened the sport to glamorous new worlds such as fashion, and manufacturer involvement also grew, led by Mercedes' success in unlocking the marketing potential of the sport in partnership with McLaren. As the new century develops, Formula One has almost turned full circle. Anchored by the passion of its participants, the sport saw the involvement of seven major automotive manufacturers in 2002. The billion-pound industry created by the vision of Bernie Ecclestone provides an addictive mix of glamour, excitement and action. For the teams, every new year marks the beginning of a fresh season of joy, despair, competition and commitment.

1. THE TECHNICAL HERITAGE

Motor racing is a combination of man and machine. Indeed, to compete at today's level the driver must be much more than just a racer. He must punch his weight in the secret technological battle, or risk losing his place in the car. In today's world of Formula One, winning on the track means winning in the lab. You don't just need the best car, you need the best engineers, the best factory, the best of everything. Or you just don't win.

In the 1930s, Mercedes-Benz produced engines of awesome power. The Germans dominated Grand Prix racing at speeds of up to 320kph – almost as fast as today's cars. A new weight limit was brought in to restrict the size, and hopefully the power, of the cars, but the engineers countered with high-strength, lightweight alloys, better streamlining and smaller components. These ultimate racing engines of the 1930s were invincible. The Mercedes-Benzes and Auto Unions always finished five minutes ahead of everyone else. Mercedes-Benz won the 1938 Tripoli Grand Prix by thirteen minutes.

The Auto Union car created by Ferdinand Porsche was an evolutionary leap in Grand Prix design. The key feature was its sixteen-cylinder supercharged engine, which, unconventionally, was mounted at the rear. Unfortunately, the revolutionary suspension and tall, heavy engines were such that they were notoriously difficult to handle. The futuristic engine-behind-the-driver idea would be neglected for two decades until one chap, John Cooper, put his motorbike engine at the back. He competed in the poor man's racing formula, Formula Three. No one could have guessed then that the future of the Formula One racing car was being laid out in a Surbiton garage. Cooper put the engine behind the driver for the simple reason that power in Formula Three cars was transmitted from motorcycle engines by a chain; the shorter the chain to the rear wheels the better. With the weight of the engine and the driver equally distributed between the wheels, Cooper's cars were inherently well balanced. He had probably seen the Auto Unions and the very few rear-engined racing cars there had been before, and thought that he could do it better. And by 1958, Cooper was doing it better. His ideas had developed into Formula Two cars, then into Formula One. Despite their having less horsepower than the competition, the Coopers had better balance and could corner faster. They were even worrying the

Italians. Little by little, Cooper finished the job Porsche had started, his Cooper-Climax ending the domination of the Ferraris and Maseratis.

The next radical idea in the evolution of the Formula One car came in 1967, when Chapman's British Lotus team made the engine part of their car's load-bearing structure by bolting it directly on to the back of the cockpit. This was a classic aircraft structure; indeed, the style that was carried over on to the Lotus 49 came straight from the aircraft industry. By this time all the teams had placed the engine, Cooper-style, behind the driver, but Chapman's innovation, using the engine as a stressed part of the car's construction, was unbeatable.

Increasingly, the emphasis in Formula One was moving from the track to the drawing board. A game of technological cat and mouse developed as the rulemakers tried to keep up with the engineers. With six wheels, the Ford-powered Tyrrell tried to reduce the drag from big tyres. Bernie Ecclestone's Brabham, plagued by an underpowered Alfa Romeo engine, used a fan to stick the car on to the road through corners, almost like a hovercraft in reverse. It had one outing, and won the race. Then it was banned.

The most exotic innovation of all came with the rise of computer use in Formula One. The Williams FW15 could change gear in less than a tenth of a second. Its onboard computer could also overrule the driver: if he called for a gear wrongly, say from sixth to second, and he did it at the wrong time, the computer would prevent it, because the wheel sensors were telling it that the car was going, say, 180mph; to actually get into second, he had to be travelling at 100mph, and as soon as that speed was reached the computer changed gear. And Williams went one step further. Constantly variable transmission, or CVT, introduced in 1993, was a perfect example of machines talking to machines. The engine was electronically linked by sensors to the gearbox. This kept the engine's speed within its peak power range, so the familiar gear-changing sound was absent and the engine revs remained constant all the way. It proved that machines worked better than men, making much smoother gear changes than a driver ever could when going into and accelerating out of corners.

There was naturally the fear that technology was changing not just the car but the role of the car. But motor racing is a combination of man and machine. Indeed, to compete at today's level the driver must be much more than just a racer. He must punch his weight in the secret technological battle, or risk losing his place in the car. In today's world of Formula One, winning on the track means winning in the lab. You don't just need the best car, you need the best engineers, the best factory, the best of everything. Or you just don't win.

The modern Formula One car is about maximum power and minimum weight and size – what's called the power-to-weight ratio. Engineers fight for every gram and every millimetre when designing each individual part, down to the smallest bolt. The engine they use these days is a three-litre V10, two thirds the size and less than half the weight of its roadgoing counterpart but ten times more powerful. It's a mechanical monster with the precision of a Swiss watch. There are 900 moving parts, most of them racing at three times the speed of a road-car engine, at around 18,000rpm. Pistons experience 7,000g – that's 7,000 times their own weight. Components such as the crankshaft are designed on the limits of tolerance. Formula One engine designers build components light enough to support high revs, but they are only just strong enough to survive.

Getting to the physical limits of the components is the secret of success. The ultimate Formula One engine would blow up as it crossed the finishing line; as it is it's always teetering on the brink of destruction. To get more power, designers will try to increase the revs as much as possible, to get the engine to spin faster. You get more power by getting more air into the engine, which at three litres has a fixed capacity. Indeed, engineers are so good at making up for lost ground, regardless of the limitations placed on them, that the modern Formula One car could exceed the speed the circuit has been built for. That is a given mathematical fact. There are corners around the world that would become totally unsafe and unusable if the cars weren't controlled in the way they use their wings, the aerodynamics, the power of the engine, traction, and so on. Even without any skirts, or active suspension, a modern Formula One car can generate enough speed and downforce to overcome its own weight. It could race on the roof of a tunnel with ease.

The requirements of Formula One cars are very similar to the aerospace industry's fighter planes. You want ultra-light weight, high levels of structural integrity within a small volume, very high engine power, systems packed within a very small space, and very high aerodynamic performance and efficiency. All these requirements tend to lead to design thinking having certain common aspects with aerospace in terms of the materials employed – aluminium alloys or titaniums – and some of the bonding and joining techniques. More recently, within the last twenty years, composites have been used a lot to increase structural integrity and reduce weight.

The level of commitment and the intensity involved in producing such a car is what makes one team better than the other. Top designers are constantly battling with the Formula One rulemakers; clever engineers are always trying to find loopholes. In the labs, Formula One is an obsessive pursuit of perfection. Competence and consistency in a Grand Prix team these days means a heavy investment in IT to keep up with the best. All the teams want to carve a permanent niche for themselves in the record books, but to achieve this the racing team of the new millennium must become a sophisticated user of IT, which it uses as a tool to create its products, run its operations and compete for sponsorship business.

Computer-aided design (CAD) and computer-aided manufacturing (CAM) technology is no longer the treasured ground of engineers, nor is it isolated from the rest of the business. It's now viewed as an important competitive weapon, as Andy Smith, a Frost & Sullivan analyst and author of the industry-watcher's report on the subject, 'European Markets for CADCAM and Related Software', explained: 'The argument for design and manufacturing firms to adopt CADCAM technology has been won. New entrants into traditional mechanical industries find it hard to match competitors if they have not invested in a CADCAM solution.' Designing and manufacturing parts using CAD-CAM software ensures that the entire design and manufacturing team has access to the same data, the common use of which reduces errors and duplication. The design and development stages of a project occur in parallel, and data can be shared with 'downstream' applications such as product analysis and manufacture, a process that cuts down lead time, or the period it takes for a part or product to reach the market from the drawing-board stage. For European companies, this is the prime reason why they adopt the technology. 'Using CADCAM software, lead times can be reduced by up to 50 per cent,' Smith claimed. Strategy consultant Clive Longbottom agreed. 'Time to market is now more important than ever,' he said.

McLaren launched its first 100 per cent CADCAM-produced racing car, the Marlboro McLaren Mercedes MP4/10, in 1995. At the time, it represented a significant technical milestone for the company, which designed and manufactured its new machine in just three months. Today, during every race and test session Sun computer systems continually monitor and measure all aspects of the car's performance. The data is then fed back to McLaren's headquarters in Woking, where the design and development team can access it on the company's network and thereby enhance the car's design and assess the performance of a component under racing conditions. The team has actually built a completely new chassis in just 33 days, a task that would normally have taken three months.

The Jaguar Racing car has been designed completely by computer since 1998 (as a Stewart Ford). The design office at Jaguar Racing's headquarters in Milton Keynes contains fifty or so graphics work-stations, all of them running EDS's Unigraphics CADCAM/CAE software to provide the design and engineering teams with an integrated design-through-to-manufacturing environment. The team also uses a host of other very specialised software applications so that the team's members can work more effectively as a unit.

The process of designing a Formula One car follows much the same path as the design of any product. It starts with a brief that defines the car in terms of its functional requirements and the regulations that govern Formula One racing. From this, the general arrangement and space envelopes for major components and assemblies can be developed in the CAD system, and the assembly structure tree for the whole car is mapped out. Where the process differs is in the lead time available – a mere four to five months from one season's car to the next. From the earliest stages of the development process, all the design engineers working on the project are able to reference other designers' areas of responsibility in order to put their own work into context, using the assembly navigation tools in Unigraphics. For example, the rear suspension designer can view the gearbox designer's model to see where the suspension assembly should connect to the gearbox housing.

In addition to this, Jaguar's Teamcenter Engineering system, which controls access to the product model and manages nongeometric data such as manufacturing information, as well as the geometric model data, provides facilities such as design history and traceability and assembly structure management. This makes it impossible for out-of-date or nonissued parts to be used in any assembly by ensuring that when a new part is up-issued to one assembly it is automatically up-issued to all other assemblies in which it appears. The ability to work collab-oratively on the geometric model is essential, because any changes to the gearbox design, for example, may well have a knock-on effect on the suspension design. Parametric modelling facilities in Unigraphics ensure that defined geometric relationships are maintained, not only within the individual models that go to make up the complete car but also between components in different assemblies. If a change is made to one model, that change is reflected in related geometry from other assemblies.

Such collaboration extends beyond Jaguar Racing's own design team to embrace suppliers as well. For example, the engine used by Jaguar Racing in its Formula One cars is developed and supplied by Cosworth Racing, another Ford subsidiary. And while the gearbox housing is designed in-house by Jaguar Racing, the internals are developed and supplied by specialist transmission company Xtrac. Both Cosworth and Xtrac are Unigraphics users. So, for example, Jaguar Racing and Cosworth are able to exchange design files with each other over the Internet using straightforward FTP links. This means that between them they can agree on the best position for engine mounts, the cooling system and oil inlets, and so on, without having to compromise the overall design of the car. It also means that Jaguar Racing's designers can obtain torsion and structural information on the engine for use in the design of, say, the suspension units. Building on the knowledge and geometric data developed over the previous years, a complete digital mock-up of the following season's Jaguar can be produced well before physical testing begins. This helps the designers to package the bodywork as tightly as possible around the working parts of the car. They can optimise the design and take into account aerodynamics test results.

The kinematics analysis software in the Unigraphics suite is also used within the assembly environment for clash detection and motion analysis, while data required for more advanced vehicle dynamics analysis, such as roll centre, pitch and acceleration loads, are exported to the Adams system simulation package from Mechanical Dynamics Inc., an EDS Unigraphics software partner.

With some 80 per cent of each car being manufactured in-house at Jaguar Racing, the integrated CAM facilities in the Unigraphics software suite have proved invaluable for cutting production timescales to an absolute minimum. Design data is used directly in the CAM environment for the development of computer numerical control (CNC) milling and turning tool path programs. For example, while gearbox casings are cast outside, the patterns for them are produced from the 3D model data in-house in Jaguar Racing's own machine shop, where the supplied castings are also finished. Teamcenter Engineering files are also translated into the correct STL format used by the team's stereo lithography machine, a 3D printer employed for making prototype parts. One of the advantages of keeping as much of the manufacturing as is practical in-house (as well as the design and analysis work) is that it provides maximum flexibility. For example, short-run batches can easily be split so that only the number of parts required to fulfil immediate needs are finished, leaving the rest to be completed quickly when required. It also means that the design and development teams can react rapidly to demands.

It's a similar tale at Jordan and Williams. Ultrapowerful workstations in the teams' design offices operate what is known as CFD (computational fluid dynamics). Aerodynamic design in Formula One has in the past posed headaches for designers, especially among the smaller teams, as testing parts while constructing a new chassis is not only expensive but time-consuming. With CFD, parts can be put through their paces without actually being physically made. After a number of successful seasons, Williams' 1998 season started badly, but a major redesign of the car in June that year marked a turning point in the company's racing fortunes. As Williams' head of marketing Jim Wright admitted, technology 'played an enormous role in getting us back up to the front end of the grid. When we changed the parameters of the car, we put these changes through a model of how the car would behave in a race, long before we ever got to the track. Such IT resources helped us to understand our problems.'

Aerodynamics is key in Formula One. It is a branch of fluid mechanics that deals with the motion of air and other gaseous fluids, and with the forces acting on bodies in motion relative to such fluids. The motion of an aircraft through the air, the wind forces exerted on a structure, and the operation of a windmill are all examples of aerodynamic action.

One of the fundamental laws governing the motion of fluids is Daniel Bernoulli's principle. If, when driving at speed on a motorway, you open a window a couple of centimetres, you can feel a rush of air entering the air vents. The air going by the window has to speed up to get out of the way of the car, and when air speeds up, it loses pressure. The lower pressure of the air speeding past the window sucks more air out of the window, increasing flow into the car through the vents, to replace the lost air. Bernoulli's principle is used in aerodynamics to explain the lift of an airplane wing in flight. A wing is so designed that air flows more rapidly over its upper surface than its lower one. This leads to a decrease in pressure on the top surface compared with the bottom, and this pressure difference provides the lift that keeps the aircraft in the air. (Blow over the top of a sheet of paper and you can establish for yourself this key scientific principle. As air speeds up over the surface, its pressure drops, and the high pressure underneath pushes the paper upwards.) If the wing is turned upside down, the resulting force is downwards. This explains how performance cars can corner at such high speeds. The downforce produced pushes the tyres into the road, which in turn gives them more grip.

In the 1960s, the use of soft rubber compounds and wider tyres, pioneered particularly by Lotus, demonstrated that good road adhesion and, as a result, cornering ability were just as important as raw engine power for producing fast lap times. The tyre-width factor came as something of a surprise, for in simple experiments on sliding friction between hard surfaces, the friction resistance force is found to be independent of the contact area. It also came as a surprise that the friction could be greater than the contact force between the two surfaces, apparently giving a coefficient greater than one.

The desire to increase tyre adhesion led to a major revolution in racing-car design, the introduction of inverted wings, which produce negative lift or downforce. Since the tyres' lateral adhesion is roughly proportional to the downloading on it, or the friction between tyre and road, adding aerodynamic downforce to the weight component improves the adhesion. As well as enhancing the cornering ability, aerodynamic downforce allows the tyres to transmit a greater thrust force without wheel spin, and thus increases acceleration. Without aerodynamic downforce, high-performance racing cars have sufficient power to produce wheel spin at more than 100mph.

Another important aspect of aerodynamics is the drag, or resistance, acting on solid bodies moving through air. The drag forces exerted by the air flowing over an aeroplane, for example, must be overcome by the thrust force developed by the engine. These drag forces can be significantly reduced by streamlining the body. For bodies that are not fully streamlined, the drag force increases approximately with the square of the speed as they move rapidly through the air. The power required, for example, to drive an automobile steadily at medium or high speed is primarily absorbed as it overcomes air resistance. The more streamlined a vehicle is, the less power it needs to obtain high speeds, and it therefore becomes more economical to run.

Motorsport is used as a proving ground for developing technologies that are subsequently applied to roadgoing vehicles, and this has inspired a great deal of aerodynamic research in recent years. Intensive aerodynamic development has since the mid-1970s been an increasingly important priority within Formula One Grand Prix car design. The techniques for investigating this crucial area of performance have evolved to such a level that every modern front-line Formula One team has exclusive access to its own wind-tunnel facilities. For more than fifty years, aeronautical engineers have used wind tunnels to help them with their aircraft designs. The wind tunnel provides the opportunity for the proposed design to be subjected to aerodynamic forces. By carefully monitoring and plotting aerodynamic pressures you can accurately obtain a clear picture of the prototype shape's aerodynamic potential.

Aerodynamic wings were originally fixed at a set angle on the car. However, a major disadvantage of a fixed wing is that it produces high drag when set for cornering, so when wings were first introduced to Formula One they came with a mechanism for controlling the incidence angle. On the straight, the wing could be feathered to a zero angle to minimise drag, but on braking and entering a corner, the angle of attack could be increased negatively to provide downforce. Front wings were soon added, and as a further refinement Brabham introduced split-wing surfaces with independently variable incidence. These enabled a greater downforce to be applied to the inside wheel to offset the effects of body roll. In early experiments in 1968, Brabham and Ferrari mounted a wing on their cars' bodies. Lotus mounted theirs directly on to the unsprung wheel assembly, so that the downforce would be transmitted directly on to the tyre and its contact with the road. In order to take the wing out of the turbulence from the body, Lotus pioneered the use of very high mounted wings, an arrangement that was taken up by a number of other competitors.

But the combination of high mounting, variable incidence mechanisms and direct connection to the unsprung wheel assembly resulted in a flimsy and vulnerable structure that was susceptible to accidental damage. Following serious accidents at the Spanish Grand Prix in 1969, stringent regulations governing the use of wings were introduced, and these are still in force. Essentially, there are three rules: the maximum height, width and locations are controlled; aerodynamic devices have to be of fixed geometry (no variable incidence); and they have to be rigidly attached to the bodywork. The last two regulations have caused significant problems. The fixed incidence means that a compromise has to be achieved between the improved cornering due to high downforce, and reduced straight-line speed resulting from the high trailing vortex drag. The optimum compromise differs according to the nature of the circuit, and during practice sessions considerable effort goes into trying to achieve the right balance.

For the 1970 season Lotus developed the new 72, which, after disappointing early performances, proved to be perhaps the outstanding car of the early years of that decade. The 72 had new features such as the 'shovel' nose with twin fins, in-board front brakes, and torsion bar suspension. The adoption of mid-mounted radiators was taken from the current practice in sports cars, and the aim was to achieve good air penetration by having as small a nose as possible. Another new feature of the 72 was its three rear aerofoils.

In 1970, Jochen Rindt joined Gold Leaf Team Lotus. After a slow start, Rindt and the 72 found winning form in June at Zandvoort in Holland, where he also took pole position. Rindt subsequently won the

French, British and German Grands Prix. As the season progressed, a number of modifications were made to the cars, including a stiffened monocoque and an air collector box above the fuel injection system – something else that was copied by other teams. During practice for the Italian Grand Prix in September, Rindt ran his car without wings to gain straight-line speed, and crashed, with fatal results. A prolonged Italian investigation finally decided that the front brakeshaft had failed, causing Rindt to lose control. Team leadership was taken by newcomer Emerson Fittipaldi, who won in only his fourth race, one month after Rindt's death.

For 1971 more minor changes were made to the car – suspension modifications, a one-piece rear wing, and low-profile tyres. In this form the car was known as the 72D. But with an inexperienced driver line-up, there were no wins that season. For 1972 the cars were painted black and gold and entered as 'John Player Specials'. Changes were few, but they now included revised air-boxes, an altered rear wing, a new oil tank design and more suspension modifications. Fittipaldi enjoyed fine success, winning that year's World Championship. At just 25 years and 8 months old he remains the youngest driver ever to become the Formula One champion.

Much credit for effective early wind-tunnel work has been attributed to Shadow designer Tony Southgate, but it was Team Lotus designer Peter Wright who made some of the most significant discoveries in the mid to late 1970s. While working with models of the still-secret Lotus 78, Wright, almost by chance, stumbled over the development that was destined to have enormous implications for Formula One car design over the next five years. Wright had been studying the complexities of airflow beneath racing cars ever since the late 1960s, when he had worked at BRM. During the course of his tests to finalise the Lotus 78's basic aerodynamic configuration, an assessment was carried out as to whether the water radiators could be incorporated within the leading edge of the inverted wing side-pods. In this configuration, Wright began to obtain nonrepeatable results with the wind-tunnel model. What followed was a breakthrough of momentous significance that would open the door to new areas of understanding of under-car airflow and establish a basic yardstick that remained valid even after wing section underbody profiles were banned in Formula One at the end of the 1982 season. On closer examination, Wright detected that the model's side-pods were sagging, and as they moved closer to the tunnel floor, so the downforce increased. The Lotus research team explored this phenomenon with a degree of fascination, quickly cutting up some makeshift cardboard sides that extended the model's pods right down to the ground. Their results indicated that the downforce had doubled, opening the way for skirted ground-effect Formula One racers.

Few at the time understood the secret hidden beneath the bodywork of the sinister black Lotus 78. The layout is universally accepted as the perfect solution for a single-seat racer. The ten-cylinder engine is low down in the middle, and there are cooling ducts on either side of the cockpit. Behind these are radiators for the engine, but there are no fans to circulate air when the car is stationary. At the back of the engine, the semi-automatic gearbox supports all the suspension, and the final drive to the rear wheels. The fuel tank is a self-sealing bag holding about 150 litres of fuel, enough for about 50 laps of a 70-lap race. Every aspect of the carbon-fibre bodywork is aerodynamic. And underneath every modern car is an upside-down wing shape that can be traced to the Lotus 78. As the car raced forwards, stationary air was forced underneath, accelerated by the wing shape. The pressure therefore dropped underneath the car, and the higher pressure above pinned the car to the road. The skirts sealed the low pressure against the outside air. The 'ground effect' Lotus 78 beat everyone. The teams knew that the Lotus contained a technical feature that was a big step forward in Formula One design, but no one knew or could guess what it might be. Lotus was very good at throwing up smokescreens. Had it come up with improvements in the car's gearbox? No, the team had discovered a way of getting twice the downforce without creating any more drag, which gave the car exceptional grip.

The Lotus 79 carried the philosophy a giant step further. The design concept called for a brand-new car with a slim monocoque, central fuel cell and inboard suspension all round. In short, every facet of its performance was predicated on excellent aerodynamics. Unfortunately, title sponsor JPS then left, and the new 80 model was too advanced to tame. Reigning champion Mario Andretti scored only fourteen points in the 1979 season, with a best of one third place, compared to sixty-four points and six wins the previous year. However, the basic layout of this revolutionary car can still be seen on Formula One machines today.

For 1981 and 1982, teams were required to run fixed aerodynamic skirts, beneath which a six-centimetre ground clearance requirement was mandatory, obliging them to run impossibly hard suspension in an effort to control the under-car aerodynamics. Throughout these seasons, spring rates gradually climbed to 1,365kg (3,000lb) as designers fought to control the fixed-skirt aerodynamics. This quickly spawned a breed of 200mph go-karts.

Having got rid of sliding skirts, the next challenge to Formula One aerodynamicists came at the start of 1983, when sculptured under-body tunnels were prohibited. With effect from the start of that season, flat bottoms were required for Formula One cars from the trailing edge of the front wheels to the leading edge of the rear wheels. At a stroke, the governing body had wiped out millions of pounds' worth of research and sent designers back to the drawing board. The new cars were totally different animals. The long side-pods now tended to produce lift, so they were kept short, as on the Tyrrell 011, the Williams FW08C and the Brabham BT-52.

The new Toleman team had entered Formula One at the end of 1982, and the major rule change had forced designer Rory Byrne's ground-effect TG183 to be totally repackaged to conform with the 1983 regulations. He opted for a full-width nose section into which the water radiators were housed. He also gained some additional rear downforce by positioning an aerofoil ahead of the rear-wing centre line, at a point where it could take advantage of the maximum chassis width regulations. It complemented the conventional rear wing, which was positioned slightly lower, behind the rear axle line.

On the face of it, getting downforce to the rear of the car does not look a particularly difficult problem, the engine and gearbox making sure that the rearward weight bias of the basic chassis helps matters considerably. However, the reality is that the front wing uses so much of the air that there is precious little energy left for the rear wing. The optimum function of a wing is achieved when the airflow to and from it is not interrupted. Clearly, the rear wing has the biggest problem from the point of view of airflow to the wing, as it is broken up and disrupted by the wheels, cockpit fairings and rollover bars. With Formula One regulations strictly limiting the height at which the rear wing can be positioned, there is a restriction on the amount of scope available to a designer for raising it to a level where there is no problem with a disrupted flow.

The result of these design problems was the low-line Brabham BT55 used in 1986. It was powered by a specially made BMW engine canted over at 72 degrees to make the back of the car as low as possible, and to smooth the airflow to the rear wing. Unfortunately, although the BT55 developed up to 30 per cent more downforce than its immediate predecessor, somewhere along the line it also picked up an excessive amount of drag, added to which there was the problem of lost power due to poor oil circulation in an angled engine. The whole package was a disaster.

Nevertheless, no Formula One designer would ever underestimate the benefit to be gained by reducing the front area of the car. This prompted 1986 Williams FW11B drivers Nelson Piquet and Nigel Mansell to try to sit in the car as low as possible, each hoping to outdo the other. Mansell discovered that by removing his seat he could lower his position in the car by 1.5 centimetres, which translated into an additional 25kg of downforce.

Running flat-bottomed cars as close to the ground as possible increases the flow rate due to the constricted space under the car. Speeding the air up causes it to lose pressure and suck the car even closer to the ground. However, nothing is ever that simple. The air must be expanded to its original pressure through a rear diffuser after it leaves the flat bottom to reduce drag. The 1990 McLaren MP4-5B had one of the most fascinating diffusers before the rules limited their width and distance behind the rear axle line.

During 1990, Tyrrell took a radical step equal to the impact Colin Chapman had made with the Lotus 79. Designer Harvey Postlethwaite and aerodynamicist Jean-Claude Migeot raised the nose of the 019 to increase airflow under the flat underbody. The front wing halves were fixed off an anhedral mounting on the nose, and the lower suspension wishbones attached underneath. This elegant and simple concept produced significantly more downforce without the need to use a larger rear wing. The straight-line performance of the admittedly very light and compact new 019 raised more than a few eyebrows throughout the season.

Following the deaths of Roland Ratzenberger and Ayrton Senna at Imola in 1994, the FIA, the governing body of motorsport, produced some rapidly imposed rule changes which had the effect of cutting back downforce quite significantly. Some rule changes were immediate, and removed a small percentage of downforce. The new rule brought in for 1995 was a large increase in the minimum permitted ground clearance over a large proportion of the underbody, creating a 'stepped floor'. This produced a substantial reduction in downforce levels (by as much as 40 per cent) and also lessened the car's sensitivity, which made it more predictable and therefore safer to drive.

During 1996, the FIA commissioned studies into the aerodynamics of cars that are following one another closely, in an apparent attempt to find a general configuration that would enable close running and overtaking to occur, therefore enhancing the spectacle of Formula One. It seems the studies indicated that if the total downforce was reduced, far from making it easier for cars to follow one another things actually got worse, and there was an adverse effect on the following car. Interestingly, the emphasis of these studies switched for a while from aerodynamics to tyres. Ultimately the FIA decided to introduce grooved tyres into Formula One in 1998, in the hope that reducing the amount of rubber in contact with the road would reduce grip, and hence cornering speeds. At the same time, the cars were 20 centimetres narrower too, which reduced the front area and increased straight-line speed, with a corresponding increase in braking distances, theoretically promoting outbraking manoeuvres.

Over the past decade, racing-car technology has reached unimaginable heights of sophistication. This development has been funded, and accelerated, largely by enormous sponsorship investment, reflecting the global television interest focused on the FIA Formula One World Championship. Motor racing is now a multi-million-dollar business. Gaining the technical edge can make the difference between being a run-of-the-mill contender and a pace-setter at the front of the field. Aerodynamics has been the turning point in the design of modern Formula One machines, and it keeps the designers busy for twelve months a year as they constantly develop the car.

Setting up a car for a Grand Prix is a tricky business as no two circuits are the same. But there is a certain amount of predictability about the process. Engineers will have worked on computer modelling back at base, with the circuit's co-ordinates plotted in, analysing the theoretical impact of set-up changes. The test team will also have put in mileage at a circuit possessing corners with similar characteristics to the one about to be visited. There are a number of 'set-up' variables engineers have to work on. Then, of course, there's that universal variable known as the weather: a car's handling is affected by changes in temperature and wind direction as well as by wet or dry conditions.

Once at the circuit, teams work towards a 'balanced' set-up (where the car is moving efficiently around the track) from which they can develop the often very different set-ups that will work in qualifying and the race. By this stage computer simulation will have reduced the car's aerodynamic settings from a potential twenty to just three or four. Allied to a car's aerodynamics are its ride height and suspension requirements. In a perfect world, engineers would run their cars as close to the track as the rulebook allows, but circuits such as Brazil's Interlagos are bumpy, and running the cars low would lead to their 'bottoming' (where the underside of the car actually hits the track's surface) and the drivers losing control, so they have to be set up high. Settings will have been tested first on a six-post testing rig – a device that simulates how the car runs on the track – at the team's base, leaving the team to work through five or six set-ups. The engineers also choose which of three or four brake materials is best suited to the characteristics of the circuit. Circuits such as Monza that ask for heavy braking require thicker discs and pads, which in turn offer the driver less feel.

Finally, engineers have to consider what gearing to use to make the most of the engine's power curve without affecting top speed. A circuit such as Monaco doesn't have a straight long enough to make top speed a factor, so gearing will be fitted for maximum acceleration.

Given that there are sixteen races to be run within some eight months in the 2003 World Championship calendar, it's easy to see why running a Formula One team is an expensive and immensely complex activity.

2. MOTORSPORT VALLEY (ENGLAND) AND AUTOTECHNIUM (WALES)

The performance engineering technology and innovation developed by the UK motorsport industry crosses over a number of related industrial sectors such as aerospace, electronics, information technology, ceramics and materials. As well as racing-car design, there is also unique expertise in the related areas of world rally car and sports car design and construction, event management, motorsport insurance and publishing, and other specialised activities.

Over the last thirty or so years the UK has developed a world-class motorsport industry 'cluster' of over 2,500 performance engineering and services companies. According to a recent survey carried out by the Motorsport Industry Association (MIA), UK motorsport engineering and services is now worth £4.6 billion (£2.9 billion is generated through engineering and £1.7 billion through services). The motorsport industry contributes £2 billion to the UK's annual export earnings, and world racing formulae are effectively dominated by British expertise. Total employment in motorsport in the UK is estimated at 150,000. Of these, 40,000 are employed in motorsport engineering and service provision, and 25,000 of them are engineers. And it's a market sector that is exhibiting phenomenal growth. According to Dr Mark Jenkins at the Cranfield School of Management, the motorsport industry has grown by over 500 per cent in ten years.

'Motorsport Valley', an area that covers the south and Midlands of Britain, dominates high-technology racing-car manufacture for the major international series such as Formula One, the World Rally Championship, CART racing and the Indy Racing League (IRL). Within the valley area 75 per cent of the world's single-seater racing cars are designed and built, and these machines have made up 80 per cent of all Formula One race victories in the last ten years. The performance engineering technology and innovation developed by the UK motorsport industry crosses over a number of related industrial sectors such as aerospace, electronics, information technology, ceramics and materials. As well as racing-car design, there is also unique expertise in the related areas of world rally car and sports car design and construction, event management, motorsport insurance and publishing, and other specialised activities. Companies not only build competition vehicles, they also supply components such as brakes, engines, transmission systems, telemetry and associated goods – clothing, accessories, and so on. There's also considerable activity associated with motorsport marketing, particularly sponsorship.

Motorsport spends approximately 20 per cent of its turnover in research and development, a level far in excess of the norm for the rest of UK industry, where the national average is just 2 per cent. The pressure for innovation and the required performance standards are much higher than for any other industry, including pharmaceuticals and aerospace.

In their book *Playing to Win*, academics Dr Beverly Aston, a lecturer in finance at the University of London, and Mark Williams, a fellow in economics at Exeter College, Oxford, revealed a fascinating story of how British ingenuity was translated into economic success and why the motor racing industry is clustered in an arc to the north of London, running from Woking in the southwest to Huntingdon in the northeast.

The clustering of firms with specialised skills is not unusual in other industries. The banking industry has long gathered in the City of London, US automobile companies are concentrated in Detroit, and film companies in Hollywood, and until fairly recently computer companies flourished in 'Silicon Valley' in San Jose, California. The origins of Motorsport Valley can be found in a post-war Britain when a generation of young engineers were growing up as racers, building their own racing machinery from kits or from parts of old cars. It was do-it-yourself motor racing. The 500cc Club and the 750 Motor Club both played an important role in this, although it was the 750 Motor Club that had access to the basic Austin Seven, which the enthusiasts regarded as 'a grown-up Meccano set' with which to create racing and rally cars. The popularity of these car clubs created commercial opportunities for those with the skills and the vision. The Cooper Car Company, for example, began building 500cc racers using components from the Fiat Topolino, and by the early 1950s was attracting large numbers of customers. Eventually the company began to build 'proper' racing cars.

As the sport grew, so did the need for car constructors, component manufacturers, engine tuners and other businesses. As they were set up by racing enthusiasts with specific aims, they tended to be dedicated to motorsport, and with no spare cash to fall back on they had to be competitive to survive. When engineers came along who felt they could do better, they were often proved right.

Colin Chapman was a leading member of the 750 Motor Club. His Austin Seven-based cars were so successful that in 1952 he established

Lotus in stables behind the Railway Hotel in Hornsey. He began to build spaceframe racing cars, and as success followed success, Lotus grew. Some of the most famous Lotus designers were also 750 Motor Club men, notably Maurice Philippe, an expert in aircraft wing structures who built his own sports car, the Maurice Philippe Special, in 1955. Philippe brought in other aerospace engineers, such as John Baldwin. Other 750 Motor Club members who worked for Lotus were Tony Southgate, John Miles, Mike Pilbeam and Len Terry. Pilbeam went on to establish Pilbeam Racing Designs in 1975 and enjoyed a great deal of success, particularly in hill climbing and sports car racing. Eric Broadley was another 750 Motor Club graduate who began to build his own cars in the late 1950s. The result was Lola Cars, which became one of the biggest racing-car production companies in the world. He also recruited from among his friends in the 750 Motor Club, notably Len Bailey, the designer of the Le Mans 24 Hours-winning Ford GT40. There were other companies, too: Mallock was the brainchild of Major Arthur Mallock, who started out racing a converted Austin Seven; and Chevron was founded in an old cotton mill in Bolton by 750 Motor Club racer Derek Bennett. Other 750 Motor Club engineers went on to work for major racing teams, including aerodynamicist Frank Costin, Brabham's Gordon Murray, Paul Owens, Richard Owen, Derrick White and even Adrian Reynard.

The growth of the British club scene in the 1960s resulted in other ambitious projects, the most famous of which was March Engineering, established in Bicester in 1969 by former McLaren engineer Robin Herd, wealthy racer Max Mosley and former racer and Winkelmann Racing team manager Alan Rees. It was March that was largely responsible for the concentration of the motor racing industry around the Bicester area, and for giving birth to Motorsport (or 'Grand Prix') Valley. Over the next twenty years the company manufactured cars for Formula One, Formula Two, Formula 3000, Formula Three, Can-Am, IMSA and IndyCars. March proved to be a very forward-thinking company and helped to develop many young engineers over the years, notably Harvey Postle-thwaite, Nigel Stroud, Tim Holloway, Tino Belli, Adrian Newey and Nick Wirth.

Williams Grand Prix Engineering was the next to set up, in Didcot in 1977. What is now Renault was established in Witney, and then Enstone. Other Oxfordshire businesses included TWR in Kidlington, Reynard (which unfortunately went out of business in 2002) at Bicester, Jordan at Silverstone (Northamptonshire) and a host of other racing concerns such as the design and engineering outfit Prodrive (based in

Banbury), Hawtal Whiting, Ricardo, Tickford (now part of Prodrive), Millbrook Proving Ground and the Motor Industry Research Association (MIRA).

As talented young engineers were nurtured, some flew the nest and set up on their own, in competition with the companies that had trained them. Before establishing Cosworth Engineering, for example, Keith Duckworth worked as a gearbox designer with Lotus. Both John Barnard and Patrick Head learned their design skills from Eric Broadley at Lola; they went on to create their own 'schools' of design. Head has been particularly successful, teaching a whole generation of engineers who have gone to work elsewhere, notably Frank Dernie, Neil Oatley, Sergio Rinland, Enrique Scalabroni and Ross Brawn. In recent years Adrian Reynard also created a school of young engineers. It was a similar story in the engine world. Coventry engines, for example, trained John Judd, who later teamed up with Jack Brabham to start Engine Developments in Rugby.

The most important of the engine companies was, without question, Cosworth Engineering, established in 1959 by former 750 Motor Club racers Mike Costin and Keith Duckworth specifically to tune Ford engines for the British club racing scene. These became the mainstay of the sport in the 1960s, and the Cosworth DFV Formula One engine enabled a number of teams to enter Grand Prix racing with a cheap and reliable engine package. Without the DFV, the likes of Williams, Shadow, Arrows, Ensign, Fittipaldi and Wolf would probably never have been formed. Over time, Cosworth spawned Brian Hart Limited and Ilmor Engineering, both of which were founded by former Cosworth engineers (although Hart had also been a member of the 750 Motor Club). Other engineering companies such as Hewland Engineering were lured into motor racing by commissions from young racing car companies such as Cooper. They in turn spawned offshoots which went into competition with them.

In all cases, it was survival of the fittest. Constant competition not only promoted technological breakthroughs, it also weeded out the companies that were not meant to succeed. As a result the industry never stagnated. Every aspect of a racing car was constantly re-examined, and from time to time another budding entrepreneur-engineer would say, 'I can do this better than that,' and would set himself up as a rival business. The immediate post-war generation of DIY enthusiasts had to learn to live in this cut-and-thrust world. Some could not cope with the unremitting advances in technology, and today their names are largely forgotten. Had things been different, today, rather than Lolas and Lotuses, we might have been discussing the exploits of the Arengo or the Marwyn, the Beagle or the Parker Special.

Constant innovation and development meant that team bosses were forever looking into new areas of specialised knowledge that might help them gain the edge over the competition. It was natural that many of these innovations would come from aerospace as there were a group of 750 Motor Club enthusiasts who worked together at De Havilland in Hatfield and, later, at the Royal Establishment at Farnborough. And when aerodynamics became more of an issue after the introduction of ground-effect technology by Peter Wright and his Lotus 78, aerodynamicists were in great demand. The current crop of French wind-tunnel experts, Jean-Claude Migeot and Henri Durand the most famous among them, came out of the European space programme in Toulouse. In Britain, Williams got ahead of the opposition thanks to work in the Imperial College wind tunnel in London, which had been used by Frank Dernie. This led to the establishment of a small school of Imperial College aerodynamicists that included Tino Belli, John Davis and, more recently, Egbahl Hamidy. The arrival in Formula One of carbon-fibre composite technology drew in more expertise. McLaren used the skills of British Aerospace's Arthur Webb, but also looked to America and hired Steve Nichols, who had been trained at the Hercules Aerospace Company in Utah. Williams responded by hiring Brian O'Rourke from the US aviation giant Northrop. There was also demand for stress analysis engineers from the aerospace companies.

The rush to carbon-fibre composites created another market, because few teams could afford to do such expensive work in their own in-house facilities. Advanced Composites of Heanor in Derbyshire became the market leader when it came to building racing-car chassis, producing an astounding 700 between 1981 and 1995, including no fewer than 100 Formula One chassis for customers Alfa Romeo, Brabham, Ligier, Arrows, Toleman, March, Onyx, Fomet, Larrousse and Pacific. The other 600 chassis included 292 IndyCars for March Engineering, Penske, Kraco and Galmer; 49 sports cars for March, TWR, Schuppan, Brun, Mazda and Konrad; and 53 Formula 3000 chassis for March. Inevitably, Advanced Composites spawned its own competition in the area, notably Astec, which became part of the TWR empire.

In recent years Grand Prix teams have worked towards having not only their own composite departments but also their own wind tunnels. There has also been considerable expansion in the electronics and hydraulic engineering sectors, while today's biggest boom sector is in advanced software development such as computational fluid dynamics (CFD).

There's no question that a number of companies have prospered by being part of Motorsport Valley. They haven't just benefited from the local area's expertise, they've also tried to innovate, to stand out from their competitors, thus creating more mini-centres of excellence all over the region. Based in Silverstone, Jordan Grand Prix makes use of around 400 suppliers in the valley. 'It's tempting to say that with modern technology and the high quality of engineering skills now spread further afield, and in other countries, that Motorsport Valley isn't as important,' said Jordan's marketing director Mark Gallagher, 'but it's still a terrific place to be based. With McLaren having brought so much of its manufacturing in-house, a lot of the suppliers now have Jordan as their biggest customer. We're now getting their quality of engineering. There's a wealth of engineering expertise in the country, and we're at the centre of it. These people work night and day to give you what you want. It is a cottage industry, but a very important one. There is an awareness of the racing pressure, and a precise understanding of our needs.'

Xtrac, founded in 1984, is such a company. It specialises in designing and manufacturing high-performance transmissions for international motorsport. Occupying a leading position in the UK market, Xtrac is one of only a handful of companies worldwide which has consistently demonstrated an ability to meet the exacting product performance demands of the motorsport industry. Formula One, IndyCar, sports cars, World Rally and touring cars are just some of the users of Xtrac products, which are designed and manufactured at the company's base near Wokingham in Berkshire.

Xtrac operates at the leading edge of the automotive industry, where precise measurement is critical. Individual components, very often supplied by different subcontractors, must comply with stringent material and dimension specifications to ensure a perfect fit and performance. Even the slightest deviation from a specification could spell disaster on race day, when the components must perform faultlessly under the most demanding driving conditions. Recent investment in state-of-the-art measurement equipment has enabled Xtrac to improve its quality control and so strengthen its relationships with its customers, produce a hi-tech product with total confidence, offer shorter lead times, and extend its competitiveness. As well as complete transmission systems and single components, the company also produces driveshaft and rack-and-pinion assemblies, engine gears, viscous differentials, remote gear-change systems and flywheel ring gears. A key challenge Xtrac faces when it has to service such a broad customer base is how to maintain trust and confidentiality. Xtrac's dedicated engineering teams working with a particular client use a complex part-numbering system which means that no component can be readily identified with a particular customer by many of those working on the project.

Unlike many companies which experience rapid growth, Xtrac has been careful to match the rate of its growth with the development of its skill base, and it is this focus on gear technologies and a healthy respect for the expertise needed to perform at the highest standards which has allowed Xtrac to become so dominant. In addition to this growth, the company has never shirked from making major investments to ensure that its equipment is always the most up-to-date and efficient.

The knowledge and skills developed by Xtrac are undoubtedly a key part of its success, and the company continually focuses on proactive ways of bringing high-quality people into its operation. Gear cutting is traditionally a Midlands and northern-based industry, but the decline in general apprenticeships began some fifteen years ago. The company has had to develop a range of initiatives to take people who were machinists and teach them how to work computer numerical control (CNC) machines, or to take someone who has worked on a computer and train them to be a machinist. Xtrac's standards of cleanliness mean that the working environment is closer to a hospital than a traditional machine shop.

The company innovates in a number of ways. Xtrac's engineers are continually coming up with ideas to make components lighter, or using modular designs to make them simpler and more reliable. A key part of the company's innovation process is the way ideas are transferred across different race series. A great deal was learned, for instance, from the process of making low-cost Indy Racing League gearboxes. Xtrac was able to pass on these savings to other designs, significantly reducing, for example, the price of a British touring car gearbox. Xtrac also brings its customers into the innovation process. More often than not the company will share the development costs of a new product with them, then use the design in some of its other race series. The customer gets exclusivity in the area in which they're competing, but Xtrac gets to spread the development costs over other race series. Xtrac's unique position across a whole range of racing activities is therefore critical to its ability to innovate and develop.

Another company that has made a success of integrating various areas of activity is Ray Mallock Limited (RML). Major Arthur Mallock, who was later joined by his sons Richard and Ray, was the first of the family to create a series of race-winning cars, the Mallock U2s. Ray developed his career as a professional racing driver and formed Ray Mallock Atlantic Racing in 1979, which had developed, by 1984, into RML.

After a stint in a consultancy role for Aston Martin, RML took responsibility for the entire design, manufacture and race management of another long-distance sports racing car, the Group C2 Ecurie Ecosse Ford. In 1985, this came second in the World Championship for Teams, and in 1986, with factory support from Austin Rover, RML won the world title. Next was an Aston Martin C1 design with carbon-composite chassis and bodywork, but when the marque withdrew suddenly from racing just before the 1990 season got under way, RML was enrolled by Nissan to develop and run its R90C Le Mans car. It was a potentially race-winning programme as the team battled with the front runners, including the eventual TWR/Jaguar victor, for over sixteen hours, leading for five hours and setting a new lap record.

Recognising its massive promotional value to automotive manufacturers, in 1992 RML moved into the BTCC (British Touring Car Championship) running the privately entered Ecurie Ecosse Vauxhall Cavaliers. In 1993, with the first RML-designed touring car, the team frequently outpaced the factory-supported cars, and in 1994 was awarded Vauxhall 'works' status. Running the Vauxhallsport team in the BTCC, and supplying and supporting eight Vauxhall/Opel teams worldwide, a string of successes followed, including the 1995 BTCC drivers' and teams' titles for Vauxhall, a drivers' championship title in Spain, and 1996 championship titles in Thailand and Australia. Then Nissan decided to return to this toughest of championships and chose to do so with RML. RML took the manufacturers' and teams' titles in 1998, the second year of the programme, thus becoming the first team to win BTCC Super Touring championships for five different manufacturers.

October 1997 marked the start of a new era for RML when it secured a contract to design and develop the Astra Formula Two rally kit car for Opel, and to run the works Astras or Vauxhalls in the British Rally Championship. The car was designed from a clean sheet to first prototype in under five months and made its competition debut at the Vauxhall Rally of Wales one month later.

Recent developments in RML's history are the alliances with Mallock Sports and Saleen Inc. RML has taken over the role of designing, building and developing the Mallock cars. The RML Mallock P20 supersports driven by Chris Ward in 1999 won the British Supersports Championship. The P21 was driven by Michael Mallock in the same championship in 2000. RML and Saleen are working together to develop cars for use on both the road and race track. Working on road and race cars from a clean sheet is a new challenge and will showcase RML's automotive engineering skills.

In all this time, RML has grown from a small family company of three people to an organisation currently employing over a hundred. Growth has been steady, and this, allied to the need for confidentiality and security between projects, led to expansion in 1998 into a second unit at its Wellingborough site to create a total facility of 40,000 square feet.

RML has focused on three core activities in the development of competition-ready sports and saloon cars. The first is design, where a team of specialised designers works to ensure that weight is kept to a minimum and performance to a maximum. The second is the building or fabrication of the cars. RML has the facilities to construct tubular chassis, and to buy in composite components when these are needed. The third is the actual racing of the cars. RML has built up a wealth of experience in setting up and developing race tactics. The company has been successful because of the way it has integrated these three areas of activity and applied them across a range of touring car, rally and supersports endurance series. It's a highly competitive area of the motorsports sector where companies win bespoke contracts to run race teams for major manufacturers. This makes it an 'all or nothing' situation with bids having to be made to ensure future stability of turnover.

Another reason for RML's success has been the way it has focused on maintaining high performance and high reliability. It's really about attention to detail. Everyone in the team concentrates on continuous improvement, not only in the way they develop the car but also in terms of the structure and processes of RML as a company. RML makes sure its people have the skills to do the job they are assigned to. Much of its key knowledge lies in the area of engineering design. The challenge is making sure that the designers are focusing on practical outcomes that will produce race-winning cars rather than the most innovative design. The better engineers tend to be those who have run their own racing cars because they will focus on designing solutions that will work; it's no good designing a component that will provide that nth extra degree of performance if it takes the mechanic another twenty minutes to put the thing on the car. It is knowledge of the whole picture that really counts at RML.

Lola is another Motorsport Valley company that has always been at the forefront of the worldwide motorsport industry. Established in 1957 by quantity surveyor Eric Broadley, Lola is Britain's longest-serving manufacturer of racing cars. After an extraordinary rise to prominence during which it mastered all spheres of the sport from humble club classes to Formula One, endurance sports racers to IndyCars, its enviable position was consolidated under the ownership of Martin Birrane from 1997, when advanced technologies were introduced to keep its products winning in the twenty-first century. Lola's roll of honour includes points scored in the Formula One World Championship from the marque's debut season in 1962 until 1997, no fewer than six IndyCar World Series titles, three Indianapolis 500 wins, three US Formula 5000 titles, victory in the 1963 Monaco Formula Junior Grand Prix, the inaugural Can-Am Challenge series of 1966, the 1969 Daytona 24 Hours, the 1973 European two-litre Sportscar Championship, five successive Can-Am titles, eight Japanese Formula 3000 crowns, numerous FIA International F3000 Championships and three sports car championships in 2001 alone. Additionally, Lolas have carried amateur and professional competitors to countless championship and race victories on every major continent.

The roots of this remarkable story were put down when Broadley built the 1172cc Ford-engined 'Broadley Special' and raced it with his cousin Graham. It was the first sports car of any engine capacity to lap Brands Hatch's club circuit in less than one minute. A year later, Eric formed Lola Cars Limited and designed and built the very first Lola. Thirty-five of the Mark 1 1100cc sports racers were built at business partner Rob Rushbrook's garage in Bromley, south London. Within five years of its establishment, Lola really started to flourish when Reg Parnell commissioned a Formula One design for his Bowmaker Finance-backed team in 1962. The Mk 4 cars were raced initially by John Surtees and Roy Salvadori. Buoyed by qualifying on pole position for the Dutch Grand Prix at Zandvoort and victory in the non-championship International 2000 Guineas race at Mallory Park, Surtees finished second in the British and German Grands Prix and fourth in the 1962 World Championship.

This considerable on-track achievement was followed by a partnership with the Ford Motor Company, which resulted in the production of the legendary GT40. A descendant of the Ford V8-powered Lola Mk 6 GT, which took Lola to Le Mans for the first time in 1963 (the car was driven there on the road from Lola's new factory in Bromley), the GT40 series dominated sports car racing until the end of the decade, winning the French 24-hour classic from 1966 to 1969 inclusive.

During the mid-1960s, Broadley's latest sports car thinking resulted in the legendary T70 series of brawny V8-engined machines which first emerged in 1965 and immediately set the pace at home and overseas. Armed with an open Mk 2 Spyder version, John Surtees won the first Can-Am Challenge in 1966, while Roger Penske's Mk 3B (the closed coupé version), driven by Mark Donohue and Chuck Parsons, won the 1969 Daytona 24 Hours, proving the design's reliability. Many other Lolas had made their mark in the US during the 1960s. The company's first IndyCar for USAC championship racing was the T80, and its successor, the T90, won the 1966 Indianapolis 500 race with 1962 Formula One world champion Graham Hill at the wheel. Lola's first 'big-banger' Formula 5000-Formula A single-seater, its suspension derived from the T70 sports car, entered the fray in 1968.

Lola moved to its current Huntingdon base at the end of 1970, and Formula 5000 continued to be a speciality. Following Australian Frank Gardner's development work with the Formula Two-based T300 prototype in 1971, Lola's T330 set new standards of design in 1972. T332 evolutions of the car, entered by US Lola importer Carl Haas, won a hat trick of SCCA/USAC titles from 1974 to 1976 in the brilliant hands of Briton Brian Redman. Bob Evans also won the Rothmans European title in 1972 in a T332. Lola had also set new parameters of excellence in the new two-litre class in sports car racing, the open-monocoque chassised T210 having taken northern rival Derek Bennett's Chevron, which was still using spaceframe coupés, by surprise in 1970. European agent Jo Bonnier, a Swiss-based Swedish veteran, won the drivers' title. Austrian Helmut Marko won it in 1971 with its successor, the T212, helping Lola to the manufacturers' crown.

The ultrasuccessful Lola T290 family of cars (and the three-litre T280 series, powered by Formula One Cosworth DFV engines) are hallowed as classics of production racing-car design. Rightly so, too, since Broadley and Bob Marston were joined on the design team by youngsters Patrick Head and John Barnard, whose genius went on to embrace Formula One and IndyCar racing, and continues to leave an indelible mark on motorsport.

In 1974, after a hiatus of some six years, Lola re-entered Formula One with its T370, commissioned by Graham Hill's Embassy-Hill team and driven by the double world champion himself, along with Guy Edwards and Rolf Stommelen. A year later, in 1975, Lola celebrated the production of its 1,000th car.

The company had, since the T200 model took it into the booming Formula Ford 1600 market in 1970, consistently supported the aspiring professional racer. Lola was also ready for the FF2000 wings and slicks category (for cars powered by Ford's two-litre Pinto engine) which followed. Drawing on its two-litre sports car experience, Lola dominated the new Sports 2000 Series from the outset in 1977.

The next major international landmark in Lola's history was achieved in 1978, when Al Unser won the Indianapolis 500. A year after the company re-entered the USAC fray, Unser became the first driver to win all three 500-mile races (the others being at Pocono and Ontario Motor Speedway) in one season. Appropriately, he drove the T500 model.

The mid-1980s saw Lola enter the new Formula 3000 category from the series' beginnings in 1985, and the Lola-built T86-10 Corvette GTP car won the IMSA's prestigious Miami Grand Prix road race the following year. Lola also built a Formula One car for Gérard Larrousse's fledgling *equipe* which finished runner-up in the 3.5-litre atmospheric class, second to the big-league teams with their 1.5-litre turbocars.

Towards the end of the 1980s Lola made a move into Japan by exporting its T87-50 F3000 car. Kazuyoshi Hoshino won the Japanese Formula Championship straight off, and Lola drivers backed this up by winning the title in 1989, 1990, 1991, 1992, 1993, 1995 and 1997. Lola was also commissioned by Nissan International Motorsport to design and manufacture a Group C1 sports car chassis which won the IMSA Championship between 1987 and 1989. Lola victories continued thick and fast into the 1990s: in Japan, Mauro Martini won the 1992 sports car title with Nova Engineering, and there were three successive European Formula 3000 Championships. In 1990, expatriate Dutchman Arie Luyendyk won the Indianapolis 500 race in a T90-00, and Mark Blundell set the new lap record at Le Mans in a Lola-built Nissan. These cars also recorded back-to-back IMSA Championship wins in 1990 and 1991. These were golden IndyCar years, too: Michael Andretti (Newman-Haas Racing) and Bobby Rahal (Rahal-Hogan) won CART's IndyCar Championship, and in 1993 Nigel Mansell won it for Lola and the Newman-Haas team. The following season Lola took a clean sweep of all four formulas entered (IndyCar, Indy Lights, FIA F3000 and F3000 Japan). Subsequently, Lola was rewarded with the contract to supply spec cars for the entire one-make FIA International F3000 series.

In its final years under Eric Broadley's stewardship, Lola won all four single-seater formulas, but its re-entry into Formula One proved ill-starred and Martin Birrane purchased the company in 1997. Birrane's enthusiasm for the marque dates back to his being an owner and entrant of the T292, in which Chris Craft won the 1973 European two-litre sports car series; he also owns and drives a classic collection of various Lola models with which he competes in historic race series. With major investment in leading-edge technology, facilities and the finest talents in the automotive industry, Lola's core business evolved under Birrane to provide a complete turnkey package. The design, engineering and manufacturing skills of Lola's workforce, which now exceeds 220 people, have assisted the company in achieving its success and have helped Lola gain international recognition as a global market leader.

Lola's operations lie within six main areas. Through its Automotive Design Consultancy, the company sells creative engineering solutions in the key areas of aerodynamics, transmission design and manufacture, vehicle dynamics, and suspension design. Lola can also manufacture composite components in-house, and its integrated operation allows it to have full control over quality and to be flexible in terms of meeting tight deadlines. Lola's composite expertise has also enabled the company to develop new customer opportunities in both the aerospace and leisure industries. With its 50 per cent moving-ground wind tunnel, Lola can offer in addition full aerodynamic testing facilities. The wind tunnel was designed to ensure that the flow quality gave a true representation of data that could be gathered under circuit conditions. Lola's Full Car Testing Facility operates in conjunction with its wind tunnel by taking data from test sessions and reproducing the suspension and aerodynamics on a seven-post dynamic testing rig. The company also has transmission engineering facilities where it uses a series of resources to produce 'right first time' engineering solutions through a process of analysis and iteration at all design stages and rigorous monitoring systems during the production of the item.

Lola has recently been branching out into new markets and introducing new product and service ranges in an attempt to establish a much wider customer base, and to back this up with strong support. Through its Xtreme Sports Technology – Lola XST – Lola now designs and produces products for waterborne sports and other extreme sports markets. The company is also supporting the British Bobsleigh Association (BBA) as part of a five-year development programme. The British national squad will benefit from using Lola's state-of-the-art facilities and resources, and Lola is developing a range of new two- and four-man bobs over the next two years in the run-up to the 2006 Winter Olympics in Turin. The company is also working on a series of Xtreme racing boats – from single skulls to pairs, fours and eights, all high-quality lightweight structures – and supplying parts for the Windjet project, a British challenge aimed at shattering the wind-powered speed records on land, ice and water.

Not only does Lola supply a product to its customers, but in order to maximise the full potential of the car a wealth of information including aerodynamic data, mechanical set-ups and technical details is made available. Lola's engineers are present at every test and race to advise on set-ups, solve problems and conduct performance-enhancing development work. At Lola, innovation is not something that occurs every now and then, it is a routine embedded in everything the company does. The basic requirement to produce competitive racing cars for demanding customers means that the company can never stand still – there is no need for any incentive. Often, the real challenge once a design has been produced is ensuring that it is continually developed to become more and more competitive. The company knows it can react very quickly, so that within weeks or even days it can come up with enhancements. Its customers don't necessarily expect to have the fastest car at the first race year on year, but they do value the company's ability as a team to react swiftly and develop the car during the season.

Lola, too, has introduced new technologies such as CAD systems and manufacturing resource planning (MRP) to ensure that everyone stays involved and aware of what's going on. Composite manufacture, suspension development and gearbox design all play key roles in Lola's operation, but aerodynamics take centre stage. It is enhancements in the aerodynamic properties of the car that can yield the greatest benefit, and it is for this reason that Lola has invested so heavily in aerodynamic testing facilities.

In 2002, Lola announced a partnership with Dome Cars to build a Formula Three car as well as an agreement with Japanese Race Promotions to supply the new generation of Formula Nippon chassis to the series that has, in the past, nurtured the driving talents of Mika Salo, Eddie Irvine, Ralf Schumacher and Heinz-Harald Frentzen. The 2003 formula runs on Honda Mugen engines, Bridgestone slick tyres and advanced wing and suspension packages. The move into Formula Nippon marks a return to Japan for Lola, the company having enjoyed great success there during the 1980s and early 1990s, before Lola then refocused on the US ChampCar Series. Recognising the successful contribution Lola had made to the export market during the previous twelve months, in 2003 the Motorsport Industry Association bestowed upon Lola its Export Achievement award. MIA praised the effectiveness of Lola's ongoing business with the ChampCar, F3000 and sports car categories, but it was the renewed strength of the company's relationship with the Japanese market that swayed the members of the judging panel.

The Motor Industry Research Association (MIRA) is another integral part of the network of performance engineering organisations which make up Motorsport Valley. MIRA was established after the Second World War to provide the British motor industry with a state-of-the-art research and development facility, and now employs over 500 staff, 350 of whom are qualified scientists and engineers, across three sites: two in Nuneaton, Warwickshire, and the European Test Operations centre in Basildon, Essex. The main site covers over 700 acres and boasts more than 50 miles of test track and some 30 laboratories. MIRA receives no grant funding and operates as a commercial company, its customers, be they from Formula One or Formula Three, multinational companies, government or privateers, paying for services.

Like many of the historic race circuits in the UK, MIRA benefited from being located on the site of a former airfield – in this case, RAF Lindley. This provided the basis of MIRA's extensive Proving Ground facilities and allowed the organisation plenty of space in which to expand as new facilities were added over the years. Today, MIRA's activities cover a wide range of transport-related engineering services and research and development, but its motorsport activities have always been a core area of its work embracing all types of technology that have an impact on transportation: body and safety engineering, calibration, computer-aided engineering, dynamics and refinement, electrical and fluids technology, systems integration, ride and handling, test facility engineering and vehicle engineering and powertrain.

Two of its business areas in particular actively benefit from the Motorsport Valley phenomenon: the Fluids Group, which includes aerodynamics, thermofluids and powertrain; and the Proving Ground, which provides a wide variety of track and road conditions for testing and development. Within the Fluids Group, the key area for motorsport is aerodynamics; as most of the motorsport companies are relatively specialised there is very little work in the area of powertrain, and only a certain amount of work within the domain of thermofluids, with rally cars and cooling systems for Formula One teams. MIRA operates the only full-scale aerodynamic wind tunnel in the UK. The real advantage of a full-scale tunnel is that it does not require the construction of scale models; actual cars can be evaluated *in situ*, anything from Formula One and Formula Three to hill climbers and dragsters. Still, despite its being the largest facility in the UK, it appeals in the main far more to the grass-roots competitor than the top Formula One teams, most of whom have their own wind tunnels, although they do use MIRA's facility to check their figures. Although the facility is forty years old and was the first dedicated automotive wind tunnel in Europe, it is still highly popular within the motorsport sector. It is far more cost-effective to do all your tweaking and testing in the wind tunnel and work out exactly what you've got rather than rely on subjective feel on the track.

As well as hiring out its wind tunnels, MIRA has a great deal of expertise in how these principles can be used to enhance racing-car performance. Recently, MIRA aerodynamicists were sent a car that was going to compete in a South American race series. The group was sent a copy of the rule book and given four months to come up with the optimum design within the rules.

As well as aerodynamics testing, the team has developed expertise in the application of computational fluid dynamics, or CFD – basically a computational equivalent of a wind tunnel where designs can be evaluated in terms of internal (in the engine compartment of a saloon car, for example) or external air flows. However, MIRA sees CFD only as a complementary tool rather than a substitute for the wind tunnel. In a recent project, the MIRA team started with considerable CFD work to evaluate a number of different options, which were then narrowed down to two styles of design. Two models were then built and tested in the wind tunnel. This procedure saved a great deal of time, and it also meant that the team was able to make more detailed comparisons as the design progressed.

MIRA has no single direct competitor in terms of an organisation that can offer such a wide range of facilities and expertise, but each area of activity does have significant levels of competition to deal with. The DMW wind tunnel in Holland, for example, can test full-sized planes, a German facility at Stuttgart University is used heavily by Mercedes, and there is also the Pininfarina facility in Turin, Italy. In the UK, there are some fifteen or more model-scale facilities, most of them in universities such as Cranfield, Imperial and Southampton. Even the Jordan Grand Prix team has constructed its own facility and is going against the Formula One trend and hiring it out when it isn't needed for Formula One development. Furthermore, MIRA's design engineering services also put it in direct competition with many of the racing-car design houses and related consultancies.

MIRA's customers range from multinational automotive manufacturers through governments to local motorsport clubs. All are important constituents of MIRA's customer base. It offers club days in the wind tunnels where groups of people can come in and bring their cars, do a bit of work on them and learn from it. One customer with a multi-wing hill-climb car had been racing for many years, gradually shaving off hundredths of a second. He brought his car to MIRA for half a day and the very simple modifications that were recommended resulted in his taking over a second off his best time. MIRA's Proving Ground customers are limited to closed-wheel vehicles due to the problems of noise pollution and other local environmental issues, but despite this constraint there is no shortage of motorsport interest ranging from GT and NASCAR through to World Rally cars, which actually make the most use of the facilities at MIRA.

MIRA attributes a lot of its success to its location in Motorsport Valley and to being part of a highly specialised network of performance engineering companies. As is the case with all companies in the area, innovation is something that occurs naturally at MIRA. Many of those working there are driven by the desire to experiment and try out new ideas which can improve the way a car performs on the track, and MIRA offers great flexibility. For example, a customer could undertake some wind-tunnel testing in the full-scale tunnel and then evaluate some of the changes on the Proving Ground. All of MIRA's specialised areas of knowledge are integrated by a common understanding of the purpose of the organisation. The association's unique core competence is not in any one knowledge sector; it revels in its ability to bring together highly technical aspects of automotive know-how to meet clear objectives. In the case of motorsport, the final objective is to consistently win races.

This is the secret that makes such a cluster successful – knowledge. It is widely recognised that the generation and dissemination of knowledge have been critical in maintaining Motorsport Valley's dominance. According to Cranfield's Dr Mark Jenkins, who has studied the valley extensively and carried out considerable research into knowledge clusters, the motorsport industry is one of a number of technology clusters that create a unique and geographically defined area of capability without equal anywhere else in the world. 'Clusters are important because they present a paradox,' he explained. 'On the one hand, in advancing technologies in microcomputing, software code and biotechnology they represent the essence of the modern knowledge-driven economy. Technology clusters are changing the way we all live our lives. However, they are also a vivid reminder that for all our wonderful "e"-technologies and instant global communication, often the most valuable knowledge does not travel at all well; that in order to stay in the game with a particular technology you have no option but to locate in a very specific geographical area.'

What is a technology cluster? Strategy guru Michael Porter defined clusters as 'geographical concentrations of interconnected companies, specialised suppliers, service providers, firms in related industries and associated institutions in particular fields that compete but also co-operate'. But why is it so important for companies to recognise such a phenomenon in their strategies? 'Using the example of Motorsport Valley,' Dr Jenkins continued, 'I suggest a more general framework for considering the potency of the cluster as a shared knowledge architecture, rooted in a particular locality. One of the real paradoxes of the globalisation which permeates the corporate mind these days is that on the one hand it encourages managers to think of universal strategies and global core competencies, yet on the other it raises the need for increasingly fine-grained views of customers and markets, and also of a more sophisticated understanding of the capability and knowledge needed to serve these markets with competitive superiority. Globalisation does not mean that all wealth-creating activities are spread universally across the world, and in fact we are now witnessing a greater specialisation of expertise in particular regions. The development of the technology cluster is one such example of how, in order to sustain innovation and technological development, firms have to locate within particular regions of the world.' A technology cluster, therefore, is not a statement of national capability; it refers to a very specific micro-region that is able to create economic value in excess of that available elsewhere.

'Technology clusters can be created by many events, including chance and the interventions of governments,' Dr Jenkins said. 'Chance can relate to radical inventions, to events that may affect demand or cost structures, and to political decisions and wars. All of these played a critical part in the development of the motorsport cluster in the UK.' Before the Second World War, the motorsport industry was dominated by two other clusters: one in the Stuttgart area of Germany, which included the Mercedes racing car factory; and one surrounding Modena and Milan in northern Italy, which included Alfa Romeo and Maserati. Significant government resources had supported both these clusters in order to bolster national pride through motor racing. After the war, however, the Allies placed heavy restrictions on the development of German and Italian infrastructure, and in particular their ability to develop aerospace industry. By contrast, Britain was left with a network of airfields that became the venues for local racing by privateers. 'This in turn created a culture of invention and private entrepreneurship that used basic car components to create highly agile and fast race cars using aerospace technology,' Dr Jenkins explained.

Governments can also promote industrial advantage with heavy-handed policies, and there are many examples of this leading to the development of particular capabilities in countries such as Japan and Korea. 'However,' Dr Jenkins pointed out, 'in the case of Motorsport

Valley it is the absence of regulation and intervention rather than the excess of it which explains the development of the cluster. A period of "benign neglect" has allowed the motorsport cluster to flourish and develop in a way which is based on informal networks and tacit knowledge rather than highly formalised processes and bureaucracy. Indeed, a lack of regulation and intervention can be seen as a policy in itself, and in this case it has helped in the development of a global centre of excellence.'

But Dr Jenkins added that to capture the value of a technology cluster it is not simply a case of locating a facility in a particular region. 'It is certainly true that building a library on a university campus does not guarantee that the students will ever use it, and it is a similar problem for firms wishing to tap into the value-generating capability of the cluster. The point is that the cluster is not simply a geographical region, it is a system of knowledge which is supported by both infrastructure and facilities and the know-how of those working within it.' For example, within the valley there is a network of moving-ground wind tunnels. These facilities have been operated largely by universities, although now firms themselves are both building their own facilities and recruiting from the network the expertise to operate them. 'But knowledge of aerodynamics is only one domain that exists within Motorsport Valley,' Dr Jenkins continued. 'Aerodynamic knowledge is not confined to any single global location, but the way in which aerodynamics is combined with other domains such as materials, computational techniques, model construction, fabrication, and so on, is the basis of the unique value of Motorsport Valley. The integration of differing areas of knowledge can be referred to as knowledge architecture, and it is this architecture that forms the basis of the technology cluster rather than any one specific kind of knowledge.'

Jenkins further pointed out that if we view the cluster as knowledge architecture then firms have to access the architecture rather than the locality. This raises a further point concerning the extent to which firms can both access and transfer knowledge. For example, new technologies such as CFD, which allows the airflow around a car to be simulated by a computer, may eventually replace wind tunnels and could therefore be far less geographically restrained, enabling the cluster to appear more like a global network than a specific region. Global automotive firms such as Ford and Honda have specifically focused on using knowledge created in motorsport to improve their development programmes for mainstream automotive products, and have seconded engineers and designers into motorsport activities within Motorsport Valley. 'All of this requires an engagement in the knowledge architecture,' Dr Jenkins maintained. 'This is knowledge which is embedded in tacit routines and the evolving practices of those working within the cluster. By finding ways to access this embedded architecture firms will be able to capture some of the value-creating processes that exist within technology clusters. However, while much is known on mechanisms for knowledge transfer at the level of data and information, we are only just beginning to recognise the value of both understanding and developing architectural knowledge.'

So, will knowledge remain in these localised pockets? Dr Jenkins' view is that it won't. 'Knowledge is a very dynamic entity and will continue to develop. Technology clusters will grow and die, but also they replicate in the way that a spider-plant replicates – by sending out a shoot which, once it finds a stable platform, grows another spider-plant. In Motorsport Valley we see firms such as Pi Technologies and Lola setting up facilities in regions of the US such as Indianopolis and Charlotte, Virginia. These pockets become offspring of Motorsport Valley which develop their own unique characteristics. For firms to stay ahead in the technology game you not only have to understand the knowledge architecture, you also have to be one step ahead of the spider-plants as they grow and evolve in different regions of the world.'

Another key issue Jenkins and his team at Cranfield identified from their own research, and that done for the MIA, was the ease with which organisations in Motorsport Valley can access a 'pool of talent'. 'There are so many talented, motivated and highly experienced and qualified employees working in the motorsport cluster that the organisations can choose someone with almost the exact skills they require. This provides the basis for the highly specialised capabilities they need to sustain in order to maintain their position in this highly competitive sector. Knowledge is often a form of shared learning across the industry as similarly trained employees usually understand the basic concepts from similar perspectives. Knowledge can become learned across the organisations and can contribute to the pool of talent because of multiple interdependencies.'

The talent of the employees was clearly shown when Ferrari relocated the design and production of its Formula One chassis from a town in northern Italy to the small village of Shalford in Surrey. The reason for this move was that Ferrari needed to access what it perceived to be the highest calibre of engineering design and expert knowledge on the subject. 'Ferrari believed that this was John Barnard,' said Dr Jenkins. 'He was established with a support team of skilled individuals as B3

Technologies [see Chapter 11]. Barnard then developed B3 Technologies as his own organisation. He has a reputation throughout the industry as one of the top designers, which has meant that many teams have accessed B3 Technologies' skills and capabilities.'

Alongside this obviously important skill base and expert knowledge, Jenkins also cited T.L. Clowes, an insurance outfit that attempts to recruit people who have an interest specifically in motorsport. 'This is because it feels those employees have more enthusiasm for and knowledge of the industry, coupled with higher levels of motivation. The skills base at T.L. Clowes is also strong, as the enthusiasm for the industry and motorsport in general develops as embedded knowledge. Some of the employees have worked for the organisation since 1985, which shows the breadth and depth of knowledge and experience available.'

Knowledge is not the sole driving factor behind the evolution of Motorsport Valley, of course. 'The technical knowledge on which the motorsport industry heavily depends has had to be balanced with commercial knowledge to ensure that the firms are run effectively and sustainably,' said Dr Jenkins. 'You need a balance of people that appreciate the sport, but who are business people first.' A hybrid knowledge comprising the very specific and relatively rare technical knowledge and the more general and relatively common commercial knowledge remains rare, but where it does exist it can be a significant advantage.

A further factor is the inherent assumption that change and innovation are ongoing requirements rather than ad hoc events. While in more mainstream firms creating the motivation to innovate is currently seen as a strategic imperative, in motorsport it is not only taken for granted, it is seen to be the reason for the whole process. 'There appears to be little need for incentives and structures around innovation,' Dr Jenkins observed. 'It just happens as everyone is striving to improve performance. The tension is more about channelling innovation into the most effective areas and ensuring that the innovative process creates practical outcomes. The desire to enhance performance through creative engineering, employing whatever fix will work and remain within the rules, is the essence of technical expertise in this area. Here the challenge lies in channelling and trading off innovations. As with the balance of technical and commercial skills, this is a particularly rare knowledge and one which is embedded in the more successful motorsport organisations. It therefore appears that the distinctive and enduring aspect of firms within knowledge clusters such as Motorsport Valley is not that they hold the greatest depth of knowledge regarding the particular disciplines needed to create success, but that they are able to integrate such knowledge, both in terms of combining it with other domains and by channelling the knowledge in effective ways.'

The loss of knowledgeable staff is clearly a cost of being active in the cluster, but one which is assumed to come with the territory. Dr Jenkins noted that the key investment these valley firms see themselves as undertaking is the way in which they provide a very specific on-the-job training. 'This experience allows individuals to apply knowledge more effectively, and it also helps to build their experience in a very specialised area, therefore making them more marketable. What is clear is that the very factors which attract individuals to one company are also those which lead them to leave, through a desire to become more experienced in the industry and to become knowledgeable in the way different firms operate. At this level it becomes an accepted way of operating, and one that firms within the cluster have to grudgingly accept.' Within the motorsport industry information tends to move freely. Direct and indirect knowledge is obtained through formal and informal interactions with suppliers and contacts who are often approached personally regarding certain queries, and sometimes poached. But if this 'firm level' knowledge is sustained, the ebb and flow of particular individuals are less critical to the organisation's success. 'This kind of knowledge can be described as architectural knowledge which both sustains and positions the individual knowledge needed to support the ongoing success of the knowledge-based firm in a knowledge-based cluster,' said Dr Jenkins. 'While architectural knowledge in isolation is insufficient, it provides a framework which allows the organisation to both capture and leverage individual knowledge.'

Creating and sustaining motorsport knowledge is exactly what AutoTechnium is all about.

In Wales, the automotive industry is represented by 200 companies employing over 25,000 people and generating £2 billion of sales every year. Technium, a revolutionary concept, aims to strengthen Wales' research and development facilities. New and existing companies are being provided with excellent support, state-of-the-art equipment and unparalleled access to academic expertise. 'We are planning to have twenty or so of these Technium facilities throughout Wales,' said chief executive Steve Davies. 'They will be places where we will have like-minded companies developing products and processes.'

Several of the Technium projects are sector specific. The £10 million AutoTechnium project, to be built at Llanelli Gate by spring 2004, will play an important role in the future of the Welsh automotive industry. Its primary aim will be to provide a research and development facility for businesses specialising in performance engineering which will enable them to embrace design, development and testing at a world-class level. Its development facilities will concentrate on industry-specific research and development and be supported by experts from the University of Wales at Swansea, the Swansea Institute of Higher Education and a number of industrial partners. It will supply highly qualified development engineers together with leading-edge computational facilities for the design, simulation, analysis and virtual prototyping of automotive component systems and subsystems. 'This resource,' Davies confirmed, 'aims to support companies in the automotive supply chain, particularly SMEs [small- to medium-sized enterprises], in product design and development. In addition, on-site business advice will be supplied via the Technium regional network.'

Swansea University has an international reputation in the field of computational engineering. In 1997, the university's researchers played a vital role in the success of the Thrust supersonic car, which smashed its own world land speed record in Nevada and broke the sound barrier at 763mph. Professor Nigel Weatherill, Professor Ken Morgan and Dr Oubay Hassan were responsible for modelling the effects of the airflow over Thrust and advising the project's design team about aerodynamic changes that would have to be made to the vehicle. The university's civil engineering department is well known for its particular expertise in the simulation of compressible airflow over aeroplanes using finite element analysis, a technique now familiar to Formula One that involves substituting several complex mathematical equations with millions of simpler ones, which can then be solved by running them through a supercomputer. The group has also worked with British Aerospace, Rolls-Royce, the Defence Evaluation and Research Agency (DERA), Dassault, Aerospatiale, McDonnell-Douglas and NASA, among others, on projects ranging from airliners to spacecraft. For NASA, the group simulated the separation of the Space Shuttle from its booster rockets.

Professor Weatherill explained that Thrust SSC project leader Richard Noble contacted the group to ask if it could apply its computer-modelling techniques to help with the design of the car. Following that, Professor Weatherill and his colleagues worked closely with Thrust SSC's aerodynamicist, Ron Ayers. 'Ron gave us drawings for an initial geometrical shape for the car and we formed them into a computer model. From that, we could model the geometry, generate a grid and simulate the airflow over the car,' said Professor Weatherill. Problems began to arise when the ground effects generated by Thrust became apparent during the simulations. 'In the transonic region, just before the vehicle goes supersonic, shockwaves are created that bounce back from the ground on to the car, which doesn't normally happen in aerospace projects. This was a problem that was particularly challenging. The transonic problems start at about 600mph. Because of the shockwaves you start to see different aerodynamic characteristics come into play. Then, as you get closer and closer to the speed of sound, the car actually catches up with the disturbances in the air that it's creating. Right at the nose of the car a bow-shock forms, which completely engulfs the car, and the drag increases.' As the car forces itself along, the air in front of it cannot move out of the way quickly enough and the vehicle ploughs through the increasing disturbances it has created causing a sonic boom normally associated with high-performance aircraft. There was a real fear that the pressure generated by the shockwaves could cause a devastating accident at such high speeds. 'The shockwaves reflecting off the ground were uppermost in our minds. If they had been incorrectly modelled, out by just a few degrees, the nose could flip up or down.' Professor Weatherill also explained that the team had made an enormous number of calculations. 'We would send data back to Ron, who would go over the figures very carefully. Then he would send back modifications to the geometry of the car. Slowly but surely, over a period of two years, we came up with the shape.'

The Thrust team then made a scale model of the car and ran it at Pendine Sands in South Wales to test the performance and the data. 'There was good agreement between the model's data and our computer predictions,' Professor Weatherill recalled. 'Everyone was very pleased about that.' After that, the process of building Thrust began and the researchers became involved in fine-tuning the final design. When Thrust finally began its record attempts in the desert, the Swansea team was 'quietly confident' that the ten-ton jet car would perform safely and break the sound barrier.

'Such expertise lends itself so much to performance engineering,' Steve Davies said. 'The Welsh Development Agency is also keen to keep the Welsh graduates it trains, and this is so synergistic with what we're trying to do. They train at Swansea, then get a job in AutoTechnium, creating wealth in Wales. That's the bottom line. Historically, Wales has been strong in manufacturing and heavy extracting industries, and the traditional trades. Now we want research and development to be part of our wealth creation. We've moved on. Twenty to thirty years ago we went into low-cost manufacturing, electronic assembly, but this is now moving out to eastern Europe where components can be produced much more cheaply. Wales was a very attractive location for inward investment, with its low labour costs and plenty of facilities and sites, but Wales is now not so competitive because of other eastern European countries such as Czechoslovakia which offer lower labour rates and equally attractive grant packages, so Wales has to move up the value chain. Technium – with its twenty sites, and its twenty or so knowledge-based, high-growth companies involved in research and development – is one of the vehicles we're going to use to achieve that. A job in a Technium facility is not going to be paying the same as one in a call centre, so they're going to be generating wealth. Formula One and rallying are leading-edge industries capable of bringing huge investment and creating a significant research and development base here. Any of these two will take these innovations because it makes them more competitive.'

AutoTechnium will work with a satellite operation at Pembrey racing circuit. There will be an efficient communication connection between the two sites to maximise the testing facilities at Pembrey and the training, research and development incubator facilities at Llanelli Gate. 'Lots of independent companies are looking to develop products or processes with the automotive sector,' Davies added. 'Because we'll have these close links with the Pembrey facility, we've been talking to a number of companies in the Formula One community, as well as those who support its infrastructure. There will be a broadband satellite link between Pembrey and AutoTechnium, so telemetry and testing can be done on the track and transferred. To be able to do all this in real time, on site, is a very attractive thing, and work done locally will save time and money.'

Llanelli Gate comprises a 7.4-hectare (eighteen-acre) secure fenced site. The main AutoTechnium building will occupy 2,200 square metres and provide eighteen incubator units for specialised SMEs, several meeting rooms, and a conference and boardroom facility. The site will also offer additional development land and serviced sites for self-build projects and further phases. The operation at Pembrey will include a 300-square-metre satellite office together with development land. The British Automobile Racing Club (BARC) will be extending the current motor racing track from 1.456 miles to 2.35 miles to create an international-standard circuit capable of supporting a calendar of motorsport events. A new pit-lane complex, kart track and bridge linking the inner and outer perimeter of the circuit will create a world-class facility. 'Pembrey's a circuit that has always been used for testing and development work,' said BARC's Dennis Carter. 'The idea came to try and formalise that more, and actually create a base where you didn't have to test here and then maybe go two hundred miles away and put it all back on computer; you could do everything close by. The idea really grew out of this, but developed even further and encompassed the whole of the automotive industry, not just the sporting side. I suspect it will make us even busier. We're busy now with people testing components and cars.'

'I see AutoTechnium as the key to providing a large part of the Welsh automotive sector, and the wider British automotive sector, with the sort of research and development back-up it requires,' said Professor Garell Rhys, director of the Centre for Automotive Industry Research at Cardiff Business School. 'What you need to do is to transfer more research and development into Wales, into the UK. This then becomes anchorage, for those facilities, those companies, become absolutely vital to the wellbeing of their customers.'

By collaborating with businesses to enhance their design and development capabilities, AutoTechnium will stimulate new business in the automotive and related sectors throughout Wales. 'We're developing new technologies, new componentry,' said Dave Pallas, managing director of system component designer and manufacturer Calsonic. 'We're always finding it difficult to find local suppliers who can take on board some of the manufacture and the design of some of these components, so we're hoping with AutoTechnium support that we can have some of the local suppliers developing and designing many of the products that supply us in the future.' Companies involved in motorsport need good support in research and development, and links with universities and their centres of excellence, as well as access to high levels of IT. AutoTechnium's team of development engineers will work with new and existing companies to develop, test and refine new products and processes, allowing them to use state-of-the art facilities such as computational modelling and design. 'Industry will benefit from the technology side of AutoTechnium, its facilities and the skill base,' Pallas added. 'But on the other hand, the academic side can learn from the needs of the business industry, particularly the fast-changing environment the automotive sector works in.'

The complex will ultimately provide up to a hundred highly skilled jobs in what will be a new centre of excellence in performance engineering in the automotive industry. 'The AutoTechnium project, as it succeeds, will require more and more skilled people to support and underpin its growth, therefore graduate employment is going to be a crucial aspect of this strategy,' observed Professor Rhys. 'The biggest scarce resource worldwide is human capital. If you can show yourself, in a sense, to be training that human capital, that really strikes a chord with the worldwide automotive sector.'

Those in the business are certainly enthused. According to vice-president of global product development and chief technical officer of the Ford Motor Company Richard Parry-Jones, the initiative is of great interest to Ford on two levels. 'First of all, there's the impact on improving the competence and the competitiveness of the supply base that's based here in Wales, upon which we in turn depend for our competitiveness. Second, it's important because of the motorsports connection, because again it will improve the competitiveness of the resources we can access to make our competition vehicles more successful.' Trevor Carling of Carling Motorsports agreed. 'It's quite an exciting project,' he said, 'a good way of bringing the institutes and universities together with mainstream industry, and the facilities they're planning to put in there would be very useful to a team such as ours which is always looking for an unfair advantage in motor racing.'

3. MCLAREN (WOKING)

'Although, like the other teams, we do try to create a technical differentiation in our product – a faster car – we are constantly looking at how we can be more innovative, more structured, more disciplined, we're always asking how our technical development process can be superior to that of our competitors.'

Martin Whitmarsh, Managing Director, McLaren Group

TAG McLaren Group chairman and CEO Ron Dennis, with McLaren International's managing director Martin Whitmarsh, oversees one of Formula One's most successful teams. Both men believe that Britain's self-sufficiency in motorsport engineering and technology means it will be many years before another country can threaten its dominance.

The McLaren Formula One team first breathed life in 1963 when New Zealander Bruce McLaren created Bruce McLaren Motor Racing Limited and set to work building a Formula One car. Three years later the team made its debut at the Monaco Grand Prix, and scored its first race win in 1968 when Bruce McLaren drove his McLaren-Ford to victory. Tragically, the New Zealander lost his life at a Can-Am testing accident at the Goodwood circuit in 1970, but the team continued, winning races in Formula One and expanding into Indy and Can-Am racing. In 1974, the team celebrated its first Formula One drivers' and constructors' championship wins with Emerson Fittipaldi in the McLaren-Ford M23. To date, the team has achieved the highest number of one-two finishes of any Formula One driver partnership: team-mates Ayrton Senna and Alain Prost notched up fourteen between them in both the 1988 and 1989 seasons. From that 1988 season to 1992 McLaren won four consecutive drivers' and constructors' championships. In all, the total in 2003 stands at eight constructors' titles and eleven drivers' titles.

Ron Dennis's career in motor racing has been just as impressive. It began in 1966 with the Cooper Racing Company. Two years later he became Sir Jack Brabham's chief mechanic with the Brabham Racing Team. In 1971, Ron launched his own business by forming Rondel Racing to compete in the European Formula Two Championship. Graham Hill and Carlos Reutemann spent three years with him as Rondel drivers. In 1974, a sponsorship agreement with Philip Morris helped set up the Ecuador-Marlboro Formula Two team, but by the close of that season Dennis had formed the Project Three team (project one was Rondel, and two a 1973 association with Motul). The team settled in Woking in 1976, and Project Four was born to compete in the European Formula Two Championship with Eddie Cheever.

In 1979, BMW awarded the team a contract for 25 M1 cars, and Marlboro sponsored the team to run a car driven by Niki Lauda in the Procar Championship, which Lauda won. In 1980, with encouragement from their mutual sponsor Marlboro, Project Four and Team McLaren Limited merged to form McLaren International, with Ron as its head. He was later joined by the then Williams team sponsor, later to become his good friend, Mansour Ojjeh, who funded the TAG (Techniques d'Avant Garde) Porsche turbo engine programme. The TAG McLaren Group, as it later became, grew quickly and built a roadgoing supercar, the McLaren F1, which won Le Mans in 1995. A new McLaren-Mercedes alliance came along in 1995. Mercedes-Benz brought to the association a pedigree well established from over a century of competition. The names of the company's drivers – Rudolf Caracciola, Juan Manuel Fangio and Stirling Moss, as well as the Silver Arrows they drove so successfully – have become legendary.

In 1998, Mika Hakkinen and David Coulthard dominated the Formula One World Championship, with Mika taking the drivers' crown and Team McLaren Mercedes claiming the constructors' title. Mika claimed back-to-back titles by securing the 1999 drivers' championship. In January 2000, Mercedes-Benz's parent company, DaimlerChrysler, acquired a 40 per cent stake in the TAG McLaren Group; Ron Dennis and the TAG Group, which became a major shareholder in 1985, continue to have operational management control, each owning 30 per cent of the group. This followed DaimlerChrysler's and McLaren Cars Limited's joint decision to develop and produce the Mercedes-Benz SLR McLaren sports car.

Dennis is now chairman and chief executive officer of the TAG McLaren Group, which these days is a collection of hi-tech companies that trade on the benefits of the global name and reputation McLaren has established over the years. The group has evolved considerably and now comprises seven businesses that operate in a range of diverse yet related areas: McLaren International (Formula One), McLaren Cars (high-performance road cars), TAG Electronic Systems (automotive electronic systems), TAG McLaren Marketing Services, McLaren Composites (advanced composite structures), Absolute Taste (haute cuisine) and Lydden Circuit (race track). McLaren maintains that the strength of the group lies in this diversity of its constituent companies and the individual contribution they make to the group overall.

Ron Dennis was made a Commander of the Order of the British Empire in 2000, and in 2003 he received a Lifetime Achievement award at the Formula One Awards held in aid of the Brain and Spine Foundation, of which Formula One's medical consultant, Professor Sid Watkins, is a patron (it recognised Ron's 'lengthy contribution to motorsport, during which time he has established one of Formula One's most successful teams'). Although he is a quietly spoken, usually mild-mannered man, he doesn't tolerate those who don't share his almost legendary passion for excellence. This is demonstrated by the sparkling new multi-million-pound communications centre, which has replaced the traditional motorhome and is the envy of the Grand Prix paddock, and by the McLaren Technology Centre, the Lord Norman Foster-designed headquarters for the TAG McLaren Group, undoubtedly Ron's pride and joy, which houses the Formula One team and builds the 200mph Mercedes-Benz SLR McLaren sports car. In short, Ron Dennis works hard to create perfection in everything he does. In fact, he's obsessive about it. He wants to be the best.

The Dennis philosophy also expects McLaren's technology partners to contribute to the team's performance rather than just be corporate sponsors. Formula One is the ultimate proving ground for any technology partnership: if you want to reach the chequered flag first, you need impossibly fast lead times combined with engineering teams and drivers who are constantly pushing the capabilities of new technology to the limit.

You might be surprised to see such a philosophy manifested in a hospitality unit, but the Team McLaren Mercedes Communications Centre has revolutionised the concept of Formula One paddock motorhomes. Communication is an aspect of Formula One in which Team McLaren Mercedes has traditionally worked hard, but it is also an area in which the team is trying to break new ground. In the split-second world of Formula One, communication is everything. Whether it's designers back at base discussing the latest hi-tech developments with the engineers at the track, or whether it's transmitting news of a strong result to the fans, getting the message across in the most effective way is vital.

The centre is a set of eight pods that are transported from race to race by six articulated trucks and erected over the week leading up to a Grand Prix. Made of anodised aluminium and glass, this portable structure amalgamates the team's previous three motorhomes into one big unit. 'The impetus for this stemmed from my thoughts that the original motorhome concept was outdated,' said Dennis. 'The team's partners and guests met, and then retreated to the privacy of their own motorhomes. Our concept was to integrate the partners into more of a team environment. We look on the Communications Centre as a tool to make us perform better, just as we'd look on a new wind tunnel or any other piece of technical equipment.' The project took three months to conceptualise, another six months to design and a further fifteen to build. In the ground-floor office on the left you can see desktop phones and other more sophisticated gizmos supplied by technology partner Siemens Mobile, as well as the latest in imaging and communications from official supplier Canon. This helps the team issue press releases, send and feed back engineering information, and dispatch features and images around the world. The centre's other rooms are full of tiny but important details that focus on functionality. Using small touch screens on each wall, you can pipe in your own choice of channel or video. Ceiling-mounted keypads control the ambient temperature of each room individually. 'This is a proper working environment,' Dennis added, 'whereas the old motorhomes were not as user-friendly. People can walk in here when they arrive in the paddock and just carry on without being interrupted.'

But it's the McLaren Technology Centre, much of it built underground and large enough to hold nine 747 jumbo jets, that best exemplifies McLaren's innovative approach to design and engineering. It is one of Europe's great construction projects. Every aspect of it has been painstakingly designed to reflect the group's commitment to the pursuit of excellence through technological innovation.

A formal lake sits in front of the space-age centre; nearby, a second 'ecology' lake contains reed beds which act as a filtration system for any rainwater that falls on the first lake before it flows back into the nearby river. Developed by Targetti and sitting 25 millimetres under the surface of the lake, a special underwater lighting system illuminates the underside of the curved canopy that overhangs the front of the centre. The overall effect is stunning: the light and shadow fall in such a way as to create the illusion that the roof is not attached to the building, but hovering just above it. Targetti also installed lighting along the edges of the VIP driveway that sweeps around the lake and up to the centre's front entrance. A variation on Targetti's airport runway lights, they are specially designed reflectors that give the impression that a continuous strip of light is outlining the edge of the driveway. When you look at the reflectors from across the lake, they also provide a decorative lighting effect at the water's edge.

Like the team's new motorhome, the centre acts as a showcase for the building's partners. The windblades that support the glass façade provide a striking example of how McLaren's engineers have been able to bring Formula One and aerospace technology into the world of architecture. It was thought that the prototype windblade supports would be too bulky and look too industrial for that all-important first impression, so McLaren, working with systems supplier Schüco and architects Foster & Partners, went back to the drawing board. The final, elegantly streamlined design was actually modelled on the rear-wing support struts of the McLaren F1 road car, and the twelve-metre aluminium windblades were produced by BAe Systems, another of the team's technology partners, using processes similar to those employed on the wing frames for the Airbus commercial jet.

Even the layout of the centre's wash basins, along with the automatic, computer-controlled functioning of the taps, soap dispensers and hot-air blow driers, has been carefully designed. These advanced systems, developed and installed by German water technologists Grohe, mean that as soon as you place your hands under the nondrip soap dispenser and trip its infrared sensor, exactly the right amount of soap is automatically delivered; the taps also dispense precisely the right amount of water you need, and at just the right temperature. The blow drier, instead of being mounted on the wall to one side as you'd expect, has been integrated into the same panel above the basin so that droplets of water do not fall on to the floor as you move across. As part of the building's water management system, hot water for all the washrooms circulates continuously through a central conditioning plant that not only controls the temperature but also passes it through an ultra-violet filter that kills bacteria.

By any standard of measurement, it's a stunning facility that acts as an impressive example of McLaren's attention to detail in its pursuit of functional perfection.

Martin Whitmarsh is Ron Dennis's right-hand man. After graduating in mechanical engineering in 1980, Whitmarsh joined British Aerospace and went to work as a structural analysis engineer at the BAe facility in Hamble-le-Rice, near Southampton, later becoming head of production for the Harrier and Hawk airframes. It was then decided that the factory should become an independent operation, and Aerostructures Hamble Limited was established as a BAe subsidiary, with Whitmarsh as its manufacturing director. Soon after that, however, he was headhunted to join McLaren International as head of operations, a position he held until September 1997 when he was appointed managing director, a move that has allowed Dennis to spend more time developing the TAG McLaren Group.

Although Whitmarsh is a relative newcomer to Formula One, his aviation engineering qualifications, experience and temperament make him a safe pair of hands in the sport's highly pressurised environment. 'Although, like the other teams, we do try to create a technical differentiation in our product – a faster car – we are constantly looking at how we can be more innovative, more structured, more disciplined,' Whitmarsh said. 'We're always asking how our technical development process can be superior to that of our competitors.'

Key to establishing this superiority is people. As one of the larger teams on the Grand Prix circuit, McLaren enjoys a low turnover of staff. Other teams train and develop ever younger engineers, but McLaren's reputation for stability attracts some of the very brightest. 'We're very fortunate,' Whitmarsh continued. 'Not only is F1 seen as an attractive career for young engineers, but McLaren's image of technical excellence, professionalism and strategic planning appeals to the more intelligent, strategically minded young engineers. They are also ambitious, and this pushes the organisation along. It's fantastic for me now to go and sit in some of the development meetings with these engineers, some twenty years younger than me, and be stimulated by their ideas.' However, Whitmarsh also knows that successful racing teams must maintain a balance between the theorists and the racers. 'The racers are engineers who address any issue that will make the car run quicker at the next race and hopefully help us win it. If an idea doesn't work in the rain then we're wasting our time thinking about long-term research and development programmes. On the other hand, if you let the racers predominantly determine all your thinking, then you don't develop the underlying technical wealth of the company. You've also got to have people focused on research, maybe several years or so out. If you don't, then you won't have a continuous stream of improvements.'

The team carries out a critical analysis of how it has performed after every race. 'We look at why we didn't win it, or if we did, why we couldn't have won it more easily. Inevitably you're faced with a list of things that need to be tackled, such as reliability, during all of the practice sessions as well as the race. These include what didn't stop the car but could have stopped it had the mechanics not found the problem.' This approach to solving problems has evolved as McLaren has grown and matured. Certainly ten years ago McLaren, like other teams, was a group of focused generalists, each of whom carried a broad range of skills that could be brought to bear on various parts of the car. 'However, the depth of study and the complexity of the tasks were increasing,' explained Whitmarsh. 'We were starting to employ materials scientists, structural dynamics experts, all the specialists, and arranging them functionally – working on vehicle design, aerodynamics, research, and control systems. From this, we were able to get a greater depth of expertise, and to manage some of our longer-term development programmes before some of our competitors.'

During the 2002 season McLaren went through its latest evolutionary phase. The organisation now has a matrix structure. 'Rather than management being purely hierarchical, disciplines now run across departments, and expertise vertically,' said Whitmarsh. 'If you're not careful, as you grow the organisation with more specialists, and the tasks themselves become more complex, you can lose some of the joined-up thinking, the total picture. Different departmental teams don't become disconnected from the task of making the car go quicker, but it's easier for them to become isolated from each other.' Within the new organisation, chief engineers have what Whitmarsh refers to as a 'total system responsibility', but they are not responsible for the functions themselves. So, for example, a chief engineer working on the suspension system will call upon and co-ordinate the activities of others in vehicle design (the physical members, or parts, of the suspension system). Before that, though, he'll have called upon the simulation engineers and liaised with McLaren's aerodynamicists, who will have given advice on what the suspension parts should look like, and how and where they should be positioned on the car.

Such an approach explains the thinking behind the new McLaren Technology Centre. Apart from technical excellence, a great deal of nous has been applied to the way it is used by the team. Some 140 engineers sit in a 104-metre by 18-metre office. 'It's open-plan,' Whitmarsh explained, 'but we've created islands where groups of engineers can stimulate creativity. Everything is within their grasp. Any engineer only has to walk fifty metres to the test section of the new wind-tunnel facility. Alongside that is the new model shop where, for example, you can look at the parts being made for the car before they're tested in the wind tunnel. A range of dynos and test rigs are also nearby, and the race cars are being built underneath. This layout supports the way the engineers are working. Different groups can collaborate with each other more easily.' Every time the engineers walk to the restaurant, they pass the race cars being built for the next race. 'In fact, all the staff do,' Whitmarsh continued. 'It might seem strange that the race cars are now where they are. It might seem logical to assemble the cars at the back end of the factory, deliver them through the factory door and load them on to the trucks waiting to transport them to the races. But the cars are at the front end of the factory so the whole company has to walk past them and see them before and after each race.' Keeping this association with the car at all times is very important to Whitmarsh. 'As we increase the size of the business and the complexity of what we're doing, we are reinforcing that McLaren is not Woking Engineering or Woking R&D, we are first and foremost a racing team.'

It may seem old-fashioned to have a public address system in an ultra-modern building, but Whitmarsh has insisted on one being installed in the Technology Centre. 'Practice sessions and live races are relayed back and played throughout the building. We talk about the team's progress, what the circuit's like, and how the other teams are doing. It is vitally important to remind people what we're about. It's great. If I'm not at a race meeting and I wander in when one of these broadcasts is in progress, the whole factory stops. It's not an excuse not to work; there is a genuine interest in what's going on, especially in the news from the paddock. They feel involved. It's a great motivational tool.'

Critics of the group's SLR road car project have called it a distraction, but it does represent the company's future and is every bit as much an exercise in achieving excellence as the Formula One programme. 'You have to look at the medium-to long-term objectives of the business, and its strategy,' Whitmarsh insisted. 'McLaren has been a leader and an innovator in the industry, largely thanks to Ron's vision. Formula One teams of twenty years ago were very different in their form from the sophisticated teams of today. It is our view that to prosper and succeed we need to be performing in and dominating the premier form of motorsport in ten to twenty years' time. There will still be an inherent interest in some form of motor racing. People will still be interested in driving vehicles fast, or seeing others driving them at their fastest, and seeing technical excellence as the pinnacle.' Whitmarsh believes that to ensure that future, the organisation needs to be more than a classical Formula One team. 'We need to be stronger industrially, and economic-ally; we need to be able to exploit synergies. Inevitably, the stakes will increase. We are now competing against major automotive companies. They are serious about motor racing, because they see it as a powerful way of differentiating their brand and their products in the market. If you're creating a premier brand, you need F1 because it captures the imagination of the customers.' Britain has a history of great innovators who didn't evolve and develop sufficiently, and Whitmarsh is deter-mined to avoid the pitfalls. 'You can either wait, after which it's generally too late, or by developing your five- to ten-year strategy for the business you can try to anticipate where the industry is going to be. If you can't foresee that, and you don't lead the way there, you won't be winning.'

The next breakthrough for McLaren will come when it produces the first Mercedes-Benz to be made of carbon fibre, the two-seater Mercedes-Benz SLR McLaren road car – the first Mercedes to be built in Britain. With its 'four eyes' headlamps and gull-wing doors (opened automatically by gas-pressure springs), this Mercedes-AMG-tuned V8 5.5-litre supercharged beast evokes memories of the legendary 1952 SLR but features Formula One-style paddle shifts to zip you from an estimated 0 to 62mph in just 4.2 seconds, with a top speed of around 198mph. Advanced aerodynamics and fibre-reinforced ceramic brakes will give the car huge road-hugging and stopping capabilities. The new SLR has been designed by legendary Formula One designer Gordon Murray, the man who created the McLaren F1.

'Customers are expecting ever-increasing levels of occupant safety,' Whitmarsh said. 'The car's crash performance should be outstanding. In the coming years, we're going to be able to achieve levels of occupant safety we haven't experienced before in production road cars. We can apply the approaches and the technologies developed in F1 to improving road-car safety. We're all used to seeing savage accidents into the barriers at very high speeds. Spectators think the driver is just going to hop out of the car uninjured every time and run over to his spare car. We've become almost blasé about the achievements in safety in F1 cars, with their crash and antipenetration systems. If you consider how small an F1 car and its crumple zones are, if you start to apply these technologies into road cars, customers will start to demand similar levels of performance.'

Road cars are also becoming heavier because of the functions they contain. Electronics has been part of automotive design and construction for the best part of twenty years. The electronic equipment inside today's vehicle is largely devoted to the car's main functions, particularly the mechanical ones, so it is now an integral part of the modern engine, brakes and gearbox. Research by McKinsey & Company shows that this will develop further in three distinct areas. In the front seat area, a mainly voiced interface will offer driving aids, safety and security, plus access to the Internet and infotainment. Remote diagnostics in the vehicle itself will provide real-time data on performance and the possibility of remote tuning and service scheduling. Web-based commerce, music, video and gaming will dominate the car's back seat area. The ability to link small computers in cars to the Internet, and to add this to positioning and navigation information from satellites (telematics), is opening up a new industry advocates are touting as a new dawn for the car, especially for those selling cars at the top end of the market. Somewhere along the line, though, all this functionality, including more basic systems such as air conditioning, now standard on most cars, will have to be delivered lighter. Ford, Audi and Jaguar have invested billions in aluminium cars and lightweight components, and the Mercedes-Benz SLR McLaren has a target weight of just 1,400kg.

The Mercedes-Benz SLR McLaren programme, along with the Technology Centre, will allow McLaren to invest in technologies and resources it couldn't justify on the F1 programme alone. 'Synergies can be carried both ways,' Whitmarsh summed up. 'This should also improve our facilities directly for F1 and create a better, more inspirational environment for our engineers that should encourage innovation. As a group we are also going to be stronger and more powerful. You've got to be striding forward as a business.'

4. WILLIAMS (WANTAGE)

Sir Frank Williams and Patrick Head are a formidable duo. 'We are always working on something new, something original,' Williams has said. 'That's how we try to stay ahead.' And since 1977 the company has built a solid reputation for engineering skills and consistently kept its cars at the front of the grid.

Sir Frank Williams and Patrick Head are a formidable duo. 'We are always working on something new, something original,' Williams has said. 'That's how we try to stay ahead.' And since 1977 the company has built a solid reputation for engineering skills and consistently kept its cars at the front of the grid.

Sir Frank Williams was born on 16 April 1942 in South Shields on the southern shores of the River Tyne. He went to boarding school in Dumfries, Scotland, where he first read about motor racing. He soon developed a very keen interest in the sport and followed the exploits of the era's racing heroes, such as Mike Hawthorn and Peter Collins. In 1958, he attended one of his very first races, the British Grand Prix at Silverstone, which was won by Collins driving a Ferrari. Williams was completely hooked after this and spent all his free time hitchhiking around the country watching racing, often spending hours on wet, cold and dark nights waiting for a lift. As soon as he was old enough for a licence, he was out racing himself, initially with an ex-Graham Hill Speedwell Austin at Oulton Park in 1961. Little did he realise then that 35 years later he would provide Graham's son Damon with the cars that would take him to his first Grand Prix victory and a World Championship crown.

Racing always proved a tough battle financially, and despite some good Formula Three results, especially in Scandinavia, Williams soon began to realise that his real talent lay in team management and the preparation of cars. He'd also moved to a flat in Pinner Road, Harrow, on the outskirts of London, which he shared with a number of other hard-up occupants who lived on their total enthusiasm for motorsport. It was crowded, so Frank slept on the settee, but he also established a spare-parts business from that address which acted as the foundation for Williams Grand Prix Engineering.

Formula One was always Williams' ambition, and this he realised in 1969. In the years leading up to that debut he had prepared a variety of cars for other people and run his own Formula Two team with close friend Piers Courage as driver. His foray into Formula One with Courage was in a private Brabham, and their efforts were rewarded with eighth overall in the 1969 drivers' championship.

Williams' technical director, Patrick Head, was born in Farnborough, Hampshire, on 5 June 1946. His interest in motor racing was sparked early by his father's racing career, principally in Jaguar sports cars in the 1950s. After graduating with a mechanical engineering degree from University College London, Patrick raced karts and competed in a number of rallies before he, too, realised that his talents were not being put to good use behind the wheel. From early 1970, Patrick worked for Lola Cars alongside John Barnard on a variety of machines including Indy, Can-Am and two-litre sports cars. He then assisted Ron Tauranac at Trojan, designing Formula 5000 and Formula One cars. As an extension of his continued interest in sailing, Patrick became involved in boat building before he teamed up with Frank Williams in 1975.

After a season with Walter Wolf Racing, in March 1977 the duo set up as Williams Grand Prix Engineering in a small industrial unit on Station Road in Didcot, Oxfordshire, with a staff of only seventeen. They competed in 1977 with a second-hand March, then knuckled down to the task of preparing their own car. By the start of the 1978 season, the first Patrick Head-designed Formula One car, the FW06, was ready, and Williams had found sufficient sponsorship to tempt the Australian driver Alan Jones to join the team. From that point on, they never looked back, for the FW06 in the hands of Jones was extremely competitive. For the 1979 season, Jones continued as team leader with Clay Regazzoni in a second car. WilliamsF1, as they were now called, truly arrived at the British Grand Prix in 1979 when, after Jones disappointingly retired from the lead, Regazzoni was able to drive to victory. The trend continued as Jones won four of the six remaining races that year.

The period also witnessed dramatic developments in racing-car design. Williams perfected what Lotus had so ably demonstrated in the Lotus 78 – ground effect, a technique that glued a car to the track. Lotus's rubber skirts sealed the lower pressure under the car against the outside air, but with the 1979 Williams FW07 engineers realised that air leaking into the underside and destroying the suction could be cured by having a sliding skirt. So the stiff skirts of the FW07 moved up and down in the side-pods, sealing the low-pressure region and maximising the ground effect. And maximum downforce, of course, meant a huge advantage in speed. Skirts were banned in 1981 and from then on aerodynamic gains had to be hunted down on every square centimetre of the car's surface. Nevertheless, WilliamsF1 emerged in the 1980s as the team to beat, and an unequalled reliability record helped them to sweep to unchallenged and crushing victories in the constructors' championships of 1980 (when Alan Jones also took the drivers' title), 1981, 1986 and 1987. In 1982, the team was aiming to become the first manufacturer to win the constructors' title for a third consecutive year. It wasn't to be, but newly signed Finn Keke Rosberg, who replaced the retiring Jones, won a closely fought drivers' championship.

Grand Prix racing's normally aspirated era was coming to an end in 1983 and winning proved an uphill struggle, although Rosberg did win in great style at Monaco. Williams then announced a new association with Honda, and the Anglo-Japanese turbo combination first appeared at Kyalami in South Africa in April 1984. That season the team was on a learning curve with turbo cars, the only highlight Rosberg's US Grand Prix win in Dallas. The team also moved into a superb new custom-built racing facility just a mile from their original home at Didcot.

In 1985, the team acquired a new colourful image, Keke Rosberg had a new team-mate in Nigel Mansell, and the car, the Honda-powered FW10, had an all-new carbon-fibre chassis. The season started slowly but reached new heights as the two drivers climbed to the top of the victory podium on no fewer than four occasions. Rosberg again won the US Grand Prix, and Mansell's two consecutive wins at Brands Hatch and Kyalami in October were particularly sweet as they were his first in Formula One. Rosberg also crossed the finishing line first in Adelaide, ensuring a team hat trick to round off the season.

Then, just before the start of the 1986 season, the team was dealt a severe blow. While driving away from pre-season testing at the Paul Ricard circuit in France, Frank Williams' car left the road and overturned. It was an accident that left him confined to a wheelchair and so nearly claimed his life, but, instead of bemoaning his fate, he fought his way back to lead the company in the only way he knew how. New to the team for 1986 was the Brazilian former world champion Nelson Piquet, a worthy replacement for Rosberg. He quickly adapted to the FW11 and took the new car to victory in the debut race in Brazil. The team went on to win nine Grands Prix in 1986, and success continued in 1987 with another nine victories (six by Mansell, three by Piquet), again with the modified FW11. This time the team made sure of not only the constructors' crown but the drivers' championship, too.

It was Piquet's third title; Mansell was runner-up for the second consecutive year.

For 1988 there were many changes. Mansell had a new team-mate in the vastly experienced Italian Riccardo Patrese, and the four-year association with Honda ended; the team used the normally aspirated 3.5-litre Judd engine in the FW12. Unfortunately, mechanical problems dogged the team's efforts, but despite this Mansell finished second at both Silverstone and Jerez, with Patrese achieving his season best with a fourth in Adelaide. Williams was aware that to win in the new era of Formula One, with everyone now running normally aspirated engines, he needed backing from a major motor manufacturer. He got his way in July 1988 by signing a three-year deal with Renault, who agreed to supply the team with its new V10 engines. The initial 'exclusive' deal was only for 1989, but at the Canadian Grand Prix Renault extended the deal to 1991. Patrick Head designed the FW13 chassis specifically to house the new Renault engine.

Belgian driver Thierry Boutsen replaced Mansell for the 1989 season, and he and Patrese recorded a creditable fifth and third in the drivers' championship. A better start was made to the 1990 season: Boutsen came in third in his FW13B in Phoenix, and then Patrese won his third Grand Prix (his last victory had come seven years earlier) in San Marino. Boutsen's turn came in Hungary, where he claimed his first ever pole position and went on to score an impressive green-light-to-chequered-flag victory. These two wins and several other podium placings meant that by the end of the season the team had finished fourth in the constructors' championship.

Halfway through that season, Mansell announced his retirement after a disappointing British Grand Prix while driving for Ferrari. Frank Williams persuaded him to change his mind, though, and Mansell re-signed for the team for whom he would win more Grands Prix than any other driver. Mansell had his first taste of the FW13B at the Estoril track on 20 November 1990, and then eagerly awaited the completion of the new FW14, the latest offering from Patrick Head (who by now also had Adrian Newey – later to become McLaren's design whizz – on his design team), with a brand-new Renault RS3 engine and a semiautomatic gearbox. The 1991 Canon-backed team proved a winning combination, with Mansell scoring five victories and Patrese two. The team proved to be the only real competition to McLaren and was runner-up in both the constructors' and drivers' championships, Mansell and Patrese second and third respectively in the latter.

The tide turned in 1992. On 1 March, at the first race in South Africa, Mansell and Patrese finished first and second with a FW14B fitted with active suspension. Mansell went on to become the first driver to win the opening five races of a season, and his record-breaking didn't stop there: he also became the first driver to win nine races in one season, and was on pole an astonishing fourteen times. When Mansell came second at the Hungaroring in mid-August he clinched the World Championship, the first British driver to do so since James Hunt in 1976; WilliamsF1 and Renault took the constructors' title, the first ever for Renault, at the next race in Belgium. To round off this dominant year, Patrese finished runner-up, beating Michael Schumacher in his Benetton-Ford by three points.

For 1993 it was all change in the driver line-up with three-times world champion Alain Prost and official test driver Damon Hill taking over from Mansell and Patrese. They carried on where Mansell and Patrese left off: Williams retained the constructors' title, Prost clinched his fourth drivers' crown, and Hill won his first Grand Prix in Hungary. They were driving the Williams FW15C, a treasure trove of computer-controlled, hydraulic hardware. It boasted traction control, electronic engine management, a semiautomatic gearbox and active suspension. Indeed, without electronics the car would have been impossible to drive. Wholesale incorporation of fighter aircraft technology made the FW15C, technically speaking, the most advanced racing car ever built. 'We were adding such a high degree of complexity to the car, with all of the suspension electronically controlled, it gave immense power to the engineer who could then literally fly this low-flying aircraft at any attitude he wanted,' Head remarked.

But again, another of Williams' leading-edge cars was stopped in its tracks after just one season by the sport's rulemaker, the FIA. The FW15, perhaps the ultimate racing car, threatened to become the first of an undesirable new breed. Track speeds would become dangerously high, the software within the cars would be impossible to police, and, worst of all, it was thought that electronics would create the perception that driving skills were no longer required. In the Williams FW15 suspension, hydraulic actuators controlled by the onboard computer absorbed the bumps and rolls of the fast-moving car. The computer processed information about the car's orientation a thousand times a second and fed it to the actuators to hold the car exactly six centimetres above the track, at its optimum height, so that it always produced the maximum amount of downforce. The driver was flying by wire. With conventional springs, as soon as you hit the brakes, weight transfers forward, the front goes down, the back goes up, and the balance of the car changes; then, as soon as you pick up the throttle in the middle of the corner, the back goes down, the front comes up and the balance is affected again. Ironing out these effects was the objective of active suspension; it could shave seconds off a lap, not tenths as today. To the engineers, the banning of active suspension for the 1994 season seemed unfair. Previous bans had been imposed on the grounds of safety; active suspension, clearly one technical idea that could apply to road cars, was banned because it was a driver aid. But the suspension itself wasn't an aid; it didn't drive the car for the driver. It raised the performance potential of the car, and the technology could have had many commercial uses, so it was a shame that Formula One had to jump on this one.

Soon after clinching his 1993 title, Prost decided to make the season his last in competitive racing, thus leaving the door open for three-times world champion Ayrton Senna. The 1994 championship battle began promisingly for the new-look Rothmans Williams Renault team, then tragedy struck. On 1 May, during the third Grand Prix of the year at Imola, Senna was killed while leading the race when his car left the circuit at the notorious Tamburello corner and crashed into a concrete wall. The world of motor racing was stunned and the close-knit team was shattered by the death of a driver many people regarded as simply the best. The fightback of the team after such an event typified the bravery and leadership of Frank Williams. As a mark of respect, only one car was entered for the next race in Monaco; then, four weeks after that tragic day in San Marino, Hill won the Spanish Grand Prix in Barcelona and promptly dedicated his victory to both Ayrton and the team. For this race Hill was partnered by official Williams test driver David Coulthard, who drove the second car for eight of the remaining races; for the other four races, in France, Spain, Japan and Australia, Nigel Mansell came back from the US where he was racing in the IndyCar series. Hill scored another five victories after Barcelona but lost the championship by a single point to Michael Schumacher following a controversial collision during the last race in Adelaide, which was eventually won by Mansell. In such a tragic year it was testimony to the strength of the team that it retained its constructors' title, successfully seeing out a season that will never be forgotten.

For 1995 it was Hill and Coulthard who drove for the team, and between them they notched up five victories in the FW17, the young Scot taking his first Grand Prix win in Portugal on 24 September. Hill was the only driver to challenge Schumacher for the drivers' title, but the German clinched the title for the second consecutive year at the Pacific Grand Prix in Aida, Japan. Although losing another title was a disappointment, Hill made sure the team went out on a high with a fine win at the last race in Adelaide.

Williams' Didcot headquarters had by now become too small to house the team. A search for a new base was made, and midway through 1995 the ideal place was found ten miles from Didcot at Grove near Wantage, Oxfordshire. Over the winter the team moved, the final phase – the transportation of the wind tunnel – taking place over the weekend of the 1996 San Marino Grand Prix. Joining the team for the 1996 season was the new IndyCar champion Jacques Villeneuve, son of the late Gilles Villeneuve. The team had achieved good results during pre-season testing, but it was not until the first race in Melbourne that the FW18's true potential was shown. Jacques was the star of the show, Damon was second on the grid, and the pair were over half a second quicker than the nearest opposition. They continued their domination in the race, which Damon won after the Canadian had to slow down in the closing laps because of an oil pipe problem. Jacques won his first Grand Prix at the Nürburgring at the end of April, and the team went on to win twelve of the season's sixteen races, Damon notching up eight of them. The constructors' championship was sewn up by mid-August, but the drivers' championship went to the wire. At the final race in Suzuka Damon needed just one point to secure the crown; for Jacques it was a win or nothing. In the end, Damon led the race from the green lights to the chequered flag while Jacques was forced to retire. It was Hill's first and the team's sixth drivers' title.

German driver Heinz-Harald Frentzen joined the team in 1997 to partner Villeneuve. The season promised to be very competitive. Indeed, the team had to fight hard and by mid-season was trailing Ferrari in the championship. Then the famous WilliamsF1 determination kicked in. There were celebrations at Silverstone in July when Williams won its 100th Grand Prix at the scene of the very first victory eighteen years earlier, and by round fourteen, the Austrian Grand Prix, the team was back at the top of the championship table. A record-breaking ninth constructors' title was sealed in October at the Japanese Grand Prix, and an emotional victory for Villeneuve in the last race at Jerez secured the drivers' championship too, to the delight of the entire team.

A change of image in 1998 coincided with a change of fortune. The competition had shifted up a gear, and by the first Grand Prix in Australia it looked like the McLaren team was going to walk away with the World Championship. A mass of new regulations, including a reduction in the width of the car from 2 to 1.8 metres, more stringent crash testing, and grooved tyres, had presented the teams with many new challenges. McLaren adapted best and the rest of the field was left to play catch-up. Moreover, WilliamsF1 had said goodbye to Renault in 1997 after a tremendously successful partnership; the team continued to race with Mecachrome-Supertec engines before new technical partner BMW made its return to Formula One racing in 2000. Without a works engine partner, the team had a hard fight on its hands to keep up with McLaren and the hard-charging Ferrari team. Towards the end of the season, the Winfield WilliamsF1 team found itself in a fight for third place. Continual developments to the FW20 gave the team the push it needed to secure that spot.

It looked as though the team was set to have another tough year in 1999. A completely new driver line-up brought Ralf Schumacher and reigning CART champion Alex Zanardi to the team. Zanardi had a difficult season adapting to Formula One. The advent of grooved tyres and narrow-track cars in 1998 had forced the drivers to change their technique to control the new machines, and Zanardi soon found himself at the bottom of a steep learning curve. On top of that, bad luck dogged his early races, but the turning point came at the Belgian Grand Prix at the end of August when he was finally on the pace. A strong performance at Monza followed, but further disappointments, the last of which was a terminal electrical problem on the first lap of the Japanese Grand Prix, meant it was a miserable season for the amiable Italian. And for Williams, of course: they finished fifth in the constructors' championship, behind the Jordan and Stewart racing teams.

For 2000, wonderkid Jenson Button was given an opportunity to shine by Frank Williams. He did, but he could manage only eighth place in the drivers' championship in a season dominated by Schumacher, Barrichello, Hakkinen and Coulthard, and although Williams improved their placing by two spots they were still a massive 116 and 134 points respectively behind McLaren and Ferrari. Now, well into the five-year partnership with BMW, a new era is truly under way for WilliamsF1 with a more settled driving pairing comprising Ralf Schumacher and 1999 CART champion Juan Pablo Montoya, both of them hungry Grand Prix winners.

5. JORDAN (SILVERSTONE)

'Our success in 1999 turned out to be a collection of poisoned chalices. It brought us a lot more sponsorship from Deutsche Post, adding to the Benson and Hedges money. Having a lot of sponsorship is a good thing, but if it isn't spent wisely, if complacency sets in in any shape or form and if that sponsorship is being spent at a time when the team is going through huge instability, then no amount of money is going to make up for a disconnected technical infrastructure.'

Mark Gallagher, Marketing Director, Jordan

A canny operator with an eye for talented drivers, Eddie Jordan has had a rough ride to the top in Formula One, but he and his loyal band remain the people's favourite. Jordan Grand Prix epitomises the nature and spirit of Formula One in terms of hard work, excitement, adrenalin and fun, and is truly a dynamic business in a dynamic sport. Behind the smiles, though, a fight for survival is going on.

What hasn't been said about Eddie Jordan, or 'EJ', as he is known? This flamboyant Irishman with a love for Deep Purple, U2, Van Morrison and Stereophonics, and a passion for Thai food, has brought colour and a sense of humour to the F1 paddock. Time away from the race track is spent at rock concerts with friends in the music business, at soccer matches and golf tournaments, or following his other great sporting love, horse racing. His charisma, energy and *joie de vivre* have made his company, Jordan Grand Prix, one of Formula One's best-loved teams.

Eddie began his career as a banker, but a prolonged strike in Dublin in the summer of 1970 prompted him to go to Jersey for work. It was there that he saw his first kart race, and he was instantly smitten. Having progressed through various motorsport categories and won several races and championships, in 1979 he drove in the European Formula Two Championship. The following year he made his second career switch from driver to team owner and set up his own team, Eddie Jordan Racing. EJ was a born salesman and charmer, and he knew how to make a race team work. All the necessary ingredients were present to give him almost immediate success. Eddie Jordan Racing scooped the International Formula 3000 title with Jean Alesi in 1989, and after a decade in the lower formulas the team made the transition to Formula One for the 1991 season. Jordan Grand Prix finished its debut year in an impressive fifth place in the World Championship and brought to the sport an energy and vibrancy previously unknown.

In the past twenty years, no one has brought on drivers quite like Eddie Jordan. Of the 22 men who lined up on the 2001 season starting grid, nine had been through Jordan's stables. It was EJ who gave Formula One the Schumacher brothers: Michael in 1991, when he made his debut racing for the newly created Jordan Grand Prix team in Spa, and Ralf in 1997, when he debuted alongside another Formula One new boy, Giancarlo Fisichella, fresh from only one year with Minardi. Damon Hill (in Formula 3000), Eddie Irvine, Johnny Herbert, Heinz-Harald Frentzen, Rubens Barrichello, Pedro de la Rosa and Ricardo Zonta are others Jordan has brought into the sport. Ralph Firman is the latest.

However, launching driver careers is only one half of the Eddie Jordan story; the astute deals he has struck with drivers and sponsors alike completes the other half, more than hinting at the steely business acumen that lies behind the flamboyant façade. When Barrichello started his Formula One career with Jordan in 1993, the man who took him on saw not only an awesome combination of talent and youth but also the money the Brazilian could bring to the team, which was critical at that stage. 'It was the same with Irvine,' explained Jordan. 'We took him on, he paid a little bit of money to help the team keep going, we got the benefit of his talent for a number of years and then we sold him off to Ferrari for around four million dollars to help pay the bills. Basically, this kept us going.' Jordan also broke new ground when he secured investment from global equity investor Warburg Pinkus, and in April 2002 he finalised details of a restructuring programme aimed at returning Jordan to the more flexible, open style of organisation that existed during the team's most successful seasons. It also helped to reduce costs, which had escalated after a period of unprecedented growth that had seen staff numbers climb to over 250. 'Jordan has always been at its best when lean and efficient,' Eddie insisted. 'This generated a more efficient structure to ensure the future success and longevity of our team.'

The Jordan story is certainly one of courage, luck, character and sheer bloody-mindedness. 'We've been through several chapters in Jordan's relatively short history, and as a company have been on a steep upwards climb over ten of those years, before suffering a two-and-a-half-year descent,' said Jordan's marketing director Mark Gallagher, who has been with Eddie from the beginning. 'When we started we had 34 staff operating out of Eddie Jordan Racing's premises at a Silverstone lock-up garage. It was a small, standard unit that Silverstone would let out to small outfits.' Because there was no manufacturing requirement in Formula Three or 3000, it was simply a rebuilding facility for a handful of racing cars, with store rooms and spare parts. 'That really was about it, but to accommodate Formula One, Eddie rented another much bigger unit [essentially, two of the Silverstone units knocked into one]. That was our first factory.'

During Jordan's first season, the team's head count increased from 34 to 45. By the end of 1991, Jordan had achieved fantastic success on the track but had incurred colossal debts – around £6 million. 'It certainly did get to the stage where winding-up orders were against the company,' Gallagher recalled. 'On one particular day Eddie had to pay a substantial sum of money to a court to prevent the company being wound up. On the Friday morning he certainly didn't have the funds he needed [around a million pounds]. That morning he spoke to a contact in the banking industry in Ireland, who said he would consider giving him the money that day. By then it was ten or eleven in the morning. This chap said that this was fine. They had their own aircraft, and they'd fly over. Sure enough, they were in Oxford and into Silverstone by lunchtime, with Eddie keeping an eye on the clock because the court had said that the BACS transfer had to be through by four-thirty. Anyway, this chap arrived with a colleague, and they quickly determined that Eddie wasn't offering any collateral. They had a chat with Eddie and assessed the prospects for sponsorship and television revenue. Eddie suggested they might be in the pipeline, agreed the loan on the spot, and had the money transferred. The rest is history. This sums up so much about Eddie as well as the company, because this particular person had raced with Eddie a long, long time previously – some 25 years ago, in fact. They'd both gone their separate ways but had stayed in firm contact, and this chap believed in Eddie. On the basis of just looking around, he thought that if he'd got this far, the Eddie Jordan story wasn't about to come to an end. Indeed, having loaned that money on an unsecured basis, the money was paid back in full within six months, and Jordan Grand Prix continued.'

Also around this time, 7-Up, which had been the team's sponsor in the first year, offered Eddie a deal to continue into a second year. But it was a smaller deal, much smaller than the already paltry amount Jordan had been offered for 1991 – and this was after the team had enjoyed incredible success. 'Of course Eddie realised that accepting smaller sponsorship at a time when he needed to pay debts off was never going to go anywhere,' Gallagher continued. 'He would only be doubling or quadrupling his debts in year two. So he turned down the 7-Up deal.' Eddie and managing director Ian Phillips walked over to the Silverstone canteen, looked at each other across the table, and wondered what the hell they'd just done. 'Mark McCormack's IMG Group then contacted Eddie within a matter of days to say that one of its clients, a very large South African petrochemicals company called Sasol, was looking to invest in something sporting. They'd been given some tax breaks by the South African government to promote South Africa abroad. Having looked at the field with four teams leading it, all of them well sponsored, they continued down the list and the first team they got to that didn't have sponsorship was the team that had finished fifth – Jordan. They put the call in and Eddie signed the deal within a few days. The evening he did the deal, I remember taking him and his wife Marie to Le Manoir aux Quatre Saisons near Oxford for a celebratory dinner. He was suddenly out of the woods.'

It was a remarkable turnaround. Sasol sponsored the team from 1992 to 1994, and you could say that was the period during which the team really established itself, proving to the world that it was going to survive. The team won its first podium placing in Japan in November 1994, and in June 1995 Eddie Irvine and Rubens Barrichello secured a double podium finish in Canada. Then there was a slight hiccup: the apartheid regime collapsed in South Africa, there were new elections, the South African Grand Prix was cancelled and Sasol ended its sponsorship. 'This left the team unsponsored for a year [1995],' said Gallagher. 'Another year left ducking and diving, as Eddie would say.'

Enter Benson and Hedges. Again, just like the banker who had bailed him out a few years back, a fellow Irishman, Nigel Northridge, whom Eddie had met in the 1980s when Northridge was marketing manager of the Gallaher brand Silk Cut (which was also sponsoring Tom Walkinshaw's Jaguar sports car team), came through for EJ. 'They'd talked to a few people and wanted to talk further with Jordan about it,' Gallagher recalled. 'They very quickly stitched together a deal which was the launch pad for greater things. It gave the team, suddenly, substantial revenue.' The Benson and Hedges money meant a healthier cash flow, money to pay drivers, and money to make the factory bigger. 'We had built a nice factory in 1991,' Gallagher continued, 'but oddly, in the first year when life was very tough, Eddie had managed to salt away money he knew he'd have to invest for the future to build this new factory. He knew that a glorified lock-up in Silverstone wouldn't impress sponsors or provide facilities for the future. So this new factory at the time looked huge, and we never thought we'd fill it, but we soon did.' Benson and Hedges' input also meant that Jordan could buy a wind tunnel in nearby Brackley. Staff numbers exploded. 'I'd rejoined the team in December 1995, at the end of that year of slightly less sponsorship,' said Gallagher, 'and I was the 74th employee. Soon it was 120, 150, up to 200, then 260.'

The company was flourishing, and this helped Jordan to employ Damon Hill, which led to the team winning its first Grand Prix in 1998 with a one-two finish for Hill and Ralf Schumacher. The next season, 1999, was Jordan's best ever. 'This [period] was the first time we'd ever continually developed the car right through to the end of the season. The adrenalin flow of being competitive, the extra work that went in, everyone just pushed hard to do as well as possible, right to the last race,' said Gallagher. But by the time that last race had finished, the Jordan team had to take a collective breath; before it knew where it was, it was into 2000, and the ball had been dropped. 'By the time we caught our breath and recovered, we were halfway through 2000,' Gallagher recalled, 'probably at the end of it, and we realised that repeating those successes was going to be tough. But there's great passion at Jordan, which has carried us through, and probably made up for other shortcomings on more occasions than we'd ever dare to admit. We can make a pound stretch further than most, and we can take a car that may not be the best on the grid and engineer it effectively.'

Despite the team's best efforts, instability set in and Jordan lost some key engineering people, including Gary Anderson, who had joined Jordan Grand Prix in 1990 and was the technical brain behind its cars for eight years. He was followed eighteen months later by technical director Mike Gascoigne. Now, after a few turbulent years, Anderson has returned to the fold as director of race and test engineering, and has been joined by Henri Durand, a Formula One veteran whose experience includes a decade heading McLaren's aerodynamics group and a year as Prost's technical director, in addition to spells at Ferrari and Ligier. It appears that the Jordan ship is back once more on an even keel.

'Rather ironically,' Gallagher observed, 'our success in 1999 turned out to be a collection of poisoned chalices. It brought us a lot more sponsorship from Deutsche Post, adding to the Benson and Hedges money. Having a lot of sponsorship is a good thing, but if it isn't spent wisely, if complacency sets in in any shape or form and if that sponsorship is being spent at a time when the team is going through huge instability, then no amount of money is going to make up for a disconnected technical infrastructure. You're just spending money on a bad process and system. Looking back on it today, you'd have to say Deutsche Post chose the worst three years to be with us, and I suspect in a year or two's time we'll run into them over a beer and discuss why they were with us just at the time when things were not working.'

A June 2000 works Honda deal only added to the team's problems. As Gallagher put it, 'Honda in the 1980s with McLaren and Williams was a very different Honda to the one we found this time round. They have incredibly clever and talented engineers, but only Honda could explain why their engine technology wasn't at the level it needed to be to guarantee success.' During the 2001 and 2002 seasons, even though Jordan finished as the top Honda team (in front of BAR), Honda had fundamental problems. 'Engines were blowing up, so to avoid blowing them up you ran them so low down on power that it really wasn't powerful enough,' Gallagher continued. 'When people ask me why we had a bad two and a half years, I say technical instability led to weaknesses on the reliability side of the operation, and the Honda situation. These two things combined meant you had a car that wasn't fast or reliable enough and didn't evolve over those three years because we had different people running the ship.'

And it had all seemed to be going so well in November 1998 when Warburg Pinkus bought 49 per cent of the company off Eddie, giving him and his family financial stability for the first time in his life. Until then he'd been mortgaged to the hilt; his house in Oxford had been guaranteed against the company. Warburg Pinkus and Eddie had a vision of building the company into something much more valuable. Both shareholders felt there was only so much you could sell on a Formula One car. Revenue would eventually plateau at a certain level, say $100 million, so if you wanted revenue of $150 to $200 million, you had to look elsewhere. Jordan embarked on a brand extension programme. Money and branding immediately created a perception and an expectation among the media and fans, which produced more pressure. They thought Jordan was on the up, but behind the scenes the reverse was true. It was always a risky adventure, with no guarantees attached. The team's core business, and the core competency of Eddie Jordan, was and is Formula One motor racing; to expect the management of Jordan to be involved in a brand extension programme, and for it to be run by someone who knew absolutely nothing about Formula One, was clearly not going to work from the start. 'There was a big explosion of ideas,' Gallagher recalled. 'Jordan would have a website, drinks, a clothing business, and so it went on. But it wasn't starting with a small business and growing into a large one. We had to think about having a big business on day one. That, of course, didn't happen. We all realised that other competitors, more experienced in these areas than we were, were always going to be better than we could be at it. We bit off more than we could chew. It was not a bad idea, though. Three or

Above Stirling Moss with proud parents (© Sporting Pictures)

Below Hill and son Damon help to push Jim Clark on the Hill family tractor. Graham's Bette (right) toasts the achievement (© Getty Images)

Left Sir Jackie Stewart (© Sutton Motorsport Images)

Below Bernie Ecclestone and Max Mosley discuss tactics at the 2002 US Grand Prix (© Getty Images)

Above Johnny Dumfries – a colourful addition to the Formula One pack
(Getty Images)

Right James Hunt, as we remember him
(Sporting Pictures)

Above 'Our Nige' on top form at the British Grand Prix (© Getty Images)

e Sir Frank Williams and Patrick Head share a quiet moment (© Sporting Pictures)

v The boys (from left to right) – Johnny Herbert, Damon Hill, Derek Warwick, in Brundle and Mark Blundell (© Getty Images)

Above Damon Hill an
wife Georgie enjoying
lighter side of life for

Left BAR's David
Richards

Right David Coulthar
pensive mode

(© Sutton Motorsport
Images)

Above Eddie Irvine surveying all he sees in Austria

Left Jenson Button – kid on the block

(© Sutton Motorsport Images)

so years later we're doing what I believe is the very thing which our then brand manager had exaggerated about, because we've grown organically.'

Current brand manager Mike Hall-Taylor, a former Gallaher executive, is making quite a success of building up the Jordan brand. The company has twenty-plus licensing agreements which at the last count (in 2002) brought in £3.5m. Jordan's drinks business is now established and growing, thanks to niche marketing where it doesn't compete with other major brands. 'The idea that Warburg Pinkus had of adding "shareholder" value by increasing the company's revenue and profitability was totally right to try to do,' Hall-Taylor said, 'but it was perhaps unfortunate that the personalities involved and the way in which Jordan tried to run before it could walk scuppered that first attempt.'

To put all this into context, it's important to know that Jordan's management had undergone a change. Former McKinsey consultant John Putt, who'd known Eddie for many years, had been brought in as chief operating officer and adviser to Eddie with the intention of running Jordan much more as a business than as a racing team. He'd spent 21 years in high-volume automotive engineering, working for Honda, Nissan, Toyota, Rover, Ford and General Motors, which had provided him with an insight into what world-class engineering and manufacturing really is and how it should be practised.

Eddie had approached Putt in 1996 and asked if he could transfer some of this knowledge to Jordan for a couple of days a week. 'Basically, Eddie's message to me was, "Look, we've now got the Benson and Hedges money, but we realise that with the number of people we have here today we will not grow a World Championship team unless we grow in a structured and orderly manner," ' Putt explained. 'So from 1996 to 1998 I supported his management team at Jordan. That gave me a good insight into how the Jordan team operated.' Eddie called Putt again in the summer of 2000 when Mike Gascoigne signed a contract to go to Renault, a contract with which Eddie couldn't compete. It was time to re-evaluate the business, which had moved on at quite a pace since Putt's previous sojourn. 'What Eddie needed was actually a chief executive officer,' Putt said. 'He claimed to be the chief executive officer, but unfortunately he didn't have the time to devote his attention to the company in the way that was needed. I therefore recommended he recruit one. I didn't actually realise that the Jordan board would come back to me and ask me to take the job.'

Putt immediately set about examining processes, profitability and longevity with a five-year business plan focusing on the direction of the company. This was an excellent approach to running a modern manufacturing operation, one which largely had never been part of the furniture at Jordan, certainly not in any formalised way. Processes at Jordan didn't exist in Putt's definition of the word. 'The company operated as a glorified cottage industry with a few guys doing all-nighters and suppliers having their ears bent to get the parts delivered on time,' said Gallagher. 'It was very much the way things were done in motor racing.'

There's no doubt that nowadays the Formula One business is a very complex one, especially for someone coming into it fresh. Although F1 teams can benefit from formal, best-practice automotive thinking, the sport also does its business very informally. It's a community, an incestuous group of people who talk. They may not talk on the phone or via email, but they will bump into one another in the pub, or they'll meet at race circuits and chat. When a team loses its technical know-how, correcting the situation may be more about getting that knowledge back into the company as quickly as possible rather than altering how things are done. You have to be careful about the changes you make as a boss because of the sensitivities that surround it, but you can't afford to be too careful. Because Formula One is a global business, it is fundamentally a very unforgiving one. It's high profile, and the mistakes teams make are very public. Something like 350 million people in 146 different countries watch this gladiatorial spectacle every fortnight, and teams are regularly humiliated by the performance of their cars. Finishing anything less than first is considered to be a failure, no matter what spin is put on the result by the team principals and their engineers through the media. Each team also has to design, build and develop its own cars, and demonstrate and manage expertise in a number of different and complex technologies. Around 3,500 new parts are designed for each car every year; of these, something like 1,500 are redesigned seven times during the year. It's a highly complex and difficult industry even for a large team with a healthy budget and infrastructure. It can cost around $1 million to find an extra tenth of a second per lap, and you can easily spend that money and never find the improvements you're looking for.

As one of the smaller outfits in the F1 paddock, Jordan therefore went through a period during which Putt tried to create two sides to the business so the company could both improve the way it ran itself and create its product, the racing car. One side focused on high-quality engineering – which delivered at the end of a production line a very competitive and reliable F1 car, far better than Jordan had been able to build it before thanks to modern manufacturing practices – and quality assurance techniques that made the whole process much more efficient. On the other side sat a commercial and brand management business designed to add further value to the company and to maximise Jordan's revenue opportunities. It was thought that such an approach would deliver the company's 'vision', as Putt referred to it: to win the World Championship, to succeed financially, and to be a great place to work. 'A lot of what John did was right,' said Gallagher, 'and he's left a legacy of better procedures, working very closely with [operational consultancy] Celerant Consulting, who are still here today and doing a formidable job for us.'

However, theoretical improvements in the way the Jordan business was being organised and managed have been dwarfed in the last few years by the substantial economic downturn in various key sponsorship markets, particularly in the US and Japan. 'In all the years we had Honda, we'd never attracted any new Japanese backing other than Brother Industries, which came to us from Williams,' said Gallagher. 'But we could see the sponsorship bubble was bursting.' Prior to this, the rise of technology and telecommunications shares on the world's stock markets had changed the face of Formula One sponsorship. 'Ours was a technology-driven business,' Gallagher pointed out, 'and the IT revolution in the 1990s transformed the way we had been able to be competitive.' HP, Compaq, Nortel, Lucent and Marconi had poured millions into the sport, but now the profits of companies in the technology sector were nose-diving and thousands of jobs were being axed. The IT downturn caused some consternation within the sport because it was widely felt that this area of business was going to replace tobacco advertising, due to be phased out by 2006; consequently, there had been a rush to sign up technology companies.

Unsurprisingly, IT sponsors began to look very carefully at their programmes and partnerships with Formula One teams. Some, whose contracts came up for review, renegotiated; others cut back or pulled out altogether, and a few went bust. The result for Jordan was that in spring 2002 EJ had to make fifty people redundant for the first time. 'It was a very painful process,' Gallagher recalled. 'He cut a slice off the company, like a cake, from top to bottom. The top end was John Putt, [joint managing director] Trevor Foster and [head of engineering] Tim Holloway – high as well as low salary earners. John was the first to offer his position. If the company was going to get smaller, then he thought there wasn't much point having a chief exec who was brought in to grow the business.' The cull left Jordan with 210 employees. 'This period was used to make the company lean, to shorten lines of communication, and to try to regain lost ground,' Gallagher added. 'Now, after the initial shock, there is a realisation that we can get the job done with 80 per cent of the people we had. Some of the younger people who'd been given new positions steamed into their jobs much more aggressively.' The company seems happier, too. 'This is what we're best at. We're not a huge corporate entity, but a lean Formula One team trying to beat the big guys. Entertainment is more important than technology. Our future is back to basics, as a company which outsources most of its manufacturing to keep its overheads under control. We have to rebuild our position as the team most likely to cause an upset, by beating the big guys in the next three years.'

Formula One is still going through a love affair with the corporate world, but the sport needs the racers who live and breathe the sport and are passionate about what they do. There's no doubt that Eddie Jordan isn't an engineer; he doesn't appreciate some of the things that need to be done to produce consistent winners. But if you step further back, you'd have to say that on the whole he's a committed racer and has done an amazing job at Jordan. It's up to the people who work for Eddie to manage Eddie, as Gallagher explained. 'The downside of Eddie is that he doesn't always understand some of the issues. But the upside is that anyone can walk in his door and explain what they honestly believe needs to be done over time, and he can be won round.' Mix this flexibility, dedication and commitment with teamwork, engineering excellence and good financial resources, and you've got a winner. 'We've learned a few hard lessons, and are much stronger for it,' Gallagher concluded. 'We need to keep our technical team together and spend money wisely, but we also need to use the legacy that John Putt and Celerant brought to us, making sure that we remain a quality engineering company.'

6. JAGUAR RACING (MILTON KEYNES), COSWORTH RACING (NORTHAMPTON) AND PI RESEARCH (CAMBRIDGE)

'I made a decision when we were coming into this business that as a brand-new team we would have a totally computer-designed F1 car. No one had done this before. Many F1 teams and motorsport teams had computer-designed component areas, but no one had done a total vehicle. We set out with not one drawing board in the factory.'

Sir Jackie Stewart

A little-known fact is that the founder of the Ford Motor Company, Henry Ford, was involved with motorsport before he began manufacturing the cars that formed the basis of his world-famous company. In 1901, Ford was challenged to race fellow automotive enthusiast Alexander Winton. Like the many Formula One design engineers who came after him, Ford had experimented with some new materials and used a ceramic casing on the ignition coil to ensure he got a better quality spark than his competitor. Needless to say, Ford won the race, established his reputation and was able to secure investors, the money from whom allowed him to establish his own company two years later. The Ford Motor Company has since played a major role in motorsport across the world. The rivalry between Ford and Chevrolet (General Motors) within NASCAR alone is legendary, but more particularly Ford has contributed greatly to the development of the UK motorsport sector. Although owned by Ford, the triumvirate featuring in this chapter are British operations that are constantly innovating. Jaguar Racing has a fine sporting pedigree, Cosworth Racing produces revolutionary engine technology, and Pi Research is respected the world over as an automotive electronics designer and manufacturer.

Jaguar Racing has longevity: the company has been involved in motorsport since the company that was to become Jaguar was founded by Sir William Lyons in Blackpool, the celebrated seaside resort in the northwest of England, in 1922. Lyons' first products were sidecars for motorcycles, and he quickly realised that if his products were seen on the racing circuit his company's profile would be raised. His Swallow sidecars were soon notching up successes in the famous TT races held on the Isle of Man, as well as other motorcycling events, and by the mid-1930s Lyons had moved his company to Coventry and was building cars. He continued in his keen support of motorsport, and the new SS

Jaguar 100 became a regular and successful competitor in circuit racing and rallying. A victory in the 1936 Alpine Rally followed by a win in Britain's 1937 RAC Rally established the SS100's performance credentials.

Britain's first production sports car race was held at the newly opened Silverstone circuit in 1949. Three recently announced Jaguar XK120 sports cars were on the starting grid, and, cheered on by coachloads of Jaguar employees, they went on to score an impressive one-two victory. The XK120 also quickly made its mark in international rallying, winning the classic Alpine Rally at its first attempt in 1950. But it was the gruelling endurance race at Le Mans that Lyons believed would be the ideal showcase for his car's performance and reliability, and during the winter of 1950/51 the Jaguar boss authorised his racing chief, F.R.W. 'Lofty' England, to build an aerodynamic version of the XK120 especially for the race. Inside Jaguar, the car was known as the XK120 C; motorsport enthusiasts the world over know it as the Jaguar C-Type. The three-car team, with a young Stirling Moss among its drivers, lined up for the traditional Le Mans start; 24 hours later, Jaguar was celebrating a historic victory. Jaguar C-Types won at Le Mans again in 1953. In 1954, the purpose-built D-Type arrived on the scene and scored victories at Le Mans in 1955, 1956 (Jaguar also won the Monte Carlo Rally in this year) and 1957. Jaguars dominated the race in this last year, also finishing second, third, fourth and sixth. The decade's race wins helped boost Jaguar sales and inspired what is to many people the definitive thoroughbred sports car, the E-Type. Introduced in 1961, it had a very successful motorsport career in Europe and North America. Many of the Formula One stars of the time sat behind its wheel. Arguably the most famous among them, racing a lightweight E-Type to many victories in 1964, was Jackie Stewart.

Something of the Le Mans spirit was rekindled in 1982 when the Jaguar XJ-S V12 began a successful three-year European Touring Car Championship campaign. The green XJ-S clinched the title in 1984, a year in which Jaguar also returned to Le Mans via the Group 44 Team of American Bob Tullius. In 1988, Jaguar clinched its sixth Le Mans win when the V12 XJR-9 driven by Jan Lammers, Johnny Dumfries and Andy Wallace took the chequered flag. Jaguar also won America's top endurance race, the Daytona 24 Hours, that year and clinched the World Sportscar Championship for the second time. A seventh Le Mans victory came in 1990 with Martin Brundle, Price Cobb and John Nielsen. As in 1988, Jaguar's victory followed on from an impressive one-two success at Daytona. The drivers who have raced Jaguars over the past fifty years read like a *Who's Who* of motorsport. Apart from Moss, Stewart and his brother Jimmy, Sir Jack Brabham, Briggs Cunningham, Graham Hill, Tom Walkinshaw, Win Percy, Derek Warwick, Patrick Tambay, John Watson, Raul Boesel, Eddie Cheever and Teo Fabi have all driven for Jaguar.

In 1996, Jaguar Racing's parent company Ford began a partnership with Stewart Grand Prix, operated by three-times world champion Sir Jackie Stewart (who had won all his world titles in Ford-powered cars) and his son Paul. The team unveiled its car just nine months after it had been put into production, and Stewart Grand Prix was the first of the teams to release its car for the 1997 season. 'It was the first Formula One car to have been designed by computer from the outset,' Jackie Stewart said. 'I made a decision when we were coming into this business that as a brand-new team we would have a totally computer-designed F1 car. No one had done this before. Many F1 teams and motorsport teams had computer-designed component areas, but no one had done a total vehicle. We set out with not one drawing board in the factory.' Ford bought Stewart Grand Prix in 1999. At the time, the deal made Ford only the second car manufacturer to run its own team, alongside the Fiat-owned Ferrari. In September 1999, Stewart-Ford registered its first win when Johnny Herbert won the European Grand Prix.

In 2000, Stewart-Ford became Jaguar Racing. The 'new' team has some 'new' faces who represent a different breed of team heads – engineers who bring a wealth of business experience into Formula One management. Lead man is group vice president of global product development and chief technical officer of the Ford Motor Company Richard Parry-Jones, a first-class graduate in mechanical engineering from Salford University who in 1985 became executive engineer of Ford's technological research in Europe. After a spell as director of vehicle concepts engineering in the US, he moved to manufacturing operations at Ford's Cologne base, and then on to vehicle engineering. In 1991, he was elected a fellow of both the Royal Academy of Engineers and the Institution of Mechanical Engineers, and he now oversees the product development activities for Ford vehicles worldwide, as well as the company's design, research and vehicle technology functions. He's also responsible for Ford's Premier Performance Division, which includes the company's Formula One racing programme.

As chief executive officer of Ford's Premier Performance Division, Tony Purnell is the man in Jaguar Racing's hot seat. He has an extensive level of experience at the very top of international motorsport, a passion for the sport flows through his veins – he started racing karts while he was still at school – and with degrees in material science, mechanical engineering, metallurgy and aerodynamics he is easily the most academically qualified man in the Formula One paddock. Another man who is no stranger to motorsport – in fact, he still races – managing director David Pitchforth is an engineer with a long association with Ford. He joined Jaguar Racing in March 2002. 'I'd been managing director of the company that had built Jaguar's wind tunnel,' he explained, 'and as such I became closely involved. I was about to join Pi [Research], but then Tony Purnell asked me as a favour to do six months helping to develop the cars.' Once drawn into the project, Pitchforth found the challenge irresistible. 'I could see lots of stuff going on in the drawing office and the rest of the company could be improved. To this end I wrote the specification for the R4 [the 2003 car] and got involved as its project manager.'

Starting in 1982 with Schwitzer, Pitchforth's career has exposed him to a world of racing formulas including CART, IRL, NHRA, NASCAR, Formula 3 and Formula 3000, and over the years he's gained extensive experience in a number of specialised areas of development such as aerodynamic/thermodynamic measurements, spectral analysis, test-equipment commissioning and correlation, and component manufacturing. From the latter half of 2002, Pitchforth took on the engineering director's role, and it is down to him to make sure that Jaguar Racing's technical and engineering departments gel together into an effective working environment. 'There are basic principles of engineering that apply in Formula One just as they apply in the real world,' Pitchforth said. 'Actually, in the bigger teams people like the technical directors of old know all the procedures and processing in their heads and have a mandate to see that it happens. What we're doing is going in with a clean piece of paper and saying we're going to formally impose all that. At the same time, you cannot pretend that Formula One is just like the real world. The big difference is that, to use a business term, our time to market is two weeks. We have to perform every two weeks, and that is how we are judged. So the development cycle is extremely tight. You can't therefore do all the things you'd do in the real world because some of the processes would bog you down. You've got to take the essence, shed all the noise, and decant it. But the basic engineering best practices still apply.'

Pitchforth is confident that such an approach will result in a steady improvement in the competitiveness of Jaguar Racing's cars after a tough couple of years. 'The R4 has been conceived to give us a good platform as we develop our understanding. We've improved a lot since last year

[2002], but if the other teams are worth their salt, they will have too. The only way you can surpass them is either to steepen your improvement curve, which is a very difficult thing to do when you're already working it all out, or begin your improvement earlier. It's for that reason that I have already written the specification for our 2004 car [the R5]. We will populate that spec with the data and improvements we find from the R4 this season.'

No matter what people say, Ford interferes with the running of the Jaguar F1 team only when things are going astray; when things are going well, Jaguar Racing's parent is extremely hands-off. The first two years of Jaguar Racing's Formula One efforts disappointed pundits and fans alike. 'The car was an embarrassment,' Tony Purnell recalled. 'It made the Ford directors cross the line and focus on the company. You can't spend that much money only to embarrass yourself. That's when they sent over one of their top management people, Richard Parry-Jones, to have a good look at the operation. Richard found that all the know-how Stewart-Ford had gleaned to produce a good product and run an efficient concern was absent at Jaguar, because the board had thought it best not to interfere, instead to empower and encourage this small company. Richard looked under the bonnet and decided the operation needed a complete leadership change, to put in people who quite frankly knew what they were doing. All we're trying to do with Jaguar is shape it into a real engineering company rather than a company that produces nice pieces of racing car at phenomenal cost. Don't forget that money can buy you out of trouble, but in the real world, the world that Pi comes from, all departments have to earn their money. It's all right getting the money to make something that's fit for purpose, but you can also do it incredibly inefficiently. A small private company would never allow this to happen because money is too tight.'

Ferrari's Ross Brawn has commented that Jaguar has the potential to become the British Ferrari, and the parallels between the two set-ups are interesting to draw. Engineering director Ian Pocock has a PhD. in control systems and has spent a long time as an engineer, but in the last ten years his number one skill has been in the man management of development efforts (read Ross Brawn). 'This may seem dry and boring,' Purnell said, 'but he will take out of the way all the barriers that people think prevent innovation. He is accompanied by Malcolm Oastler [read Rory Byrne], who in our structure is a pure engineer. He has no management responsibilities at all. His job is solely to innovate. So we've taken all the bureaucratic load off him, all the things he's not good at, and created an environment in which he can do what he's brilliant at.'

Purnell admitted that this has worked at Ferrari. 'I also had a look round Rolls-Royce Aero Engines when I was working for Pi last year, and I was very impressed. The company is operating in an environment where the bureaucracy and the barriers to do anything different, ever, are almost insurmountable, because the engines have to be so staggeringly safe. But the innovation they've allowed to flourish is fantastic. Look at the blade designs they are coming up with inside the turboprop engines. They are stunning.'

In September 2003, Cosworth Racing celebrated the 45th anniversary of Mike Costin and Keith Duckworth's decision to go into partnership together at a garage in Shaftesbury Mews, London, combining their surnames and talents to create what was to become famed as Cosworth Engineering. Despite the two founders having now retired, the legendary name of Cosworth remains respected throughout the world for the design and precision engineering of high-performance race, rally and road engines. According to Duckworth, the pair had thought it must be possible to make an 'interesting living messing about with racing cars and engines'. Little could he have dreamed back then that the venture would record 175 Grands Prix, 214 CART and 45 WRC wins plus numerous constructors' and drivers' titles in Formula One, CART, WRC and Touring Cars.

The first work carried out by the company was the development of the famous Ford 105E engine. In 1960, a rising young Scotsman by the name of Jim Clark claimed a Formula Junior victory in a Lotus 18, the first Ford-based production unit for Formula Junior racing at Goodwood. It was the first race win for a car powered by a Cosworth engine and the starting point for an incredible four decades of motorsport success for the company.

By 1964, Cosworth had moved to bigger premises in Northampton, to a site where the current facility resides, as an increasing range of Ford- and Lotus-based engines were developed for competition, notably the hugely successful Lotus twin-cam unit. But much bigger projects were just around the corner. In 1966, Duckworth signed a contract with Ford to develop a new engine for the three-litre Formula One era, and the DFV was born. Even given Cosworth's growing reputation, no one could have envisaged just what an impact the engine would have at the pinnacle of motorsport. For the next sixteen years, the DFV was the top engine in Formula One. From the day in 1967 when Jim Clark's Lotus 49 gave the engine a debut win at Zandvoort through to Keke Rosberg's world title in 1983, the DFV was dominant. Graham Hill, Jackie Stewart,

James Hunt, Mario Andretti, Emerson Fittipaldi and Nelson Piquet all won world crowns with the aid of a Cosworth DFV. At the same time, the DFX derivative of the DFV was beginning to clean up in America on the Indy Series circuits. The DFX reign encompassed twelve drivers' titles and twelve victories in the Indianapolis 500.

As the 1980s moved into the 1990s, Cosworth excellence was applied to high-performance Ford saloon road cars. Off the road, on the race track, the Ford Sierra RS500 Cosworth claimed the 1987 Touring Cars world title. That association continued through the 1990s as the Mondeo became the centre of Ford's touring car racing with Australian Paul Radisich winning the drivers' title in 1993 and 1994. In Grand Prix racing, the HB V8 unit won eleven races between 1989 and 1993, and Nigel Mansell's 1993 CART-winning car used Cosworth XB engines. For 1994, the new Zetec V8 engine was introduced into Formula One, and it powered Michael Schumacher to his first world title with Benetton. The Ford Escort Cosworth claimed World Rally victories throughout the mid-1990s, and the Duratec-R-powered Focus has taken Colin McRae to an all-time record of World Rally Championship wins. At the same time, Stewart Grand Prix was sold to Ford, soon after the 'Blue Oval' had purchased the glamorous racing arm of Cosworth. A new era for Cosworth Racing had begun. The Stewart-Ford team turned into Jaguar Racing, and was soon joined by Arrows. Bringing the Formula One story right up to date for 2003, Minardi and Jordan have filled the hole left by the famous fall of Arrows, which means a total of six F1 cars are currently powered by Cosworth's new breed of engines – more than any other engine manufacturer.

But not just in Formula One is Cosworth returning to dominate the grid. In 2003, the XFE engine was supplied to the entire twenty-strong line-up in the CART series. The company is also preparing for the Cosworth brand to return to the roads with a range of exciting Ford products with Cosworth-engineered powerplants. 'They deserve a big pat on the back for the CART engine deal,' Purnell said. 'That's an example of how a motor racing company can be at its best. On the one hand we have a very competent engine supply company which has a good handle on the cost of things and what people want; on the other, it is imaginative enough to have some very entrepreneurial people in its sales department. This has been done in the true small-company, entrepreneurial British motor racing style, but backed up by a really solid company.'

As a result of the countless international and national races and rallies that have been won using Cosworth engines over the past four decades, the company enjoys an almost iconic status. Evidence of this can be seen every weekend when hundreds of historic vehicles are raced using Cosworth powerplants. It is estimated that over 70 DFV engines are used regularly on race tracks the world over.

Cosworth's managing director Nick Hayes developed a passion for Formula One while still at school, and with a future in the sport in mind he gained an engineering degree from Salford University. Hayes' ascension to the role of Cosworth director of engineering has been a rapid one. He worked for Rolls-Royce Aero Engines before joining Cosworth Engineering in 1984 and held a variety of liaison roles with the Ford-supported Benetton team before becoming a dedicated engine designer. In 1997, he took overall control of the works' Formula One project and led the development of the Zetec-R used by Stewart Grand Prix in its debut year. Hayes took control of all technical development at Cosworth Racing in 2001 when he became managing director, and it has been his job to make the company's new and radical 90-degree CR-5 engine a powerful and competitive unit. 'The reason we've gone to ninety degrees is in the interests of improving the centre of gravity,' Hayes explained, 'and I have to say we've achieved a very significant step in terms of lowering the C of G.'

The company is split into teams, each of which is dedicated to just one type of engine. Each engine is hand-built by one technician, but other technicians who overhaul and calibrate the specialist systems on the engine support him. Some of the components may appear similar to those found in normal engines, but they are not. The valves, for example, must accelerate from 0 to 30mph and back over 130 times per second and still get within a twentieth of a millimetre of hitting the piston, which is itself accelerating at 8,000g. 'Therefore,' Hayes said, 'attention to detail is paramount, and this is achieved with a combination of old-fashioned craftsmanship, sophisticated measurement and CNC machining techniques. Even the smallest particle of dirt can cause an engine to fail, so the workshop is meticulously clean.' When the engine is built, it is run in at 8,000rpm on a dynamometer and then power-tested. The precision of the build is displayed by the results: variation from one engine to the next will be as little as 2bhp in over 850bhp. By the time the engine is dispatched to the track the build will have cost more than £20,000 and taken 150 man-hours. For all this, it wouldn't be able to get you from London to Edinburgh before wearing out.

Unfortunately, Jaguar's poor performance in recent years has prompted speculation that Cosworth may be losing its touch. Tony

Purnell was adamant that this was not the case. 'Any accusation that Cosworth doesn't innovate is ludicrous,' he said. 'Back in the Stewart Grand Prix days, Cosworth was the first company to come up with a "micro" engine for Formula One. The company made an engine that was 35kg lighter than the previous one. In its last year as Stewart Grand Prix, the team had a very good season, winning one Grand Prix. This was mostly down to the engine, although everyone missed it. The reason why that car was so successful was because it had an unfair advantage over most of the rest of the grid in the engine.' The engine has evolved since then, and in 2003 Cosworth made another bold step with a magnificent piece of engineering that oozed innovation. 'If there's a gem,' Purnell insisted, 'it's Cosworth's Formula One engine development. It's every bit as good as Ferrari or Mercedes. A little bit behind BMW, but only a little bit, and for one third of the spend. So in terms of bang per buck, it's head and shoulders above everyone else in Formula One.'

It is Purnell's job to recognise and hire the right people and structure an environment where he can get the most out of their abilities. 'One area in which I think I can be pretty effective is strategic thinking. I think I'm pretty good at showing people how to work with one another and monitoring the whole process afterwards,' he said. However, Purnell feels he has gone beyond the thought that brilliant engineering comes from creative individuals. 'That's true, of course, but creative ways of working and a creative management approach also work. The designer must consider what the specification for the part is. Next, he should consider the specification for the test procedure, the test rigs, whereby we're going to know that that part is fit for service, and it can be inspected, so that when it's machined and made up we know it's to a standard. Some may say this is bureaucratic and slow, but with the right leadership and with the people who know where to put the right emphasis, this approach will produce a better piece of engineering.'

According to Purnell, when management reads a book or hires a consultant, it gets really evangelical about putting in some quality system, 'but that misses the point that these systems are there to serve the effort, not the other way around. What Cosworth has done is to get a management system and way of working which would tick all the boxes for an ISO expert, but there wouldn't be any cynicism surrounding it. Cosworth's engineers are so encouraged by it that they are interested in improving it. They don't just have an interest in designing the parts, they also have an interest in designing the way they work. This is something Cosworth has done well, and it is difficult to convey to people that it's different. And it's working. If you look at the company's turnover of staff, it's low because it's a good place to work.'

Although he's now in the spotlight as head of Jaguar Racing, Tony Purnell is perhaps best known in the sport as the founder of Pi Research. Started in the basement of his house in Cambridge, this innovative company created what were at the time revolutionary wind-tunnel controls and instrumentation before developing a 'black box' for Formula One cars. This system was the first data logger and electronic instrumentation console, and among its innovations was displaying results against distance rather than time.

From those relatively small beginnings, Pi Research has grown into a global electronics business with an impressive track record in the general automotive and motorsport businesses and a strong reputation for excellence. Its range of products is diverse, and it provides state-of-the-art solutions for individuals and racing teams competing at all levels, from budget-conscious kart and club competitors through to the sophisticated requirements of Formula One and ChampCar teams. Still based north of Cambridge, within Motorsport Valley, Pi Research now has over ten years' experience at the pinnacle of motorsport technology, and it's an integral part of the Premier Performance Division alongside Cosworth Racing and Jaguar Racing. Since 1989, its data acquisition products have evolved to become the industry standard for race teams.

The company's early growth was stimulated mainly by Purnell's determination and vision. Pi started out in instrumentation design, and it was this, together with Purnell's contacts, that took the company to the US and an initial involvement with the then IndyCar Series. Pi targeted its sophisticated data acquisition and instrumentation systems at those who were keen to really understand what was happening inside their racing cars, and word soon spread. Although many of the company's early systems were semi-customised, Pi did end up with a number of standard configurations, and their success led to Pi developing cheaper, less sophisticated products aimed at less technical customers – those who raced karts and competed at club level.

Pi Research enjoys a unique position in the motorsport industry. It is the only supplier to offer such a broad range of products and services, and when working with teams in Formula One Pi offers a bespoke consultancy service, working to specific design requirements to solve a problem that is particular to one team. Sometimes these developments become more generic products and are offered for wider sale, usually after a period of exclusivity with the original customer. What all Pi's customers have in common, though, is that they are all serious competitors. They care about the performance of their chassis, engine and driver. They also know they must have Pi systems because their competitors on the starting grid do.

It's a challenging environment for Pi to work in. The extreme nature of motorsport, particularly where it relates to electronics, means there's every likelihood that a first design won't get out of the starting blocks because of a variety of development obstacles, from radio interference and heat to vibration, G-forces and a host of other considerations. A racing car is probably one of the most extreme environments into which you can put electronics. Circuit design is one thing, but implementing it so that it isn't destroyed is another.

Pi's real value lies in the collective skill of its employees. In the mid-1990s, virtually everyone working for Pi was fanatical about racing to the point where most of them had either done it or been involved with it for so long that they lived and breathed it. It was part of the corporate culture. Since then, as the company has grown, the racer element has been diluted by those with different skills. These days, if the company is looking for a software engineer, it needs someone who can write efficient code and also design and implement a user interface suitable for use by a race engineer.

Motor racing accounts for 60 per cent of Pi's revenue, the automotive industry claims the balance. 'You've got to look beyond Formula One and use your technical excellence in the sport to innovate into new markets. This is also the way you can get talent back into your own market,' said Purnell.

An early development for Detroit Diesel, as well as other customers, led to the formation of Pi Technology, which operates as part of the Pi Group in the general automotive electronics market. Cars are fast becoming computers on wheels; engine, brake, gearbox and stability control electronics are widely used in production vehicles, and guidance, collision avoidance and adaptive cruise control systems are appearing on prototype vehicles. The Internet and information revolution is coming to cars in ways that will transform the way we use our vehicles. Even the conventional engine is not immune from change, with ecofriendly, electric- and fuel-cell-powered vehicles becoming a reality. Pi Technology is a leading developer in this field. The company is currently involved in a range of projects from 50cc scooter engines through to motorbikes, cars, trucks, buses and 300-litre stationary industrial engines, as well as other agricultural, construction and marine applications. More recently, Pi Technology has been working in the exploding field of vehicle interior electronics, which covers the areas of audio and multimedia, navigation systems, telematics and the Internet.

One in four trucks in North America, Canada and Mexico now relies on Pi software for its engine control systems. The majority of gas and oil pumping stations installed in the last three or so years are regulated by Pi electronic control technology. These engines are the size of a small house, and they pump fuel and gas out of the ground. 'They also run off the fuel they pump out of the ground, which is constantly changing. They run 24 hours, 365 days a year,' Purnell added. 'They also phone home if they are going wrong.' Such deals have been secured because of Pi's reputation for technical excellence. Its repeat business is strong.

7. BAR (BRACKLEY)

'Formula One is entertainment. We are competing for the entertainment time of consumers. They've got lots of other things they can do if Formula One becomes boring, if it doesn't provide a spectacle. We don't want to become a bland, grey industry run by bland, grey business people who've come out of admirable business structures but who don't have personalities. This industry was built on not just the drivers but the likes of Enzo Ferrari, Colin Chapman, Eddie Jordan, larger than life people in the best tradition of the football club manager who is as big a personality as the football players themselves. That's terribly important. If we make this business too structured and too dull, it will lose some of its magic. If you separate out those people responsible for running the business as a business, and those people who are the public face, the representatives of the team, you can then afford to have that flamboyance which is essential to the sport.'

Hugh Chambers, Group Managing Director, BAR

British American Racing was formed in November 1997 by Craig Pollock, Reynard Racing Cars and British American Tobacco, and was launched to the world's media on 2 December. BAR bought up Tyrrell Racing shortly afterwards and moved to a state-of-the-art, 86,000-square-foot headquarters in Brackley, near Northampton, just down the road from Jordan Grand Prix. The then reigning Formula One world champion Jacques Villeneuve signed to drive for the fledgling team in July 1998; Ricardo Zonta joined three months later, and the inaugural driver line-up was complete. With everything in place, BAR staged its first team launch at Brackley in January 1999, and completed its first ever Formula One race in Melbourne in March.

Lessons learned from a tough first season were put to good effect. The new Honda-powered BAR002 came fourth and sixth on its first competitive outing in 2000 and went on to finish the season equal on points with fourth-placed Benetton. However, after this successful second year, BAR Honda couldn't keep the momentum going into 2001, and the year petered out into mediocrity. Villeneuve had been joined by the highly experienced and versatile Olivier Panis to form a solid driver line-up, but despite grabbing the team's first podiums in Spain and Germany, not even the mercurial French-Canadian was able to fully conquer a hard-to-handle car.

On 18 December 2001 came the announcement that David Richards, founder of Prodrive, had been appointed the new team principal of BAR Honda, taking over the reins from Pollock. Richards set about making a detailed and extensive review of the team, as a result of which he created a new structure to improve lines of reporting and make the organisation itself leaner. Designer Malcolm Oastler and Andy Green left the team and the workforce was cut by 15 per cent. Richards felt his task was clear: to take a team high on potential and resources but low on results and esteem out of Formula One's midfield and into the elite group of challengers for the World Championship. 'I have the greatest respect for the people who created this team, and the dedication they have shown to the task, but at the end of the day the organisation has not delivered,' Richards said at the time. 'I know that Malcolm and Andy recognise that their results have been below their expectations and I appreciate their disappointment, and thank them for their efforts. But we need to build a team with a very clear structure, with the very best people, and give them the responsibility to deliver against precisely determined goals. As I have said from the beginning, BAR has many extremely talented people, and what we are now doing is giving them the framework within which they can fulfil their true potential.'

Richards' track record in motorsport includes Prodrive's World Rally Championship-winning success with Subaru, a current FIA GT programme with Ferrari, and ownership of the rights to the World Rally Championship through ISC. He started his career in motorsport as a highly successful rally co-driver, and ended it by winning the 1981 World Rally Championship in a Rothmans Escort alongside Finland's Ari Vatanen. After retiring from active competition at the end of that season, he devoted all his time and energy to developing the motorsport consultancy he'd started in the mid-1970s. Perhaps not surprisingly for a driven man, Richards eventually formed his own rally team, creating Prodrive in 1984. The company moved from Silverstone to its present site in Banbury, Oxfordshire, where it has grown into a £100 million-plus motorsport and automotive technology concern. During the late 1980s, Prodrive managed successful race and rally programmes with Porsche, BMW and MG, and in 1990 the company formed its most successful and longest-standing partnership with Subaru. Since then, Prodrive has won a handful of world titles: three manufacturers' in 1995, 1996 and 1997 and two drivers' for Colin McRae in 1995 and Richard Burns in 2001. During the 1990s, Prodrive also formed partnerships with BMW, Honda, Alfa Romeo and Ford in touring car racing, securing the British Touring Car Championship five times. In 2001, Prodrive entered sports car racing, netting victories in the FIA GT Championship with its Ferrari 550 GT Maranello. For 2002, Prodrive masterminded Volvo's entry into the European Touring Car Championship.

In addition to his Prodrive chairmanship, Richards also became chief executive of the Benetton Formula One team for the 1998 season, and in April 2000 he purchased International Sportsworld Communicators (ISC), acquiring the television and commercial rights to the FIA World

Rally Championship. Richards has now built a team that is focused on transforming the championship into a mainstream entertainment package.

Richards succeeded BAR founder Craig Pollock at the helm the day before the launch of the team's 2002 car. The team finished that season eighth in the constructors' championship with seven points, even though the operation was being completely overhauled at the time. 'When we came here,' Richards said, 'there were around 430 people without a clear focus or direction about them. We needed to restructure the operation so that their performance could be made far more accountable. The aim is to be in a championship-winning position by 2005. All the in-fighting has been knocked on the head, but you can imagine how hard it was to build everything up from scratch. I sympathise with the people who lived through that period. They had the stuffing knocked out of them. But we have only one task now, and that is to win.' By the beginning of the 2003 season Richards believed the process to be complete and was looking for an immediate improvement in the team's performance on the track. 'We have to make sure that the team here shows some sign of its potential [in 2003], which it has grossly underachieved to date. If it does that, then the next stage is to really be a challenger to the leading teams in 2004, and by 2005 be a potential championship-winning team, which I think is realistic.' It's quite a challenge, but, based solely on his achievements with Prodrive, you have to believe him.

So, how does BAR compare with Richards' time at Benetton? 'It was a very different scenario,' he said. 'I was there with far less experience than I have today. They wanted me in there almost just to give the company a face. It was a well-established infrastructure that had won World Championships, so the shareholders assumed Benetton didn't need much doing to it. It was very clear to me after a short period of time that it did need to change, but no one was willing to accept that view. [BAR] was a new team which hadn't achieved, and everyone was aware that something fundamental was wrong and it had to change if it was to deliver. I've therefore had the full support of British American Tobacco, the shareholder, and we've gone about it with some rigour. We will see the results of this pan out over the next couple of years.'

Despite his forecasts, Richards is well aware that he can't just wave a magic wand, no matter how much money he's got to do the job and no matter how talented his people are individually, especially when he's up against teams with more resources who've been involved with the Formula One game for years. 'You can't just put it together overnight,' he admitted. 'It's like building an effective football team. Every single one of them plays a vital part, to work with each other, to compensate for the weaknesses in the organisation, to play to their strengths. It takes time for such organisations to gel. It's no coincidence that the likes of Ferrari, McLaren and Williams, the longest-standing teams, got better through an iterative process. Every year you improve a little bit. We can arrive at a certain point quite quickly, but after that you just have to wait.'

There has been some criticism that Richards is too thinly spread over his three companies to be really effective at BAR, but Richards dismissed such observations. 'I have a very different view and style of doing things than the traditional team principals. If you look at Frank Williams, Eddie Jordan, Peter Sauber or Ron Dennis to a certain extent, they are very focused on the Formula One aspect of their business. That's what they have been brought up in. They have a very hands-on approach to it as well, very detailed, very involved; they are highly competitive people. I'm often in awe of their attention to detail and their focus on things, but I know where I'm strong and where I'm weak, and I therefore employ appropriate people with the strengths I don't have to sort those things out for me. I delegate very effectively. I let those people get on with the task in hand, and as a result of that I can create the ideas, move things forward, give the company direction and leadership. But for a lot of the day-to-day functioning of the business I rely on a very solid management team, not just in Formula One but in all the businesses I'm involved with.'

Business is an evolution, and Richards believes Formula One companies are no different. They are moving on from the entrepreneurial stage, where one individual managed all the disciplines, to a far more corporate culture. This environment has to be more process-driven, authority must be delegated, and the company must have a clearly defined structure. 'We all have to go there,' he said. 'Companies of this size with such different disciplines, from the high-skill end of the technology side to manufacturing and marketing and all the other issues we face every day, cannot be properly managed at an efficient, professional level by one individual. We have to have skill in each individual area. The skill set becomes different because it's now about managing the organisation, not its activities. That's what we're putting in place here. I believe it will be very sustainable, and that I will re-engineer myself out of this job in four to five years. That is my objective. From then on, it will be a business that will flourish.'

But isn't this formal corporate approach to running a Fomula One team going to stifle innovation and kill its racing spirit?

'No. If you try to lead an organisation as one individual, yes, you can keep everyone going, but it becomes a personality cult. Cults are very fragile, and volatile. In an organisation which has proper delegated authority, where everyone knows their role, knows that they play a key part, and knows that they are acknowledged and rewarded for it, it's a far more inspiring and rewarding environment to work in. It's the way I've been brought up, an approach that explains my whole behaviour in life. I couldn't run an organisation in any other way, without acknowledging the people around me. Teamwork is in my blood.'

So, what of the future?

'We are looking at joint ventures with our partners to develop other products, a whole raft of ideas. Assuming everything carries on according to our plans, three years down the line this company's revenue will be split equally with 33 per cent of its income coming from sponsorship, another 33 per cent from the FOA and TV rights, and the last third from alternative business streams that we've created, whether through merchandising in the conventional sense or through genuinely alternative business streams that are spin-offs from our skills base or the intellectual property we've developed within the business. Our skill set lies in applying ourselves to different activities, whether it's motor racing, automotive technology or the raft of other businesses we're involved in. The fact that we're running a Formula One team is irrelevant; we could just as easily be a sports car team, an automotive product or an aviation business. The technical skills are certainly unique to the actual activity, but the application, the way we manage them, is what makes the difference. McLaren has certain similarities with us because it has diverse businesses. But they are more focused with the single-stream product, the Mercedes road car, other semiautonomous businesses such as TAG Electronics. We tend to revolve around automotive, from motorsport over to high-performance road cars through to specialist areas such as automotive engines and other developments. That spread makes us unique.'

A key member of Prodrive and BAR's management team, and one of Richards' right-hand men, is group marketing director Hugh Chambers. It was perhaps destiny that he ended up in motor racing. His father Marcus was a leading figure in the industry for more than thirty years, a competitions director of BMC and MG during the golden age of rallying. He revealed just how Prodrive and BAR work and support each other. 'Prodrive is in the business of providing motorsport programmes and automotive engineering consulting to vehicle manufacturers and top suppliers,' he said. 'Clearly, there is a relationship between those two elements. We're about providing engineering solutions to vehicle manufacturers,' who approach Prodrive because they want to promote their products and boost their image through racing. 'We think of ourselves as a company that is focused on creating cars which people are more likely to buy, either through enhancing their brand image or their technology. That's the fundamental fulcrum of everything we do. The sponsors we have in motorsport are generally there to facilitate the activities of the vehicle manufacturers.'

Within this picture, BAR is a specific motorsport contract. Prodrive has been contracted by British American Tobacco, BAR's owner, to manage the team in such a way that it wins on the track and makes money. Prodrive has worked with BAT since 1993 and the Subaru World Rally programme. 'They have a brand called 555 which is sold in the Far East, principally in China,' Chambers explained. 'We had a successful five years of using the rally team as a promotional vehicle for that brand. In so doing we built up a very close relationship with the board of directors at BAT, and they gained a lot of confidence in our style of management, our ability to clearly identify the goals, to explain the strategy, and to deliver against it, rather than wave some magic dust over things, which a lot of motor racing has been historically – boffins in a back room who may or may not conjure up a win. We have a track record of delivering what we say we will do. We're winners. What people want in the motorsport arena are successful companies. We identify what needs to be done, how we're going to do it, and how to budget and run it as a proper business, rather than by the seat of the pants which is how some motorsport companies have been traditionally run.'

Is Formula One, then, entering a different era of management? Is today's team to be run just like any other business? Do you need someone with corporate experience to run a team now?

'Well, Martin Whitmarsh has come from British Aerospace; Nick Fry, the managing director of both Prodrive and BAR, has come out of Ford; Jaguar's Tony Purnell has come most recently out of his own business, Pi Research, but he also has an impressive background. The reality is that these are very complex businesses now, employing 400-plus people, with budgets in excess of $100 million a year. To bring all these strands together in the most efficient manner you need to have a very strong industry background. Those who used to manage the older teams were passionate racers. They were doing it more for their personal enjoyment of going racing rather than approaching it as a business. Those days are gone. You simply can't survive with just that approach any more.'

BAT started BAR in 1998. BAR essentially grew out of BAT's desire to do things differently to Philip Morris, which had been sponsoring McLaren and then Ferrari with the Marlboro brand for a number of years. BAT changed its constitution in the 1990s and became BAT plc – one company. 'They wanted something that would symbolise a different approach,' said Chambers. 'Starting their own team from scratch certainly symbolised that, so they put their backing behind a consortium of Craig Pollock, Adrian Reynard and others who had a good track record in various other aspects of the industry. But they'd never worked together as a company, or as a team. Some of them had very little industry experience. Craig Pollock had been a successful driver manager but had never run an organisation of even a dozen people, let alone several hundred. There was an enormous motivation to be successful, but there wasn't really the expertise, so after four years of this collection of people running it, it had had a pretty miserable time. BAT found it very expensive, too. They put a lot of money in to bolster it, and success wasn't coming, so they turned to us as an established business with a clear infrastructure and all the resources and know-how to come in and take over the management of the business.

'Last year [2002] you could say we had a miserable first year. Finishing eighth in the championship was probably worse than we thought it would be. But the reality is that in Formula One the lead times are such that you are not going to make any impact within twelve months in a way that is visible to the outside world.' The performance of the 2002 car had been set by the design work that had been done the previous year, so the new BAR team will be measured on results in 2003. 'There was a colossal amount of work to be done,' Chambers added. 'There is no one in the senior twelve people within the organisation now who was there before we took over. We have completely moved on from the old management structure and style. The whole of the organisation's structure is different now. BAR [like McLaren] uses a matrix management structure, which we employed at Prodrive. Rather than manage purely hierarchically, disciplines run across the structure, and expertise runs vertically. Take mechanical engineering. That will be an expertise that runs across all the different aspects of the car, from the suspension and gearbox design to other areas of the car. Before, it would all have been separated into its different pockets, so there is much greater continuity with the engineering of the car in all its different elements.' There is also more technical depth in the company now. Current technical director Geoff Willis has over a decade's experience honed at Williams. Previous director Malcolm Oastler had never designed a Formula One car before his arrival at BAR.

The commercial side of the business, as David Richards pointed out, is equally important. 'A Formula One team is a commercial entity,' Chambers insisted. 'It has to stand on its own two feet. There are a number of different ways in which you can create the revenue that is required. A very large part of it tends to come from the vehicle manufacturers. Certainly Honda is investing several hundred million dollars into the development of the engine. But the team itself still needs to be self-funded – and we're talking budgets of something in excess of a hundred million dollars a year.' Of course, as Richards and Chambers well know, on-track performance is fundamental to this. Everyone wants to be associated with a winner. Teams nearer the front of the grid attract airtime, media, publicity; it tends to be easier for them to get more income, more sponsorship. When you are coming from the back of the grid and you don't have that advantage of performance-derived sponsorship income, you have to have something else up your sleeve. You need to have a magnetic appeal; sponsors must want to be associated with you, whatever the reason, be it sex and glamour or a reputation for hi-tech wizardry. You need to stand for something.

So, what does BAR stand for? When Prodrive took over the BAR operation in 2002, BAR didn't really epitomise anything. It was an adjunct to BAT, and to the outside world it appeared to be the Jacques Villeneuve team or the Lucky Strike team. 'The team itself didn't really mean anything,' said Chambers. 'So we recognised that there was a task to do, to really distil what the team was all about. Any good brand should be an external manifestation of a company's core cultural values – what you believe in. So we're single-minded. Clearly, in order to be focused on the end goal, you need to have a very clear vision of where you're going. The team, partly in the way it came about and partly through its ownership, has a certain independent *esprit de corps*. It's slightly apart from some of the big teams. Individual, independent, stand-alone, prepared to take its own path. It's not going to follow fashion, just do things because that's the way they've always been done. We're also very genuine. We have a culture of openness, like Prodrive. David Richards is very open and tells it like it is. We're down to earth and honest. Another element is bravery. To be successful, you've got to take some risks. Bringing this all together into the essence of what we believe in internally, and what we should stand for, we come to two simple words: pure racing. Unless we are providing a spectacle for the fans which appeals to their core requirements, we're not going to be a magnetic brand or a popular and successful team.'

In order to effect such a transformation, the management team spent a period contemplating a name change for BAR, perhaps to distance itself from the previous team's underachievements. 'We had a candidate name that everyone was very happy with,' Chambers explained, 'but when it really came down to the crunch it was agreed by all the parties involved that it wasn't the right time to change the name. We'd stay with BAR, but simplify and clarify it. It was sometimes British American Racing, sometimes BAR. Now it's B-A-R, but we want to move it one step away from its origins with BAT. The old speeding leaf logo was a derivation of the old plc logo. We've now moved to a very simple and clean black-and-white logo which is simply B-A-R. That's a reflection of this no-nonsense, down-to-earth quality of ours. In time, the team name may evolve to something else, but in the short term we didn't want to hide behind a new façade. There was a certain genuineness about acknowledging we were now the new BAR. We had been unsuccessful in the past, but in the future we were going to stand on our own two feet and be successful.'

There's clearly a lot going on in the team, and in the portfolio of companies Richards manages. But has he bitten off more than he can chew?

'The reality is that Formula One is now a business,' Chambers reiterated. 'It is typical in business that the chairman or chief executive officer has a very diverse portfolio of responsibilities. So the connectivity between Prodrive, ISC and BAR actually helps David because he's dealing with, for example, [FIA president] Max Mosley as much on issues to do with the World Rally Championship as with Formula One. That gives him a lot of exposure with the FIA to deal with many different issues. It broadens his perspective and brings fresh ideas to the table. If he was involved only with Formula One and was narrowly focused on that, the organisation would also be cast very narrow. David has expert managers underneath him who are much more focused. You obviously don't have to travel that far down the structure to find people who are 100 per cent focused on just BAR and Formula One. But we do have the best of both worlds: a very focused operational management core based at Brackley [BAR] and people such as David, myself and Nick [Fry] who have an office here in Banbury [Prodrive], just six miles down the road from our Brackley office. It works pretty well.'

However, despite the emphasis on sound management practice, Chambers is under no illusion about what they all must never lose sight of. 'We are in the entertainment business,' he said. 'Formula One is entertainment. We are competing for the entertainment time of consumers. They've got lots of other things they can do if Formula One becomes boring, if it doesn't provide a spectacle. We don't want to become a bland, grey industry run by bland, grey business people who've come out of admirable business structures but who don't have personalities. This industry was built on not just the drivers but the likes of Enzo Ferrari, Colin Chapman, Eddie Jordan, larger than life people in the best tradition of the football club manager who is as big a personality as the football players themselves. That's terribly important. If we make this business too structured and too dull, it will lose some of its magic. If you separate out those people responsible for running the business as a business, and those people who are the public face, the representatives of the team, you can then afford to have that flamboyance which is essential to the sport.'

8. FERRARI

'Every individual who works for Ferrari plays a very important role. You have several hundred people working behind the scenes to achieve that success. If one individual, for instance a chap working in the inspections department, doesn't see a problem with a component and that component goes on the car and the car fails, then that is a race lost, so everybody is vital. Obviously there are some people in Ferrari who have a higher profile than others, but around 90 per cent of my time is spent away from the race track. I am responsible for the manufacturing at Ferrari, so my role is really two different roles. When I come to the race track, I perform the role you see on television; then I go back and have a series of meetings and discussions to get the cars designed.'

Ross Braun, Technical Director, Ferrari

Until 1997, even the cars for this symbol of Italian identity were designed and developed near Guildford, then shipped to Maranello to have their engines fitted. The work is now done in-house, but the most prestigious team in racing still relies heavily on British expertise.

Ferrari's technical director Ross Brawn is at the heart of Ferrari's new-found resurgence in Formula One, but his journey to the pinnacle of his profession has been achieved, like many of the older guard of designers and technical directors before him, by learning the craft, by doing the time. Born on 23 November 1954 in Manchester, this Reading Grammar School boy began his working career at the British Atomic Energy Research Establishment at Harwell, near Didcot, Oxfordshire. The young Brawn spent five years there in the 1970s studying instrumentation. Having acquired a passion for racing, in 1976 he enrolled at March Engineering in Bicester as a milling machine operator. This led to a job in Formula Three as a mechanic. Brawn then moved over to Frank Williams' newly formed Williams Grand Prix Engineering, based in an old carpet warehouse in Didcot, once again as a machinist. When Williams found success with the FW07, Brawn gradually moved up within the company, becoming a technician in the renowned Frank Dernie's research and development department. After the team had moved to its new factory in Basil Hill Road, Brawn became an aerodynamicist, working on the team's own wind tunnel. After eight years with Williams, during which time he gained valuable experience in all aspects of design and construction, he followed fellow Williams man Neil Oatley (later to become technical director at McLaren) to Carl Haas's FORCE-Beatrice team, where he developed his aerodynamic skills further.

The team folded at the end of 1986, and Brawn was offered the chief designer's job at Arrows. Arrows had a good budget from American investment company USF&G and was using Megatron (ex-BMW turbo) engines. The A10 and the 1988 A10B were very successful, and the team finished fourth in the World Championship in 1988. This caught the eye of Tom Walkinshaw, who was looking for someone to design a Jaguar sports car for him at nearby Kidlington. Brawn joined Tom's TWR in 1989 and built up a design team to produce the XJR-14, an innovation at the time because it was the first sports car to use state-of-the-art Formula One technology. The Brawn-designed Jaguars won the 1991 Sportscar World Championship, and in July of that year Walkinshaw bought into the Benetton Formula One team. Brawn was appointed technical director of Benetton that autumn to co-ordinate all the technical aspects of the team. Under Brawn, Rory Byrne designed the cars in which Michael Schumacher won two successive championships in 1994 and 1995.

Brawn took up the technical director's role at Ferrari in December 1996 and played an important role in building up the team towards Schumacher's hat trick of World Championship successes in 2000, 2001 and 2002. But Brawn is much better known these days for the strategic decisions he makes from the pit wall during Grands Prix. He can take the credit for many of Ferrari's victories thanks to his quick thinking. No strategy can be set in stone; its effectiveness depends on the flow of the race itself. Brawn seems to have a solution for almost every scenario that is thrown at him. His strength appears to lie in his flexibility, in his ability to sit on the pit wall and make sense of the chaos around him. He makes meticulous pre-race plans, devising a stratagem to which Schumacher can drive, but once the Grand Prix has settled down he rereads the situation and, if necessary, changes tack to give his man a better chance. He and Schuey have nicked many a race from their rivals this way. Only on a handful of occasions have they been on the receiving end.

'My philosophy is to get everything you can organised, and then, when the unanswered questions come along, you can cope with them,' he said. 'I like to get all the variables out of the way so we can be ready for whatever happens. If you have a feeling about how a race may pan out, you prepare around that, but you always have a plan B and plan C, so if it all goes wrong you have other solutions. Sometimes I have to think very quickly; on other occasions it's better to slow things down and examine them properly. Some say it's better to have any decision than none at all, but I'd rather have the right decision, even a lap late. It's great working with Michael because he trusts what I see from the pit wall and I trust what he sees from the track.' Brawn is certainly one of the most self-effacing people you could wish to meet. 'We don't chase records,' he said. 'What evolves, evolves. We don't set out to win World Championships, we set out to win the next race. And if you win enough of them, you win a championship.'

The Benetton 'dream team' of Brawn, Byrne and Schumacher was lifted lock, stock and smouldering barrel into Ferrari, but Brawn does not view himself as a key player. He knows there is more to Ferrari than the front men, and he makes sure the team knows they are all important. 'It is something that we tell them all the time, that they are an intrinsic and vital part of the success of Ferrari. A lot of the guys have been there twenty or so years. They have been through some very tough times, and they are now getting the rewards for the hard work they have done. They are a vital part of our success and every individual who works for Ferrari plays a very important role. You have several hundred people working behind the scenes to achieve that success. If one individual, for instance a chap working in the inspections department, doesn't see a problem with a component and that component goes on the car and the car fails, then that is a race lost, so everybody is vital. Obviously there are some people in Ferrari who have a higher profile than others, but around 90 per cent of my time is spent away from the race track. I am responsible for the manufacturing at Ferrari, so my role is really two different roles. When I come to the race track, I perform the role you see on television; then I go back and have a series of meetings and discussions to get the cars designed.'

However, Brawn does believe that the driver is the crucial cog in the team's machinery, a point often overlooked by the critics. 'I have often said that, as well as being a fantastic driver, Michael has been a very good catalyst for Ferrari because he has made the effort, very often, to come to the factory and meet the people. When we have won the championships Michael has spent a lot of time personally thanking them for their efforts. He recognises very much that it is a team effort.' The *tifosi* are important too: 'The atmosphere and feeling you get when you win a race for Ferrari are not comparable with what you would get in England. It's something English teams miss. If I go out to a restaurant in Italy, someone will buy me a meal. That doesn't happen in England. It gives you a little extra impetus and makes winning a bit special.'

Brawn is also acutely aware of the debt the team owes to technology. 'Technical partnerships are essential for a successful Formula One team. They can provide knowledge, expertise and resources beyond the capacity of the team alone. We need committed partners in all areas – fuel, lubricants, tyres, bearings, dampers, and so on. This is the commitment needed in Formula One, and without the special efforts of our technical partners we could not succeed. There are new and stronger tools to analyse the behaviour and performance of our car. Vehicle dynamics, stress analysis and computational fluid dynamics are becoming more and more important, and they are all areas where we have increased both our human resources and our technical capacity. But, of course, the most important technical partnership at Ferrari is that between the engine and the chassis. It is a tribute to the attitude and approach of our staff that this partnership becomes stronger and stronger. This is why I am very pleased that we have maintained a stable organisation. Every team strives to improve, and the value of stability cannot be underestimated.'

Brawn's life is intense. During the week, he is based at the team's Maranello headquarters, overseeing the design, development and production of the racing cars. He is always at the sharp end. If he takes his eye off the ball and the opposition gain an advantage, the whole championship might be lost. Given all the pressures that he has to face, how does Ross Brawn relax? It is well known that he likes his moments of solitude and tranquillity, in contrast to others in the paddock who have a more energetic way of letting off steam. A release of pressure is necessary from time to time, and on his weekends off he escapes to rural Oxfordshire where he and his wife Jean keep a home. His favourite way to unwind is fly-fishing. To the uninitiated, this may seem a boring way to relax, but it is an intensely challenging sport. It also relies heavily on strategy. The angler needs to know what kind of fly is attracting the trout at any one time and at what depth they are feeding. Each fly pattern must be fished in its own way; a poor imitation will always be ignored. Conditions can change rapidly during the day and, without warning, the fish will move on to different flies, so fast changes of strategy are required. Luring your prey with different movements of the line, reading the water and wind, and then getting a fish to strike is all a question of timing, tactics and instinct.

'I find I have to have activities to take my mind off Formula One,' Brawn said in an interview with the Racing Horse website. 'If I just have a quiet time doing nothing, my mind always strays back to racing. The great thing about fishing is I don't think about F1, even when I'm not catching. I like the contrast with what I do the rest of the time. In F1, there is intense pressure wherever you are on the grid. If you are too hyper, you are going to suffer. You need periods away from racing. It's a stressful job, twenty-four hours a day, seven days a week. If you are burned out and jaded, you don't perform as you should. Everybody has his own way of unwinding. [Ferrari boss] Jean Todt is very sociable. He goes home to Paris at the weekends and he has a strong network of friends. Rory Byrne likes to play cricket. I like to fly-fish.'

Interestingly, although Brawn admits that Schumacher was a major factor in his decision to join Ferrari, he insists that whenever the German champion decides to retire he will not necessarily follow him. 'Michael is an important ingredient in the team, but it is not solely dependent on him,' he said. 'Michael came to Ferrari before me. That was one of the reasons [I joined]. For sure, it was a very strong reason, but it was not the only reason. I am very happy at Ferrari, and 2004 is the end of my current agreement, but at the moment I see no reason why that shouldn't continue. I enjoy Ferrari a great deal, I am probably happier here than I have ever been in my career, so if that continues there is no reason why I shouldn't continue. Michael has also reaped the rewards of his investment over the last few years, and from what I know he is going to keep going for many years. Of course there is going to come a day when he is going to say, "Now is the time to stop," but right now I see huge enthusiasm in him.'

9. RENAULT (ENSTONE)

'I am a great believer in continuity in anything you do – getting a team to work together, getting everybody to know one another's little foibles – but above all it's about the mentality of winning. Some people have it, some don't, and people who have been involved in it definitely have it. Even if they didn't have it, they soon believe. Mechanics, engineers, whoever they might be, they think, "Yeah, I have won the World Championship and I can do it again." It is the mind-set that's important. This is what we had at Benetton in the successful years. We had a team that was working together and pushing in the same direction.'

Pat Symonds, Executive Director of Engineering, Renault F1

There isn't a great deal RenaultF1's executive director of engineering Pat Symonds has missed in his 27-year career in Formula One. Many a head has come and gone, but Pat has remained. He's a wise old owl, and perfectly qualified to talk about British Formula One.

Symonds started his career in the automotive world as an apprentice with the Ford Motor Company. He went on to study automotive engineering at the Cranfield Institute of Technology, graduating in 1976 with an MSc. He joined the Hawke racing car company as a designer of Formula Ford racing cars, but after two years moved to Royale, where he worked with South African designer Rory Byrne. Pat's talent was soon spotted, and in 1981 it was time for Formula Two with Toleman, where he worked in the wind tunnel and became a chassis engineer. The Toleman-Hart combination was very competitive, with Brian Henton and Derek Warwick winning four races and finishing one-two in the 1980 European Formula Two Championship. The team then moved on to Formula One in 1981 with Symonds working on research and development while also engineering Stefan Johansson in a Formula Two Toleman run by Docking Spitzley Racing. The following season, Symonds became a full-time member of the Toleman Formula One team, engineering Teo Fabi and Derek Warwick in 1982, Bruno Giacomelli in 1983, and Ayrton Senna in his first season of Formula One in 1984.

When Benetton took over the Toleman team, Symonds continued as a race engineer, working once again with Fabi and then with Alessandro Nannini. When in 1991 Benetton decided to hire John Barnard as its technical director, Byrne and Symonds quit the team and signed up with Adrian Reynard to design a Reynard F1 car. That project failed to get off the ground, but then Barnard fell out with Flavio Briatore and Byrne and Symonds returned to Benetton. Pat became Michael Schumacher's race engineer, as well as fulfilling the role of head of research and development. He engineered Schumacher during the controversial 1994 season when the German won the title, and continued when Schumacher won his second title in 1995. When Schumacher moved to Ferrari, Symonds stayed at Benetton, and after the departure of Ross Brawn at the end of 1996 he was appointed technical director. Pat became director of engineering for Benetton in 2000, and remained so when Renault returned to Formula One. Today, as executive director, he is one of the key members of the RenaultF1 team, with overall responsibility for running the cars at Grands Prix and during testing, as well as for calculating race strategies.

'There are an awful lot of people still around from that era, and going back way before that,' Symonds commented. 'I am a great believer in continuity in anything you do – getting a team to work together, getting everybody to know one another's little foibles – but above all it's about the mentality of winning. Some people have it, some don't, and people who have been involved in it definitely have it. Even if they didn't have it, they soon believe. Mechanics, engineers, whoever they might be, they think, "Yeah, I have won the World Championship and I can do it again." It is the mind-set that's important. This is what we had at Benetton in the successful years. We had a team that was working together and pushing in the same direction, with reasonable access to technology and budgets. There are lots of things that make a team work, but the one thing we had was continuity. Michael, Ross, Rory, myself and the others. We won because we had the same drivers, engineers and designer. Ross did a fantastic job of pulling that team together. We managed to generate success quite quickly. When Michael went off to Ferrari, it took the Italian team quite a while to achieve the dominance they've got now. The very scary thing about their current dominance is that they've kept their continuity. The 2003 team is exactly the same as it was in 2001 and 2002, which makes it all the more difficult for people to beat them. If any one major element of that team was to disappear, it would make life a lot easier for the rest of us.'

The 'winning' mind-set is still very much alive and kicking at Renault, both at the Enstone factory, out of which came the title-winning Benetton cars, and at the Viry-Chatillon factory which produced the engines that powered them and the Williams machines to titles through the 1990s. But the means of achieving success are different. In the late 1980s, Formula One cars took shape on a drawing board and were modelled by hand; today's four-wheeled power machines move on from concept to race track using a battery of sophisticated technologies.

'Information technology has transformed design,' Symonds confirmed. 'You can't really produce a Formula One car without it these days. The technology we use to help us with the design process is therefore not an add-on, it's at the core of the business.' The RenaultF1 cars are designed with modelling software running on the latest computer work stations. Design tasks are split between the team's engineers who are connected to one another by computer. They share information about the latest design revisions for each of the car's components. 'Back when we still used drawing boards,' Symonds recalled, 'there was always an element of surprise when you came to finally build the first car. Today, we can put together a prototype car in around one week because we know the parts will fit together as the computer will have checked this aspect of the design package.'

Making sure parts were aerodynamic used to be about building wooden models and testing them in a wind tunnel. Ultrapowerful work stations in the RenaultF1 team's design office now operate computational fluid dynamics software to test the aerodynamics of the car's chassis and wing designs. There are still many aspects of car development which need wind-tunnel testing, but computers control the wind tunnel's operations, and the information gathered through the hundreds of test runs held every day is stored and shared with key aerodynamic and design engineering personnel. 'Because our computers are linked together,' Symonds said, 'I can sit in my office and see the results of the wind-tunnel testing as they arrive.' Once designs are finalised, they are passed for manufacture, and the focus of operations shifts to the test track. Engineers use desktop and portable technology to analyse how the car behaves, and thousands of kilometres are covered to hone the car's design and find the best set-up.

'Applying technology to the car's design, testing and manufacture doesn't simplify the car creation process,' Symonds concluded. 'It takes us more man-hours to design a car now than it did ten years ago, but in our quest for perfection the final product's quality is an order of magnitude better.'

10. MERCEDES-ILMOR (BRIXWORTH)

The domination of Ferrari in recent years has put a lot of pressure on Ilmor, and things were not helped in May 2001 when Morgan was killed while flying a Hawker Sea Fury, one of his vintage planes. This led to a deal at the end of 2002 which saw Mercedes-Benz increase its shareholding in Ilmor Engineering; this will lead to a full takeover of the entire company by 2005.

Paul Morgan had been tinkering with cars since the age of fifteen. His father was managing director of an automotive component company, and the young Paul learned the basics of engineering by helping him to restore vintage cars such as a 1904 De Dion-Bouton, a Lagonda Rapier and a Talbot Lago in his spare time. Morgan developed his interest by going on to study mechanical engineering at Birmingham's Aston University. In 1970, he set up the in-house piston-making department at Cosworth and co-ordinated the development of the Cosworth DFX Indy engine which dominated IndyCar racing for almost a decade.

Also a mechanical engineering graduate, Mario Illien was born in Switzerland where motor racing had been banned since the 1955 Le Mans disaster. Nevertheless, Illien developed a passion for racing and trained as a draughtsman with Swedish driver Paul Bonnier. After Bonnier was killed at Le Mans, Illien was hired by former racer Fred Stalder to modify a Chrysler-Simca four-cylinder engine for Le Mans. This would go on to be used in Formula Two in the mid-1970s, but by then Illien had enrolled to study mechanical engineering at the famous Biel University Engineering School. He graduated in 1977 and joined the Mowag company in Kreuzlingen, designing diesel engines for tanks and armoured vehicles. He joined Cosworth in 1979, where his main projects included designing the DFY Formula One engine and the powerful Ford Sierra Cosworth engine.

Having decided they could build a better IndyCar engine themselves, Morgan and Illien broke away and started their own business, Ilmor Engineering Limited (the name comes from a meeting of their surnames – Il-Mor). But where would the financial backing they required come from? They approached US racing great Roger Penske, whose IndyCar team was using the Cosworth engine at the time. Funding was agreed, in exchange for Penske taking shares in the company, and Morgan and

Illien left Cosworth to start the project in January 1984, Mario designing the engine in his bedroom while Paul searched for suitable land for a factory. The factory was eventually built at Brixworth in Northampton-shire, and the duo completed their first engine in the summer of 1985. The following year the engine took two pole positions, and in April 1987 Mario Andretti scored one of the engine's first victories at Long Beach. It was the first of 86 wins between 1987 and 1993, including six Indianapolis 500 victories and five CART titles.

In 1989, Illien and Morgan took the decision to expand into Formula One and built a 3.5-litre V10 engine. This was used in 1991 by Leyton House Racing, and by March and Tyrrell in 1992. That year the company was commissioned by Mercedes-Benz to design an engine for the Sauber Formula One team. It was quite successful, and in 1993 it was christened the Sauber V10. At the end of that year, Mercedes-Benz decided to enter Formula One officially, buying Chevrolet's share of Ilmor and supplying Sauber with engines. A Mercedes CART engine was built for the Indianapolis 500 and Al Unser Junior won the 1994 race with ease. For 1995, Mercedes dropped Sauber and went into partnership with McLaren. The relationship was immediately successful, and in the US Ilmor-designed Mercedes engines scored six wins that year. The following year the engines didn't win anything in either Formula One or CART, but in 1997 the Penske, Forsythe and PacWest teams collected nine wins in CART and at the end of the year Mika Hakkinen won the European Grand Prix at Jerez to give Mercedes its first Formula One victory in the modern era.

The McLaren-Mercedes combination went on to dominate the 1998 and 1999 seasons, although Ferrari was able to sneak a victory in the constructors' championship in 1999. But the success in America tailed off, Greg Moore winning only three times in 1998 and 1999. The domination of Ferrari in recent years has put a lot of pressure on Ilmor, and things were not helped in May 2001 when Morgan was killed while flying a Hawker Sea Fury, one of his vintage planes. This led to a deal at the end of 2002 which saw Mercedes-Benz increase its shareholding in Ilmor Engineering; this will lead to a full takeover of the entire company by 2005. The engines have since become known as Mercedes-Ilmor V10s.

An interesting branch of the company, the Mercedes-Ilmor Special Projects Group (SPG), undertakes development work for other indus-tries, as well as its traditional markets. Recent projects include work for Triumph Designs. The first quarter of 2001 witnessed the launch of the three-cylinder Triumph 955 bike, which owed a good deal of its 147bhp to the group's high-performance engine design and development expertise. Triumph had earlier involved Mercedes-Ilmor in the development of its four-cylinder 600cc engine. SPG was also called in to design an engine for an unmanned high-speed target aircraft for Meggitt, which eventually chose the 955 Triumph engine as its base because of Mercedes-Ilmor's earlier involvement in its development.

In addition to this, SPG is running the non-Formula One racing programme Ilmor is involved in – the Indy Racing League (IRL), which runs the Indianapolis 500. At the 2001 race, Ilmor-developed engines took pole with Scott Sharp, driving for Kelley Racing, and a spectacular race win and second place for Helio Castroneves and Gil de Ferran, both driving for Penske. Ilmor engines also took one further race win with Kelley Racing at the Texas Casino Magic 500, and four more pole positions.

11. B3 TECHNOLOGIES (GUILDFORD)

'It is just as important to me to create something that looks right, since the old adage "if it looks right, it usually is right" holds much truth. Every racing car is designed and built to a specific set of rules and regulations, and it is the designer's job to manipulate these to the best of his advantage. In racing, your design ideas and solutions will be very quickly measured against your contemporaries. An original idea, if successful, can immediately leapfrog you ahead of your competitors. However, one can be sure that it will not be long before another designer sees the benefits and starts along the new path. Therefore the pressure to be original, to make that step forward before anyone else, is continuous and intense.'

John Barnard, Head of B3 Technologies

The head of B3 Technologies, John Barnard, is Mr Innovation, a vastly experienced Formula One designer, and a legend. The Englishman made his name designing Grand Prix cars for McLaren and Ferrari, but in a 35-year career in Formula One he has also worked for Benetton, Arrows and Prost. He was the brains behind two of the most significant and lasting innovations of the last two decades: the first carbon-fibre monocoque for the 1981 McLaren, and the first semiautomatic gearbox, operated by paddles on the steering wheel, for the 1989 Ferrari. Barnard has certainly come a long way since his days tinkering with an Austin Healey Sprite and its souped-up engine.

Having been fascinated since childhood by cars, and racing cars in particular, Barnard finally managed to secure a position in the design office of Lola Cars in 1969. Here, as a newly qualified mechanical engineer, Barnard discovered that he no longer had a hobby but an all-consuming passion for designing racing cars. 'On reflection,' he recalled, 'those early years were irreplaceable for the experience and knowledge I gained in all areas of racing-car design and operation. In those days, the design office did not consist of many dedicated specialists, but a few enthusiasts like myself who were expected to do everything from producing quarter-scale clay models to driving the finished product, with van and trailer, to Earls Court to sit on a stand – and helping to sell the product we had designed.'

In 1972, Barnard was invited to join McLaren. He carried out much of the detailed design work on the team's M23 car that in 1974 took Emerson Fittipaldi to the World Championship. In 1975, the US beckoned when the Vels Parnelli Jones Racing Team, based in Torrance, Los Angeles, offered Barnard the chief designer's position. There he pioneered the development of the turbocharged Cosworth engine for IndyCar racing, and the following year the VPJ 6B was the first IndyCar to win using the turbocharged Cosworth engine in the American USAC (United States Auto Club) Championship. Barnard was fast building himself a reputation in IndyCar design, and in 1978, 'after a handshake agreement with Jim Hall', owner of the Chaparral team, Barnard returned to England where he designed and built the Chaparral 2K, the first to introduce full ground-effect aerodynamics to American open-wheeled racing cars. The car's immediate success and its revolutionary ideas won Barnard the Louis Schwitzer Design Award in 1979, a gong presented by the American Society of Automotive Engineers for Innovation and Excellence in the Field of Race Car Design.

The design of a racing car is defined by a number of factors. First, there are the rules and regulations that govern its basic size and weight. Then there are performance factors to consider – its aerodynamics, suspension parameters, weight distribution, and so on. The designer's job is to combine all these factors with the minimum compromise to achieve maximum performance. 'However,' Barnard added, 'it is just as important to me to create something that looks right, since the old adage "if it looks right, it usually is right" holds much truth. Every racing car is designed and built to a specific set of rules and regulations, and it is the designer's job to manipulate these to the best of his advantage. In racing, your design ideas and solutions will be very quickly measured against your contemporaries. An original idea, if successful, can immediately leapfrog you ahead of your competitors. However, one can be sure that it will not be long before another designer sees the benefits and starts along the new path. Therefore the pressure to be original, to make that step forward before anyone else, is continuous and intense.'

After the Chaparral project, Barnard looked for a return to Formula One, and at the end of 1979 he joined Ron Dennis at his small Project Four team based in Woking. The Chaparral had been revolutionary, and Barnard was determined to do something else that would be seen as a fundamental step. This objective, coupled with the self-belief he had gained during his American experience, convinced him to embark on an ambitious carbon-fibre monocoque design (the McLaren MP4/1). It was a world first, and such a step forward in the use of the material that most British companies already working with carbon fibre refused to participate in the project because they thought it might be too ambitious. 'Through contacts made while racing in America,' Barnard explained, 'I found Hercules, a company based in Salt Lake City, which volunteered the use of its special projects division for building the first monocoques. Working with carbon fibre required a very different approach in terms of design and manufacture. New methods of attaching components and defining shapes and surfaces had to be thought of and perfected. Today, virtually all open-wheeled racing cars use carbon-fibre monocoques. Initially, safety was a great concern when using this material, but after several major accidents where the drivers walked away unscathed it became an essential part of the safety mechanism of a modern racing car.' Barnard's revolutionary design led to Project Four and Team McLaren joining forces to become the new company McLaren International, of which Barnard was appointed technical director.

As well as manufacturing, Barnard was also taking a fresh look at aerodynamics. In 1980, the number of wind tunnels with a rolling road (a large machine with a moving belt underneath the model which simulates airflow under the car) capable of running a scale-model racing car were few – maybe only one or two at university teaching facilities. 'So, at the start of the McLaren International period I was forced to create a new facility that would allow us to conduct sufficient testing,' said Barnard. 'This meant laying down the design for a new rolling road and then converting an aircraft wind tunnel to accept it. The need to improve these facilities and create new ones has been a constant factor with each team I have worked with. To date, I have converted four aircraft wind tunnels with the design and installation of purpose-designed rolling roads to allow them to be used to run scale-model racing cars, each design taking a step forward in size and capability.'

By the mid-1980s, therefore, Barnard had started to gain a 'no compromise' reputation for design and engineering quality. In 1984, he was responsible for the first Formula One car to win a World Championship using carbon brakes. 'This required me to design special brake callipers that would work with the high temperatures generated by carbon brakes. Each component has to be thought about in the greatest detail. Even small brackets have to look right and function with the minimum compromise. I hammered this message constantly into my designers and engineers. Indeed, such was my desire to see everything as near perfect as possible, a magazine reported that secretly I was known as the "Prince of Darkness", probably because of my continuing criticism of anything I saw as falling short of what I considered the optimum. From my early time at Lola, the appreciation of flowing lines and smooth shapes that belonged together had become firmly planted. Over the years I have tried to incorporate this approach and concept right through to the smallest component, even though it may rarely be seen except by the mechanics handling it.' In 1994, Carbone Industrie, the manufacturer of the carbon material used for the brakes, recognised

Barnard's pioneering work by presenting him with a special trophy to commemorate the 150th win of a Formula One car using carbon brakes.

During his time at McLaren, Barnard's cars won three consecutive World Championships. This is perhaps the reason why at the end of 1986 a significant event occurred in the history of Italian racing-car production: Ferrari approached Barnard and asked if he would like to set up a design and manufacturing studio in England. Of course, Barnard was renowned as the best designer in Formula One in the 1980s with a reputation for creativity and revolutionary thinking, and Ferrari had been without a win for some time, but such a decision was unprecedented. It was made by Enzo Ferrari himself, but considering the heritage of Ferrari and its ownership by Fiat, such a move cannot have been made lightly.

Barnard's first season with the team in 1987 brought two wins, and in 1989 Barnard introduced the type 640 Ferrari which was again a radical departure from the established traditions at the time. This car introduced the electrohydraulic gearbox which eliminated conventional gear changing, and allied to a new aerodynamic shape it won three races in 1989. 'This was a risky move,' Barnard explained, 'since the car had been designed to accept only this type of gearbox and a return to the conventional type was not possible. But I was so sure it was the way to go that I was prepared to suffer a number of heated discussions with the Ferrari top management in order to race this system on the car. Fortunately, it won its first race [in the hands of Nigel Mansell].' Indeed, the system has been so successful that all Formula One cars now run this type of gearbox, and the idea of gear shifting with paddles on the steering wheel and an automatic clutch has now migrated across to road cars. The Ferrari 640's direct descendant, the type 641 that took Alain Prost close to the 1990 World Championship, was exhibited in New York's Museum of Modern Art because it bridged the gap between designing for function and creating style and beauty, and was therefore deemed a work of art.

That same year, 1989, Barnard moved to work for the up-and-coming Benetton team with a brief to establish a new technical centre and start a long-term development programme to produce a winning car. In 1991, he produced the B191 which won in its first year and burnished Barnard's reputation for producing winning Formula One designs. The foundations had been laid for the team's successes over the following seasons.

During the early part of 1992, Barnard took a short-term contract with the Toms GB Team to advise and assist them in setting up a new

Formula One-level facility in Norfolk. 'By the end of this contract I had been out of front-line Formula One for about ten months and was beginning to miss the pace of design and development,' Barnard recalled. He was then approached again by Ferrari and asked to re-establish a UK technical base from which he was to head a design and manufacturing group. The concept was to establish a research and development centre that would work purely on designing and building cars rather than on racing and developing them. This was an important shift, as the tradition within Formula One was for the same engineering team to be involved with designing and building a new car while they were racing and developing the existing one. The facilities included a wind tunnel and the equipment needed to construct models for use in the tunnel. The operation designed and built Ferrari Formula One cars up to 1997, when Ferrari finished second in both the drivers' and constructors' championships, its best result for almost twenty years.

At the end of the five-year contract, Barnard was looking for a respite from the pressures and intensity of Formula One involvement. Faced with the choice of closing the operation or keeping it going and finding work to keep it viable, he decided on the latter, and renamed it B3 Technologies. B3's first contract was with the Arrows team in 1997. This relationship included design work and fabricating specialised components such as a revolutionary carbon-fibre gearbox. In 1998, B3 started to supply the newly formed Prost team with titanium components for its cars. This developed into a more comprehensive relationship including designing, producing and assembling an increasing proportion of the components for their F1 cars.

B3 Technologies has no direct competitor in the sense of a company that offers the range of capabilities B3 has developed, and generally machine shops avoid the particular problems associated with working with composite materials. Barnard's reputation as a top Formula One designer has meant there has never been a shortage of teams interested in accessing B3's skills. However, B3 has been very selective when it comes to the types of relationship it enters into. The company has a history of very close alliances with single customers rather than supplying a range of people with components. This means that, although B3 is trying to develop a much wider customer base these days, it doesn't labour under the larger overheads needed to service a huge number of them. The philosophy at B3 is centred on becoming a supplier of dedicated expertise to support a particular team. 'The reason why a team like Prost came and made a deal with us was because it wanted to learn from us,' said Barnard. 'It sent people over here to work with us, so they took back some of the way we did it. We didn't want to give too much away, but at the same time it was going to learn something through its involvement with us.'

But it's B3's high-quality design and manufacturing projects that have been the basis of its success. There is always pressure to grow and increase capacity, but the B3 approach is to keep the organisation focused and flexible. It describes itself as 'a design house with exceptional manufacturing capabilities' and prides itself on its ability to integrate composites and machining better than anyone else. The secret lies not in terms of composite knowledge or design or machine skills, but in the way it integrates these areas to produce high-performance components. Rather than doing things at minimum cost, B3 has its own test lab where all its components are rigorously tested before being sent out to customers. This is not a stipulation of its contracts, it is simply something B3 does so it can produce the highest quality output. The areas of knowledge within B3 are design (including use of state-of-the-art CAD systems), composites, fabrication and machining. In other words, it can both design and manufacture specialised materials to the highest standards. For example, for a carbon-composite gearbox case it can make all the tooling needed to shape the composite materials, and can also make the composite component and then machine it, if necessary halfway through a composite stage. It can design the composite, mould it, machine it into a part, go back and perfect it. It is this kind of interaction that is essential for producing leading-edge components that are able to achieve the highest possible levels of reliability.

'The classic thing is that people believe a successful designer sits in a nice office producing lots of nice drawings, but it doesn't really work like that,' said Barnard. 'If you're trying to take a new step, then you have to go and get something made to determine that you're going to be able to design the component in the way you have in mind. Sometimes you've got to go and do a lot of tests. We've got a very good materials guy here and we produce our own data for FE [finite element analysis] work, such as work on composites. And sometimes you can't design without having that manufacturing [expertise] to hand. That's why we have all the disciplines. This means that we can make the initial pieces which confirm to us as designers that we know we can make it, or we know we can manufacture it.'

B3 invests in bringing on young people, but Formula One grows all the time and B3's reputation as a provider of one of the best technical apprenticeships in the industry means it suffers from skilled technicians being poached by F1 teams. Interestingly, Barnard finds that growing his own is the best way for the company to develop staff. 'In the past we've recruited good people from hi-tech industries, but we've struggled with getting them into the mind-set to do things "now". You're not teaching them about the job, about composites or anything like that, you're teaching them to make quick decisions and to solve problems. In their old companies things would take three or four days to reach a decision. We just need to get on with it, and that's what we have to instil.'

B3's biggest opportunity lies in taking its unique skills into other markets where the focus is on leading-edge development of specialised materials. As with many Motorsport Valley companies, innovation is not something that happens now and again at B3, it's part of the basic routine. All those working in the company are motivated by a constant desire to push the limits and develop new ideas. The aerospace sector therefore obviously has potential. 'We have already applied our thinking and technology to a project which involved the redesign of some aircraft seating components,' Barnard said. 'We reduced the weight of the component from 3kg down to 1.5kg, which in aircraft terms is real money in the pocket. We also simplified the way it was made, using fewer pieces in its construction. The company was extremely impressed that we'd actually done it, and in a couple of months, too, which in their terms was next to no time for a redesign and development project. The material we used was carbon, with the addition of a little bit of titanium, but fundamentally we used new thinking on the project, took a different approach. That really was the key to the project's success. We don't just take an existing solution and tinker with it. We try to throw it away and take a completely fresh look at it.' Barnard also quoted another example involving a helicopter rescue hook. 'These are massive things made from steel. Again, the client wanted to save a lot of weight, and asked if it could be done in titanium. We sat down, looked at the design, played around with it, and concluded that we could cut half the weight.'

Another exciting area B3 is moving into is motorbike design. In doing so, Barnard is following in the footsteps of Alan Jenkins, a former colleague of Barnard's at McLaren and formerly of the Arrows and Stewart teams, who designed the bike that debuted with Ducati in 2003. 'There are a lot of things that can be done with motorcycles,' Barnard insisted. 'There are new ways to make things as well as new ways to approach things in general.' The fact that Barnard has retained respect within the industry as a man with a superb eye for engineering detail and packaging ideally qualifies him for motorbike design. He switched to two wheels at the beginning of 2003 by agreeing to join the Proton KR MotoGP team as technical director. He will be responsible for all technical aspects of the team that's headed by former world champion Kenny Roberts, including the new Proton KR V-5 four-stroke Grand Prix bike, Britain's first home-grown MotoGP championship contender for more than half a century. The bike, the fastest ever built in Britain, should be capable of challenging for the championship in 2004. The Proton KR was designed at Roberts' Banbury headquarters in Oxfordshire, in the heart of Motorsport Valley. 'Bringing John into our organisation is another step in our quest to achieve a higher level of engineering, overall expertise and competitiveness,' said Roberts. 'Britain is the perfect country to do this because of your cottage industry in making racing components. I've known John for a lot of years and have complete faith in his ability to help us evolve our company and our team to a higher level.'

The furniture industry is another that has caught Barnard's eye (perhaps inspired by his work on aircraft seating). 'We don't want to be in the mainstream furniture design business,' he maintained, 'but we could certainly experiment, design and manufacture different kinds of modern furniture using carbon. The fact that we have almost every discipline here – a design office, good machine and fabrication shops, a composites facility, test machines, inspection expertise, and so on – is one of our great pluses. It's a one-stop shop, and that's what we try to sell. If you want a carbon chair and present us with a concept design, we'll take it from there and produce for you.' As an RDI (Royal Designer for Industry), Barnard recently contacted other RDI colleagues, established names in the furniture design industry, and asked them why there wasn't any carbon furniture on the market and would they be interested in developing new products. 'They all came down and had a look around B3. They were quite impressed with what we did. However, I was staggered to find out from one that mine was only the second letter he'd ever had from a British company talking about design and trying to advance it using new materials and concepts. A true innovator goes across industries, sharing ideas with other like-minded individuals. You have to explore new areas to be able to innovate. I can always find something to which I can add my opinion, or possibly suggest an alternative way of looking. It doesn't matter what it is. If you can think laterally enough, and apply good, basic principles, I guarantee you that there are lots of areas where you could make an impact. We just need to get to people out there and persuade them to come to us with these solution requests.'

12. THE POWERS ON THE THRONE

The secret of Ecclestone's success has been to make Formula One entertaining. In fact, you could say that without Bernie Ecclestone, the conditions that have allowed the sport to grow so fast would not have been created.

Bernie Ecclestone and the Paris-based Fédération Internationale de l'Automobile's president Max Mosley comprise another formidable British duo with a vicelike grip on Formula One motorsport worldwide. Ecclestone and Mosley are undoubtedly the two most powerful men in Formula One. It was they who set about improving contracts with circuit owners and television broadcasters. They also encouraged and cajoled the teams into taking the sport more seriously. In earlier days, UK constructors needed sponsors to survive, but sponsors weren't prepared to waste thousands of pounds on a sport whose members, they thought, weren't behaving professionally. Incredibly, before the Formula One Constructors Association (FOCA) imposed order on the way the sport was run, constructors were under no obligation to turn up for every Grand Prix. Ecclestone's companies hold the licences that 'exploit' Formula One on behalf of the sport's governing body, the FIA, but the secret of Ecclestone's success has been to make Formula One entertaining. In fact, you could say that without Bernie Ecclestone, the conditions that have allowed the sport to grow so fast would not have been created.

Born in Ipswich, Suffolk, though the family later moved to Bexleyheath in southeast London, Ecclestone left school at sixteen, by which time he'd acquired a passion for motorcycle scrambling. He began racing just after the war. Because machinery was scarce at the time he began to buy and sell spare parts for motorcycles, doing deals during his lunch break. In this way he built up a spares business and then went into partnership with Fred Compton to form the Compton & Ecclestone motorcycle dealership. He later bought Fred out and built up the business into one of Britain's biggest motorcycle dealers. In 1949, Bernie had a go at racing on four wheels in the 500cc Formula Three series, but after a big accident at Brands Hatch he decided to call it a day and concentrate instead on his business, which grew to include the

Weekend Car Auctions company (which he eventually sold to British Car Auctions), loan financing and property.

In 1957, Ecclestone returned to the sport to manage Welsh racing driver Stuart Lewis-Evans. He bought the Formula One Connaught team and ran cars for Lewis-Evans, Roy Salvadori, Archie Scott-Brown and Ivor Bueb. He even tried to qualify one of the cars himself at Monaco in 1958. At the end of that year, Lewis-Evans, who was by then driving a Vanwall, suffered serious burns when his engine blew up during the Moroccan Grand Prix. He later died from his injuries. This led to Ecclestone abandoning the sport again, but he returned once more in the early 1960s. His friendship with Salvadori, who was by then running the Cooper team, eventually led to a meeting with Austrian driver Jochen Rindt. Ecclestone became Rindt's manager and business partner, and in 1968 and 1969 he helped to run the Lotus Formula Two factory team, whose drivers were Rindt and Graham Hill. In September 1970, Rindt was most of the way through his championship-winning season for Lotus when, tragically, he was killed in an accident at Monza. Again Ecclestone quit the sport, only to return for a third time in early 1972 when he decided to buy the Brabham team from Ron Tauranac and set about turning it into a winning force.

Two years later, while trying to get the sport more organised, Ecclestone became one of the founders of the Formula One Constructors Association (FOCA), alongside Colin Chapman, Teddy Mayer, Max Mosley, Ken Tyrrell and Frank Williams. In 1975, he led the team owners in a battle with the FIA for a new system of entries and appearance money which would be paid to all teams. The teams had won the battle by the following year, but soon afterwards a second battle brewed over the sale of television rights. In January 1978, Ecclestone became chief executive of FOCA with Mosley as his legal adviser, and a fresh conflict was sparked with the FIA's new affiliate FISA, the brainchild of Frenchman Jean-Marie Balestre. The battle for commercial control of the sport continued until March 1981, when the 'Concorde Agreement' gave FOCA the right to negotiate television contracts. In the same year, Brabham won the World Championship with Nelson Piquet as its driver. A second victory followed in 1983.

When the first Concorde Agreement expired in 1987, Ecclestone became the FIA's vice president in charge of promotional affairs, and he began to spend less of his time managing Brabham. At the end of the year the team lost its sponsorship and Ecclestone decided to take a year out of racing, selling the team to Alfa Romeo so that he could prepare for the new Procar Championship. When this series failed to get off the ground, Alfa Romeo had no use for the team and it was sold to a Swiss businessman.

The proceeds from the sale of Formula One's television rights originally belonged to all the teams, but in the early days the business appeared to be a risky and not very profitable proposition. Bit by bit, Ecclestone began to distance himself from the sport's team owners, and eventually they allowed him to establish Formula One Promotions and Administration (FOPA) to manage their rights. As part of the deal, 47 per cent of the television revenues went to the teams, 30 per cent to the FIA and 23 per cent to FOPA. FOPA, however, received all the fees paid by promoters, in exchange for which it agreed to pay prize money to the teams.

In 1995, the FIA decided to grant Formula One's commercial rights to Ecclestone's Formula One management company for fourteen years in exchange for an annual payment from Ecclestone, but this upset the Formula One teams. McLaren, Williams and Tyrrell refused to sign the new 1997 Concorde Agreement, though the other teams backed down. They eventually signed an agreement spanning ten years.

This, then, in brief, is how Bernie Ecclestone became the most powerful man in Formula One. Like many of his generation and before, he has seen enough death in the sport to last a lifetime. Many forget when they meet him that this kind of experience breeds toughness. To his enemies, he's a formidable opponent; to loyal friends, he's a brick. He also holds a realistic view of what the sport has become. 'The way the whole thing is set up now, there's no necessity to be like the daredevil guys of the past,' he said. 'It's like today's fighter pilots compared to the Battle of Britain boys. Those guys went into the sky thinking they weren't going to come back. Maybe that meant they were prepared to push the envelope. That said, we have as many accidents today as we ever had, but they walk away. Which is good.' Having said that, he does miss the less formal, more characterful atmosphere of former days. 'Today, someone like James Hunt would never be tolerated by Marlboro the way he was when he was driving for them. They are looking for a different image. If I were a sponsor I'd rather have a character than just another guy that pitches up and says thanks to the sponsors, thanks to the engine company, thanks to the tyre manufacturers.'

Ecclestone remains an enigma to many, but one thing's for sure: he's a tough cookie and a smooth operator. In his book *The Piranha Club*, Tim Collings described an episode in Ecclestone's life which epitomises this aspect of Bernie the man: 'Those who have known him for a long time are full of admiration and respect. Frank Williams recalled him buying Brabham and running the early meetings of the 1970s. He remembered one incident in particular, at the Watkins Glen Motor Inn. "He was there negotiating with the organiser from Mexico, and the man literally excused himself to go to the lavatory . . . and never came back. He went out of the back window!" That, as Williams conceded with a smile, stuck in his mind. Of Ecclestone the achiever, he said: "In the big picture, we all know, and respect, that Bernie saw Formula One for what it could be. Over 30 years, he has moulded it into the activity that he thought would earn an important place in the world and a strong commercial base for the teams as well as creating a side of the business for himself. He has achieved his objectives very successfully. I think he has the admiration of all the teams for that. He really is a formidable individual in every sense of the word, and he has created a worldwide sport pretty much single-handedly . . . [He has] a gifted business brain . . . He is intellectually very clever and level-headed. Clearly, he is very determined. He can also be very persuasive when putting his deals together in the order in which he wanted them to stack up." ' Could anyone else have done what Bernie did? ' "Probably, but he wasn't in this part of the universe at the right time . . . I've always known it is impossible to second-guess Bernard. Like many clever businessmen, you don't know what he is thinking." '

The second son of the notorious politican Sir Oswald Mosley and his second wife Diana Mitford, Max Mosley spent his childhood in Ireland before being sent to school in France, and later in Germany. In 1958, he won a place at Christ Church College, Oxford, where he became secretary of the Oxford Union and from where he graduated in 1961 with a degree in physics. He then read law at Gray's Inn, and in 1964 qualified as a solicitor.

Mosley got involved in racing after a visit to Silverstone in the early 1960s. He raced mainly at club events, but in 1968 graduated to Formula Two, having founded the London Racing Team with Chris Lambert. When Lambert was killed in an accident with Clay Regazzoni at Zandvoort in August 1968, Mosley became Piers Courage's team-mate in Frank Williams' Formula Two team. A year later Mosley decided to retire from driving and established March Engineering with Robin Herd, Alan Rees and Graham Coaker. The outfit was a great success as a racing-car production company in the early years of what was to become Motorsport Valley. March cars won many championships, but the company never really lived up to its potential in Formula One. Jackie

Stewart drove one to victory at the 1970 Spanish Grand Prix, but March won only two more Grands Prix, with Vittorio Brambilla at a soaking wet Osterreichring in 1975, and with Ronnie Peterson at Monza in 1976.

By this time Mosley was becoming increasingly involved in the activities of FOCA, and he withdrew from Formula One at the end of 1977 to become a legal adviser to FOCA and a member of the FISA Formula One Commission. Mosley was a leading light in the FISA–FOCA war of the late 1970s and early 1980s which led to the Concorde Agreement, of which he was one of the architects. After the political battles were over, Mosley took three years out of the sport before becoming president of the Manufacturers Commission at the FIA in 1986. He had another crack at motorsport by becoming involved with Simtek Research in 1989, although he sold his shareholding in the company when he became president of FISA (the sporting subsidiary of the FIA) in 1991, ousting Jean-Marie Balestre. Mosley announced that he would resign after a year so he could be judged on his merits, and twelve months later he was re-elected for four years. He then engineered the merger between the FIA and FISA, and in October 1993 became the FIA's president for four years. He was re-elected in October 1997 and again in 2001.

As is the case with Ecclestone, it's difficult to assess Mosley the man, but in an exclusive interview carried out by Tim Urquhart for itv.com in 2003 the general public were given a taste of what the FIA president, a powerful man in terms of altering and generating the sport's rules, thinks about Formula One today. Urquhart began by asking about the last major technical rule change to be pushed through: the move to grooved tyres, which was introduced back in 1998 in the teeth of a fair amount of opposition from the teams. Was that regulation change also agreed by the Formula One Commission?

'Well,' Mosley replied, 'if they hadn't agreed to it we couldn't have brought it in. They agreed it for two reasons. Number one was that we agreed that for four years we would not ask them to change the chassis regulations. The second reason was that they thought we could never make it work, or that it would be such a disaster that we would have had to abandon it. So in their minds it was a win-win situation because they got their four-year-rule stability in return for something that we would have to abandon. Don't forget that when we first brought the grooved tyres in, all the experts, including the drivers, said, "It will be completely undriveable and the cars will be at least ten seconds a lap slower. They'll be slower than Formula 3000 and that is going to be a disaster." This was all obvious nonsense – well, to me it was nonsense – but I think they really believed it. Now, of course, without grooved tyres we would have massive problems with corner speed. Always what happens is that they say, "Don't let's interfere with the tyres, let's reduce downforce." I completely agree with that. Now, in an ideal world we would have big sticky tyres and very little downforce. That would help in all sorts of ways. But the problem is, it's easy enough to put the big sticky tyres on, but it's difficult to get the downforce off. The engineers will come along and say, "This change is going to add one point five to two seconds a lap to the lap times." And they probably believe that at the time. But by the time they've finished in the wind tunnel over the winter, things have got back to where they were. I've just said to the teams recently, "If you allow us [the FIA] to do what we like with the aerodynamics with a few months' notice, you can have tyres that are as big and sticky as you want, but we must be free to act." Then you can do it, but you would have to be able to do dramatic things with the aerodynamics.'

Urquhart then switched to the question of Formula One as entertainment. 'You've said in the past that lots and lots of overtaking is not necessary for exciting motor racing, using the analogy of a football match requiring only one or two goals to make the spectacle. Do you still stand by that?'

Mosley did. 'When you had massive amounts of overtaking, when you had the "slipstreamers", what happened then was at Monza, if you had a car in the race, you would watch the start, go and have lunch, and come back later because really all that mattered was the order in which they came out of the Parabolica on the last lap. They'd all be there swapping places.'

Urquhart: I'm too young to remember those classic races at Monza in the 1960s and 1970s, but wasn't it fun to watch them racing so closely for such long periods of time?

Mosley: Well, they were great to take part in because a very mediocre driver could keep up with a very quick driver – speaking as a mediocre driver [laughs]. But the thing is I think they were quite pointless compared to modern racing. The real test is this. Formula One has been available on television all over the world for about the last 30 years. It's only really in the last five to ten years where we have seen this massive boom, and it has coincided with overtaking being difficult but not impossible, pit stops and strategy. The races are more interesting now than they were in the 1980s. It doesn't matter what all the old boys say, they remember the good races but forget about the bad ones.

Urquhart: I've heard you use this argument in the past. That Formula One has never been more popular and that the television audience has never been so high, ergo, we must be doing quite a good job. However, is this not linked to the fact that Bernie Ecclestone has done a very good job in promoting and selling the sport to the global television networks rather than the product being inherently better now?

Mosley: Not really. You can get the television network to show it, but you can't make the public watch it. That's what you get in all sections of motorsport. They always come to us and say, 'You must do more to get us on television, we don't have enough television.' Well, quite apart from the fact that if everyone who was saying that was on the television you would have 24 hours of motorsport, the fact is that people don't want to watch it. The reason they watch F1 is that it is interesting. There are two categories of people. There are the anoraks – and, with all respect, most journalists fit into that category – and then there is the public. The anoraks and the enthusiasts who want to see wheel-to-wheel racing and overtaking continually say to us how much better oval racing in America is, for example. Well, it is for them. The public could watch oval racing for hours if they wanted to, but they don't. What they watch is the tactics and strategy of Formula One. That should not make one complacent, but it does tend to refute the argument that what the anorak likes is what the wider public likes.

Urquhart then addressed another perennial point of debate in modern Formula One, the balance of the relationship between driver skill and electronic aids such as launch control, traction control and automatic gearshifts. 'Is there any chance,' he asked, 'that the driver, as opposed to the software engineer, is going to become a more integral part of things?'

'Well, we would like to get away from a lot of these sophistications, for example have a standard ECU [engine control unit],' said Mosley. 'The difficulty is that electronics are more and more an essential element of the road car, and the big manufacturers are really into their electronics, and especially the electronics on the engines. If you went back to fully manual gearboxes, for example, it would certainly create more overtaking opportunities as people would make mistakes which they don't at the moment. But as a practical matter you would have to make completely new gearboxes and so on. A modern gearbox is tiny because it's all run by computer, and you don't have to deal with a ham-fisted driver. So that would be quite difficult. There are other things we don't like, such as pre-loading the transmission for launch control. They wind the whole thing up before the car goes, they then press the button and release it. It's unnecessarily expensive and entirely pointless, and I think we're going to outlaw that on the grounds that it is an energy storage system. That's what we have told the teams, but it's quite difficult to check.'

Urquhart: If you want to police these things, surely you need to go with sealed FIA electronics and engine control units?

Mosley: If we could do it, we would do it. The problem is getting them all to agree. Worse than that, if it's something to do with the engines or the transmission we can't interfere for the length of the Concorde Agreement [which expires at the end of 2007] without unanimous agreement.

Urquhart: I think almost every Formula One fan is happy about the fact that you've banned team orders. These things are of course hard to police too, so how do you intend to police them, and what punishments will be available for anyone trying to pull off an A1-Ring-style stunt in the future?

Mosley: Well, if you're policing it you have to catch somebody. Obviously if it's an absolutely in-your-face thing like Austria [in May 2002, when Barrichello, having led virtually the entire race, allowed team-mate Schumacher to pass him on the finishing line], it is an open-and-shut case. But if people try to do it subtly, if the public can see it, we can see it. If you see something suspicious, like one of two drivers has been fast all through the weekend and he's been leading the race until two-thirds distance, comes in for his second pit stop and they lose one of the rear wheels, then the race director would probably report this to the stewards. The stewards would be tempted to draw the inference that this was deliberate and this was team orders being implemented secretly. The team would be given a hearing, we would listen to their defence and the stewards would then decide. If the team weren't happy with the decision they could go to the court of appeal. In real life, most crimes are convicted because you can draw an inference from all the circumstances.

Urquhart: OK, what happens if someone has been caught?

Mosley: They would get a race suspension, but that would be a matter for the stewards, and the court of appeal if there was one. But the most obvious thing would be a race suspension, depending on how serious the case was. That's why we don't have fixed penalties. It's very tempting to have them, but each case is different and there are often mitigating circumstances. To fix a race at the beginning of the season in favour of one driver is very different from fixing it at the end of the season when the championship is at stake.

Urquhart ended his interview by comparing Mosley's racing past with that of the second half of the Formula One power base. 'You and Bernie Ecclestone both started out as team bosses. Are you sad that the era of the entrepreneurial team boss seems to have come to an end?'

'I'm not sure that it has, really,' Mosley countered. 'We have still got a lot of entrepreneurs. In the end, practically everyone around the table is an entrepreneurial team boss, even, for example, Renault, which is completely owned by a manufacturer, and as far as I know Flavio [Briatore] works for Renault. But he's still an entrepreneurial team boss, he's completely out of that mould. And then, of course, you've got people like Eddie Jordan and [Minardi boss] Paul Stoddart.'

'But if you were to start a team now, it would surely be a lot more difficult than it was back in 1970.'

'You'd certainly have to have a big backer. But then you had to have a big backer in 1970. It's just that we didn't!'

13. THE BRITISH BOYS

'The fact that we've had so many British champions makes you think there must be something in the water that makes them great natural drivers.'

Tony Jardine, Formula One Analyst

Formula One analyst Tony Jardine knows a thing or two about Formula One drivers. He's been around most of them since his days clambering into Aintree to see Stirling Moss. Tony worked for Brabham, alongside Niki Lauda, as race co-ordinator for all races and tests before moving into the drawing office with the legendary designer Gordon Murray. He then moved to Marlboro McLaren where, as assistant team manager, he worked closely with Alain Prost and John Watson. He's also worked with Nigel Mansell, Elio de Angelis and Ayrton Senna. 'Britain still leads the world, not just in motorsport technology, but also in motor racing drivers throughout history,' Jardine said. 'The fact that we've had so many British champions makes you think there must be something in the water that makes them great natural drivers.'

But what did make the likes of Stirling Moss, Jim Clark, Jackie Stewart, Graham Hill, James Hunt, Nigel Mansell and Damon Hill so special? 'It's because there's such a passion in this country,' Jardine replied. 'A daredevil breed came through that pre- and post-war period. Motor racing was nurtured here, and in turn it nurtured the heroes themselves. They've benefited from Britain's home-grown facilities and the teams themselves, as well as the encouragement of its people. It's in their blood. Take Stirling Moss. Both parents were racers. He was able to hill-climb from a very early age and people were able to spot his natural talent. He drove just about everything on four wheels, and although he never won the World Championship he is acknowledged as one of the true greats of the track.' For Jardine, though, Jim Clark sits at the top of the mountain of fame. 'He is level with Ayrton Senna in terms of his greatness. He had this unique talent which quickly developed. He was swiftly followed by another great, Jackie Stewart, who had the same natural ability, although not quite to the same level as Clark. Stewart wanted to make it as a top sports car driver, just as his brother Jimmy had done, but his natural talent took him a lot further.'

Jardine also believes that the British temperament is suited to Formula One. 'The enthusiasm, the facilities, the technical know-how, a great feel for the car and the most incredible determination all mix together. You have to put drivers like Nigel Mansell and Graham Hill under the "determined" label. They really worked hard at their motor racing and exemplified real British bulldog spirit. Nigel Mansell never had the talent of Jim Clark, nor did Graham Hill have the talent of Jackie Stewart, but they worked so hard at it. They won races, became world champions, and they were exciting to watch. Mansell had this never-say-die attitude, an incredible confidence on the track that earned him the loyalty of thousands of British and Italian fans as well as many millions of fans around the world. He had this win-at-all-costs attitude that runs through the British psyche.'

Of the current crop of British drivers, Jardine thinks Jenson Button is the one to watch. 'He is a great natural talent. Watching him on the limit on his first flying lap in a Williams a few years ago when he was ahead of Michael Schumacher was awe-inspiring. He really showed that he had it. Since then he's struggled, mainly due to uncompetitive equipment. Hopefully he's got a better chance now with BAR. He is potentially one of the great British heroes in the making.'

For many years, the route to the top of the treacherously tall motor racing ladder for a young driver was a conventional one, determined more often than not simply by ability. Many of the Formula One greats started in 100cc karts when still in short trousers, moving swiftly through Formula Ford, Formula Three and Formula Two (F3000 in post-1985 money) before arriving in Formula One. This guaranteed maximum experience and exposure to the business of racing before becoming involved in a full-blown manufacturer effort at the top level. Jenson Button skipped F3000 altogether on his way into Formula One, arriving in 2000 straight from the British Formula Three series, but Minardi's Justin Wilson tasted success in the junior single-seater categories, proving that the conventional path to the top still enjoys much appeal. In fact, only four of the eighteen F3000 champions since 1985 have not raced a Grand Prix car. But it's Button's experience that will be more familiar in years to come, for life is very different for drivers in today's technology-fuelled, high-profile Formula One. The current crop of superstars have to be fitter and hungrier than ever. Team bosses are now starting to look for their next hot property while he's still wearing those short trousers and washing his hair with two-stroke oil. The best ones will miss out several rungs of the ladder so that team bosses, manufacturers, sponsors and talent scouts get their way. The

2003 Formula One line-up may well be the youngest grid of Grand Prix drivers ever. Many of these young men in a hurry have found themselves in the world's motorsporting spotlight only a few years after learning the Highway Code.

There's no proven formula for success when it comes to driver selection in Formula One. Purists still correctly point out that age, financial backing and experience count almost for nothing; what is needed in abundance is pure ability. Much enthusiasm and hard work added to the mix will work wonders, though, as Jaguar Racing hoped to demonstrate in 2003 with its talented, enthusiastic and hard-working duo Mark Webber and Antonio Pizzonia. These days, of course, drivers have more sophisticated wizardry to cope with alongside the driving; they're more like jet-age pilots than the sporting heroes of the pre-1970s.

Like most technologies, the brand of sophisticated IT used by Formula One teams relies on a human being, the driver, to analyse the data produced by the telemetry systems that monitor the car's performance, and to interpret the information correctly to get the most out of the car. Former world champion Damon Hill, a smooth, consistent driver, gained a reputation for his testing and development ability. 'Technology is another aspect of the job that the drivers have to adapt to,' he said. 'It works to your advantage and you have to know how to exploit it. IT can back up your instincts, or prove you wrong. Sometimes that's quite humbling, but at least you've got the right answer, which is obviously what we need.' At the same time, the modern Formula One car with its power steering and clever software controls has become a much easier beast to control. 'This makes it impossible for a driver to hide,' observed former Toyota driver and current Renault test driver Allan McNish. 'If I do something correct, everyone will see it and learn from it; if I do something wrong, it can be quickly identified and corrected. IT is not going to usurp the driver's judgement. It doesn't matter what regulations or technology you have, if the driver's clever, he's going to use that technology to his advantage rather than fight it.' Former Jaguar and Jordan driver Eddie Irvine agreed. 'At the end of the day, telemetry is just a tool to help you come to a conclusion. But just like business, you have to make sure the right information is coming in to get the proper information out to make a decision on. There's so much going on in F1 it becomes difficult to just look at a computer and assume it's going to provide you with answers – it just doesn't work like that. Drivers' feedback is still very important. Within five laps of driving the [Jaguar R3] car in our first test I said things about its performance, but it took ten months looking at telemetry data to prove I was right.'

Another aspect of performance today's crop of drivers must be on top of is fitness. Controlling a modern Formula One car is a gruelling, physical challenge. Drivers have to be very tough and extremely fit to cope with being jet-propelled around a track at average speeds of around 160mph and being buffeted by G-forces equal to three times their own weight. Just the act of turning the steering requires an effort of some 20kg, then drivers find their line, hit the apex and floor the throttle, changing up through the gears as they exit a bend. Their neck muscles strain to keep their head upright as massive centrifugal forces batter against them. The track temperature may be around 35°C, and with a cloudless sky above and the sun beating down, it is going to get hotter. Very soon, they'll be sitting in a carbon-fibre box in temperatures of around 50°C. A circuit has many corners and they'll have to get around them 70-odd times before it's all over. Over the course of those two or so hours their bodies will suffer extreme fluid loss, and even a momentary lapse of concentration could embed them in the scenery. If they want to handle the stresses and strains effectively, if they want to have even the slightest chance of finishing a race, they must devote around three hours of every day to some form of physical training. Working to an individual schedule, F1 drivers run, swim, cycle and lift weights, with an emphasis on developing the muscles around the arms, shoulders and neck.

All of this is a far cry from the lifestyles of past drivers. The public perception of a racing driver was for a long time that of the playboy, with a girl on each arm and a big cigar to go with the ubiquitous bottle of bubbly. In the 1950s, that was a relatively accurate view. Drivers such as Mike Hawthorn and Peter Collins, a handsome and congenial pair, actively cultivated the playboy image, and it was often the reason behind their occasional poor showing on the track. The situation during the 1960s and 1970s was not totally dissimilar; world champions such as Emerson Fittipaldi and James Hunt would normally scrounge a cigarette the moment they got out of the car. While performing his laid-back broadcasts for BBC television, Hunt would often pop out of the commentary box for a quick joint, leaving Murray Walker to cover up the fact, often claiming that 'James has just nipped out to have a look at the far side of the circuit.' Eating habits, too, have changed. Gilles Villeneuve, for instance, lived on a diet of milkshakes and burgers. He had to be physically dragged to the car just to get him to go for a run. Nigel Mansell was another whose aversion to training and fondness for fried breakfasts eventually resulted in his getting too portly to fit into a McLaren car. Today's Grand Prix drivers concentrate on eating healthy, balanced diets and steering clear of stimulants such as alcohol or coffee. Fat intake is kept to a minimum, and drugs are certainly not on the menu. The job of a driver in a modern Formula One team is literally no picnic.

There have been many good British racers over the years, and one can never hope to do justice to them all. Each would be worthy of his own book, but a handful do stand out from the rest.

SIR STIRLING MOSS (1929–)

What hasn't been said about Sir Stirling Moss? The name and image is synonymous with all that is British and motor racing, even to generations of ardent followers of the sport who have never seen him race, even to those who've never been interested in the sport but who think they know the man ('Who d'you think you are – Stirling Moss?'). The ten-times British champion is often referred to as the greatest Formula One driver never to have won the World Championship. He was indeed one of the most versatile drivers in the history of the sport, competing and winning not only in Formula One, Two and Three, but in hill climbs, sports and touring car races, rallies and world speed record events.

His skill and daring may well have been in the blood. His father raced at Brooklands and twice contested the Indianapolis 500, where he drove a Fronty-Ford to sixteenth place in 1924; his mother, too, competed frequently in British rallies and trials. In 1936, she won the Ladies Experts Trials.

When he'd reached the tender age of eighteen Moss drove a Formula Three Cooper-JAP and notched up eleven wins out of fifteen starts in his first full year of racing and hill-climbing. In 1949, seven more wins followed, including a 'foreign' victory, the Formula Three race at Zandvoort, which captured the attention of the British motor racing public. But it was his sports car win the following year that really launched Moss's professional career. Driving Tommy Wisdom's privately entered Jaguar XK120, Moss won the Tourist Trophy. He beat not only all the foreign entries but Jaguar's works cars as well. That year, at the age of twenty, Moss won the first of his ten British championships and was hired by Sir William Lyons to lead the Jaguar team in 1951.

Moss's success in sports cars continued, and his popularity grew. Although he had a miserable run of luck with British Formula cars, he showed enough talent to get an offer (which he rejected) from no less a man than the great Enzo Ferrari. Finally, in 1954, Moss relented and looked outside Britain for a proper Grand Prix ride. In his new mount, a privately entered Maserati 250F, Moss did battle with the works Ferraris, Maseratis and Mercedes, finishing third at Spa and qualifying on the front row four times. At Monza, Moss overtook Fangio and Ascari to lead the race and held it easily until his Maserati broke down ten laps from the finish. The victorious Fangio hailed Moss as the moral victor that day.

Though he never won the World Championship, his form in Maseratis, Vanwalls, Coopers and Lotuses was never less than impressive: he finished second to Fangio in 1955, 1956 and 1957, and to Mike Hawthorn in 1958, and from then until his horrific career-ending crash at Goodwood in 1962 he never dipped below third place in the drivers' championship.

MIKE HAWTHORN (1929–1958)

Known locally as the 'Farnham Flyer', Mike Hawthorn was truly one of Britain's great drivers. He was born on 10 April 1929 in Hexborough, Yorkshire. In 1931, the family moved to Farnham, Surrey, where Mike's father Leslie went into partnership with motorcycle racer C.W. 'Paddy' Johnstone and set up the Tourist Trophy Garage (now renamed Hawthorn's), selling and tuning motorcycles and cars. Late in 1946, Mike began a four-year apprenticeship at Dennis Bros. of Guildford, which he did not much care for, for it restricted the time he could spend having fun with cars and bikes, and his gang of friends known as the 'Members'.

Hawthorn made his competition debut on 2 September 1950 at the Brighton Speed Trials, and by the end of his first season he had notched up several wins, including the Brooklands Memorial Trophy. But Hawthorn's main successes came at the beginning of the 1952 season. The majority of motor racing fans didn't really know him at this point, but the Goodwood meeting soon changed that. After the race all the talk was about the blond-haired young driver who'd just won the first two races and come second in the Formula One race. Mike was driving the Cooper-Bristol Special Brew for the first time, and he caused quite a stir. Suddenly he was England's great hope, a racing driver who could outdrive established champions.

Success after success followed. By the end of that 1952 season he had so impressed Enzo Ferrari that he offered him a drive. It was an average start, though, for Hawthorn was one of Ferrari's junior drivers, and the established Italian drivers were offered the best cars. But again Hawthorn upset the odds and changed everyone's views, this time at the French Grand Prix where he beat the legendary Fangio to the chequered flag by one second.

Hawthorn became one of Britain's most famous racing drivers during his short career. He recorded wins in Jaguar D-Types at the Le Mans 24 Hours endurance race and at Sebring, and crowned his career in 1958 by becoming the Formula One world champion, after which he announced his retirement, partly as a result of the death of his team-mate Peter Collins. Tragically, Hawthorn was killed in a road accident just a few months later.

GRAHAM HILL (1929–1975) AND DAMON HILL (1960–)

Mr Hill senior came late to motor racing; he didn't even drive a car until he was 24. However, one of the first cars he owned, a 1929 Austin, was to prepare him for Grand Prix competition. It was a wreck, with no brakes; Hill had to rub the car's tyres against kerbs in order to stop. He later remarked that all budding racing drivers should own such a car. 'The chief qualities of a racing driver are concentration, determination and anticipation. A 1929 Austin without brakes develops all three – anticipation rather more than the first two, perhaps.'

Graham Hill joined Smiths, the instrument makers, at the age of sixteen. He served a five-year apprenticeship and was then called up into the Royal Navy. Two years later he returned to Smiths, during which time he met his future wife Bette. One day he saw an advertisement in a magazine for a new racing school which stated that anyone interested could drive a racing car at Brands Hatch for five shillings a lap. Hill went down, raced four laps, and then, as he later commented, 'everything changed'.

The school was the Universal Motor Racing Club, and Hill asked the owner if he would be willing to let Hill work for him as a mechanic if he could drive one of the race cars. Unfortunately, the club's owner took advantage of Hill, and he left soon afterwards without ever getting close to driving a racing car. But Hill stuck to his guns and would not give up on his dream. He struck up a similar arrangement with another person he had only just met. This time he actually did race one of the cars, and soon this new school had its first group of students; Hill, as the only employee, and with a handful of races under his belt, would be their instructor.

Soon, Hill was ready for bigger and better opportunities. After one of his races he hitched a ride back to London with another entrant, a man by the name of Colin Chapman, and got himself a job at Lotus working as a mechanic for one pound a day. He actually had to quit Lotus temporarily before finally convincing Chapman he was worth a bet, and in 1958, after much cajoling, he started to drive full time, making his debut in Formula One that year. A driver could only do this today if he had a few million pounds in his back pocket.

After limited success and too many mechanical failures, Hill left for BRM in 1960. Just two years later he won his first race at Zandvoort and went on to claim the World Championship. He continued to battle closely for the title over the next few years, but again, too many mechanical failures scuppered his chances. In 1967, he returned to Lotus to form a 'super team' with double world champion Jim Clark. After Clark's tragic death at Hockenheim in 1968, Graham Hill scored victories in the next two Grands Prix and was crowned world champion for a second time.

The last year of the decade was not a good one for Hill. He recorded a fifth win at Monaco – a record on this difficult circuit that was not surpassed until Ayrton Senna captured his sixth victory in 1993 – but at Watkins Glen he was injured in a terrible accident that resulted in his being confined to a wheelchair. After he recovered from his injuries he continued racing, but without any further success. He eventually started his own team, but was killed in 1975 when the plane he was piloting went down after getting lost in fog. The world would never again see the famous helmet with the rowing stripes – until 1993, when his son Damon resurrected that famous icon in Formula One.

Hill junior (OBE) is the last British world drivers' champion. He'd been absorbing the thrill of speed from the age of eleven when his father gave him his first motorbike for passing his eleven-plus. You could say that racing is in his blood thanks to his father, who became world champion for the first time when Damon was barely two years old. He's still the only man to have won a Formula One World Championship, the Le Mans 24 Hours and the Indy 500. Damon certainly had a lot to live up to, and it is a mark of the man that not only did he emerge from the shadow, he also forged a career that placed him close to the hearts of millions of Formula One fans. He gave the Hill dynasty in the 1990s every bit as much notoriety and success as it had attracted in the 1960s by driving in 115 Grands Prix and recording 22 victories, 21 pole positions, 360 World Championship points and one World Championship title. In other words, he won 19 per cent of the Grands Prix he contested and scored an average of over three points a race during a career spanning eight seasons.

Such impressive statistics tell only half the story, for Damon Hill's Formula One career was about many things, and the hard facts barely scratch the surface. 'Whatever one thinks of Damon Hill – and, like every great driver, he has attracted both critics and fans – there is no denying that he produced some unforgettable Formula One moments,' said Jordan's Mark Gallagher. 'It may have been his emotional debut, in the 1992 British Grand Prix at Silverstone, when he finally qualified the recalcitrant Brabham-Judd during the dying days of that once great team. Or perhaps it was his first win, for Williams, in Hungary one year later, as team-mate to Alain Prost. Then there was the emotional tidal wave that followed the death of Ayrton Senna at Imola. Hill took up the reins to lead the Williams championship challenge. It ended only when he was apparently "taken out" by Michael Schumacher's wayward Benetton while dicing for the lead, and the title, in Adelaide.'

Unlike most Formula One drivers who start their careers very early with karts, Damon's began later, on motorbikes. At the age of eleven he tried a 50cc Honda monkey bike in the paddock at the Silverstone circuit, and was immediately hooked. He pestered his father to get him one, and shortly after seeing an advertisement in a motorcycle magazine he got his wish. His real enthusiasm for speed, however, started when he was allowed to try out his dad's 350cc Bultaco off-road bike. But it wasn't until 1981, six years after his father's death, that Damon began to race bikes seriously. At the age of 21 he was earning money as a motorcycle dispatch rider during the week in order to fund his racing. It was a hectic schedule, leaving him barely enough time (or energy) to race his Kawasaki.

In 1984, with funds low again, Damon chose to concentrate on the Brands Hatch track, and his efforts paid off. Scoring over forty wins on a Yamaha, he became 'Champion of Brands' before turning his attention to Formula Ford 1600. He managed one first place and finished fifth in the end-of-term Formula Ford Festival. After only half a season of single-seater racing he was voted best newcomer, and this and his results helped him find the backing to do a full season in 1985. Racing against other future Formula One drivers Mark Blundell, Johnny Herbert and Bertrand Gachot, Damon won six races and finished third in the Esso FF1600 and fifth in the Townsend Thoresen Championship. He also recorded a third place in the Formula Ford Festival.

The 'normal' path is to progress from FF1600 to FF2000 and then to Formula Three, but Damon decided to bypass the 2000 series and go straight on to F3. It was a risk that didn't pay off. After overcoming initial sponsorship problems, Damon finished ninth in the 1986 British Formula Three Championship. The next season he won two races and finished fifth, then in 1988 he won the British Grand Prix support race and went on to finish third in the championship.

Damon now desperately wanted to move up to Formula 3000, but he had married his long-time girlfriend Georgie and things were looking financially bleak for 1989; he didn't have anywhere near the £70,000 needed to fund a drive in the European Formula 3000 Championship. Instead, he accepted a few paid drives in the British Formula 3000 series, at Le Mans, and in the British Touring Cars Championship. His break came when the Japanese Footwork team offered him a paid drive in the International F3000 series. The unspoken catch was that the car was next to useless, but Damon managed to qualify it for every race. It was his qualifying effort at the legendary Spa Francorchamps circuit in Belgium that made people sit up and wonder what he could do in a competitive car, and in 1990 he moved to the Middlebridge team. That season Damon led over 50 per cent of the races, starting most of them from the front row, including three consecutive pole positions. Sadly, mechanical retirements meant his best result was a second at Brands Hatch. Clearly his joint thirteenth position in the championship did not reflect his driving ability.

Damon continued to give it his all in 1991, and even though his Formula 3000 car was worse than the previous year's model and was being beaten hands down by the competition, Damon's dogged determination and raw speed meant he was the only driver to lead a race in a Lola. This attitude was exactly what Frank Williams was looking for in a test driver for his Formula One team, and so it was that Damon took over from Mark Blundell. Damon fitted into the team perfectly and immediately began to impress; it was rumoured that some said he was Williams' best test driver ever. It was Damon Hill who helped evolve the car that would eventually give Nigel Mansell a World Championship. Damon was not only fast – sometimes lapping and running race simulations quicker than the Formula One drivers could manage on race day – he was also consistent, which meant that any performance increase was due to mechanical modifications rather than the driver.

In 1992, while still testing for Williams, Damon was offered the opportunity to drive for the Brabham Formula One team. They were experiencing financial difficulties at the time and Damon was just the sort of driver they needed, one who would perform to his maximum under trying circumstances without complaining. Damon made his Formula One debut at the British Grand Prix in July. It must have been demoralising for Hill to see Nigel Mansell streak ahead and lap him in a car he had helped to develop, but nevertheless Damon finished the race in sixteenth place, and went on to finish eleventh in Hungary in what proved to be Brabham's last outing.

A few months later Frank Williams signed Alain Prost, Mansell left for the American IndyCar series, and Riccardo Patrese joined Benetton, so there was a spare seat up for grabs in 1993, and Damon wanted it. He had matured considerably as a driver, certainly enough to persuade the team to give him the drive. Damon was quick to tell the press not to expect too much of him – he was, after all, racing alongside the driver who had won the most Grands Prix ever – but still he was billed 'the next Nigel Mansell'. Damon wasn't prepared for the intense media interest in him; all he wanted to do was get on with the job of learning to be a full-time Grand Prix driver, so 1993 was quite a culture shock for him, a year of considerable stress and pressure. Even so, he repaid the faith Frank Williams had shown in him with two pole positions, three wins and 69 World Championship points, seventeen more than Michael Schumacher in his Benetton. His final position in the drivers' championship was bettered only by Prost and Senna, arguably the best drivers at that time.

In 1994, the title went right down to the line. Surprisingly, it was neither Schumacher nor Hill who took pole position at the mid-November Australian Grand Prix, but Nigel Mansell. He failed to make a good start, though, and both Michael and Damon got ahead of him, the German in the lead. The two of them pulled away and were nose to tail as they fought their way past back markers. Both came in to the pits at the same time, but with similar stops the positions remained the same. Schumacher managed to open up a bit of a gap, but then on lap 36 Damon saw the Benetton slithering across the grass back towards the track. The German swerved from side to side, blocking Damon along the run to the next corner, and in a split-second judgement Damon attempted to go down the inside of the Benetton as he thought there was no way Michael could turn in quickly enough. But he did turn in, and the two of them collided. Schumacher was momentarily airborne and went out of the race; Damon moved on, but his front suspension had been terminally damaged. The race was over, the championship settled by one point in Schumacher's favour. Had Damon known that Schumacher's car was damaged before he came upon it, he could have held back and won the race, but he couldn't have known. It was a bitter pill to swallow, but Damon accepted it like the true gentleman he is. The team certainly had nothing but praise for him; Williams had still won the constructors' title.

The following year again belonged to Benetton and Schumacher, and it was clear that Damon – and Williams – had a lot to think about during the winter break. But the season hadn't been an entire failure: another seven pole positions, four wins, four fastest laps and 69 World Championship points had been added to Damon's Formula One career total, he'd learned some more valuable lessons, and his rivalry with the German was gripping people in the paddock and in the stands. 'Hill versus Schumacher, Britain versus Germany – it was a great story and the Formula One public, particularly in the UK, loved it,' Mark Gallagher recalled. 'That he took second place in the World Championship in 1994 and 1995, then won it with a controlled drive in Suzuka in 1996, confirmed Hill as Britain's top driver of the decade, a worthy successor to Nigel Mansell.'

The 1996 season was indeed unforgettable. Frank Williams had selected IndyCar champion Jacques Villeneuve to partner Damon, so it was the two sons of famous racing fathers who took their seats in the FW18. Damon scored maximum points in the first three races of the season, so including the last race of 1995 he won four in a row, a personal-best winning streak and only one short of the record. Then, between the Belgian Grand Prix in late August and the Italian Grand Prix in early September, it was confirmed by Williams that Heinz-Harald Frentzen – who had compared favourably with Michael Schumacher when the two had been team-mates in their pre-Formula One days – would be driving alongside Jacques Villeneuve in 1997. Naturally this upset Damon who had been led to believe that he would be staying with the team, and at Monza he was out to prove a point. This he did by claiming a superb pole position and blasting away at the start, aggressively regaining first place and then defending it from Jean Alesi, who had also got off well. Damon won the race and ended the season as world champion, with sixteen front-row starts, eight victories, five fastest laps and 97 points to his name. 'It was an apparently unfathomable decision by Williams to drop Hill at the end of his championship-winning year,' Gallagher commented. Damon himself reflected, 'It wasn't something I was particularly happy about at the time, but now I look back and, hand on heart, it does not bother me. You just have to accept that what happens, happens.'

There was more head-scratching in Formula One circles when it was announced that the world champion would be moving, not to McLaren, Ferrari or Benetton, nor even to Jordan, but to Tom Walkinshaw's Arrows, with the unfashionable Yamaha engines and the then untried Bridgestone tyres. And then in August 1997 he oh-so-nearly won the Hungarian Grand Prix. It was an unforgettable drive that provided the thrilling sight of an Arrows overtaking Michael Schumacher's Ferrari and scampering away into a comfortable lead. 'No one at the Hungaroring could believe their eyes,' Gallagher recalled. 'Hill's decision to drive for Arrows, and Tom Walkinshaw's investment in him, it seemed, were about to be fully justified. Then, with two laps remaining, electronic gremlins interfered with the Yamaha V10 and Hill limped home second. The dream was over.'

It was a year later, at Spa Francorchamps, that Hill produced arguably his greatest win. Having signed for Benson and Hedges Jordan, the first half of his season had been marred by poor car performance, but by the time Spa came round things were all very different. The team was on a roll and the car was improving. 'On a weekend when all assumed Schumacher would be invincible, it was Hill who beat him fair and square during qualifying,' Gallagher said. 'With both cars on the same lap, the Jordan blew the Ferrari away to line up third on the grid behind the McLarens. If ever there was a sign of things to come, that was it. Hill, in full flow, driving the lap of his life in qualifying.'

The race itself has been well documented: that first, dreadful start when the mother of all pile-ups occurred on the run down to Eau Rouge, leaving Jordan the only team with both drivers unscathed; the restart, when Hill nipped in between the McLarens to take the lead, only to be passed by Schumacher who promptly drove straight into the back of Coulthard's McLaren. Back in the lead, Hill had to keep his team-mate Ralf Schumacher at bay after the safety car had bunched everyone up, but he held on to win. It was his 22nd career victory and the first ever for Jordan Grand Prix. Who could blame him for emulating Schumacher senior with a victory leap on the podium? His smile that day said it all. 'That was a defining moment for both Hill and Jordan,' said Gallagher. 'Hill showed his critics that he could win in something other than a Williams, in a car that was not the best in the field. It also gave the entire Jordan team, and in particular Eddie, the long-awaited win.'

'There can only ever be one first time for everything,' Hill said, 'and, until Jordan wins a championship, the win in Spa will be special. I think there was only one thing left for me to show [by 1997] – that I could win a race in whatever car I drove. I mean, I nearly won a race in an Arrows, but that win in Spa was special. I got a fax from Frank Williams saying that was my best race ever. It was all the more satisfying because I had taken responsibility for delivering the result to Jordan, and I saw the delight on the faces of the guys. They were just ecstatic, almost in awe of what had happened. But now they are Grand Prix victory veterans and there are expectations of being among the front-running teams. I knew what effect the win would have. I've seen it often enough, with drivers and race teams. Until they have crossed that threshold they are never really sure whether they can do it. It was a bit like when McLaren's Ron Dennis engineered a race win for Mika Hakkinen in Jerez in 1997 by persuading team-mate David Coulthard to let him win. He started to believe in himself. I think the same thing happened with Jordan. You do that – you win a race and you believe in yourself. You believe that the people you are racing against are beatable. The change in your philosophy and perception is powerful. Once the genie is out of the bottle, it's not unstoppable, but it will always be there. You always want to win again.'

Hill's arrival at Jordan in the winter of 1997/98 had certainly concentrated people's minds. The Benson and Hedges Jordan 197 had been moderately successful with Ralf Schumacher and Giancarlo Fisichella as drivers, but there was a sense that the team had failed to maximise its potential, partly due to lack of driver experience. With a former world champion on board, a man whose very *raison d'être* at Jordan was to bring the team its first Grand Prix win, the pressure had been on. 'I think I was a catalyst in raising the team's game,' Hill said, 'not through design but simply by being in the team. I think Eddie said as much. He said I'd won twenty-one races and a World Championship, therefore if the team couldn't win with me in the car then they were doing something wrong. It put pressure on ensuring that the design of the car and the engine was up to the job. It was a question that needed answering about the Jordan team because they had never had such an experienced driver. The question was starting to be asked within the team: "Is it the drivers or is it us?" '

When talking to Jordan's Gallagher about the final race of his career, in 1999 at Suzuka, Hill became more pensive. He admitted he'd been in a reflective mood, as was his wife Georgie, his greatest supporter. He took her on the drivers' parade lap, waving to the massive crowds and noting the large banners which said 'Thank you, Damon, we'll never forget you' and 'Well done, Damon'. They seemed to adorn every grandstand. It was, without a doubt, an emotional day for both of them. 'I had some fantastic moments in Formula One,' Hill said, 'but everyone has to stop some time. You have to make a decision to do something else and get satisfaction from whatever else life has to offer. I don't miss all the travelling we did because if you have a family it is very difficult. I certainly achieved more than I set out to. There were lots of good races, such as 1994 in Suzuka, which was very special, and I am proud of that performance. Being a Grand Prix driver is a very special thing. It's a rare achievement just to be one, and I do miss the environment, the excitement and the thrill of competing.'

Damon thinks that Formula One has now become very 'corporate'. He would like to see more of a driver championship, with the skills and characters of drivers shining through rather than the sponsorship money of the large motor companies. He rates Jim Clark as the greatest driver 'because it did not seem to be a difficult thing for him to do. He accepted his abilities and didn't have an answer about why he was so good. Champions know what they have to do and just go out and do it.' Nowadays he enjoys a variety of things in life, including performing with his group the Conrods, which he founded in 2001. The group has appeared at international gigs in support of charitable causes. More recently he has founded a supercar club, P1 – the perfect antidote to boredom, even for Damon Hill.

PETER COLLINS (1931–1958)

A contemporary of Sir Stirling Moss, Peter cut his single-seater teeth in the rough and tumble of 500cc Formula Three racing before becoming Moss's partner in the HWM team for the 1952 season. He drove briefly for BRM and Vanwall, too, before signing up with Ferrari for 1956. The following year he was joined at Ferrari by Mike Hawthorn, and the two men became the closest of friends. They used to indulge in outrageous pranks, and both derived huge fun from their motor racing. They nicknamed each other 'Mon Ami Mate' after a contemporary newspaper cartoon-strip character.

In 1958, Collins emerged as a serious championship contender after winning the British Grand Prix at Silverstone. Yet the Ferrari Dino 246s faced an uphill struggle against Tony Brooks' Vanwall at the Nürburgring a fortnight later, and in an effort to keep pace with Brooks, Collins lost control and slid off the circuit. He died later that evening from head injuries.

JOHN SURTEES (1934–)

A familiar sight driving his vintage cars at modern Grands Prix, Surtees achieved greatness on two wheels as well as four. He rode his MV Agusta to countless victories and World Championships in 1956 (500cc class), 1958, 1959 and 1960 (350 and 500cc) before switching full-time to cars in 1960, though he'd driven Vanwalls and Aston Martins in 1959. He drove for Ken Tyrrell in that first season, moved to Lotus, and then on to Ferrari, with whom he won the World Championship in 1964. He left in 1966 to join BRM, but after a dismal 1969 season he retired from racing to set up his own team, Surtees Racing Organisation, which raced Can-Am sports cars in the US.

One R.D.B. Jones wrote in the early 1960s, 'John Surtees, a man of great skill in motor cycling, has for the last two years performed with startling ability in the world of motor-car racing. We know, of course, that Stirling Moss and Jack Brabham are the "old boys" of the game, and they are at present at their peak point. Surtees, however, a man of great courage and ambition, who is also very young, is giving these same "old boys" keen competition.' Surtees was indeed a fearless, tough but fair competitor. He was also deeply interested in how his machines worked, and his quest for technical perfection would have suited the modern Formula One world perfectly.

JIM CLARK (1936–1968)

I remember the impact that fateful day in 1968 had on my parents. It was the day Jim Clark died during a Formula Two race at Hockenheim. My mother had followed his progress throughout the 1960s and it was the first time a 'hero' of ours had died. To a war generation used to the exploits of fighter pilots, Jim the brave fitted the bill perfectly. His good humour and consummate skill seemed indestructible to my parents. He was only 32 when he passed away. I was twelve. It was the first time I'd really been made aware of motor racing. From then on it became a 'dangerous sport'.

In the years that have gone by since, Jim Clark's reputation has remained as strong as ever. Former race engineers and Team Lotus colleagues still recall with warmth his sportsmanship and enormous ability, and Clark's contribution to Formula One, as well as a host of other competitions, deserves to be remembered and passed on to future generations whose view of Formula One in the new millennium is in danger of being sanitised. He conquered the World Drivers' Championship, the Indianapolis 500, IndyCar racing, the British and European Touring Car Championships, the Tasman Cup and the British and European Formula Two Championships, winning races in the Lotus 23B and some 30 sports cars. He also proved adept at rallying, even at NASCAR racing. At a Grand Prix meeting, he could race in a number of classes. He stayed loyal to Lotus and its mercurial leader and founder, Colin Chapman. Apparently, the two were unlike in many ways, but they proved to be a formidable combination. Chapman once remarked, 'I felt from the start that he was such a good driver, a man with whom I was so completely at one, that I could retire from driving myself and concentrate purely on producing cars for Jimmy to drive. And that is what I did.'

Clark was born in Kilmany, Fife, to a Scottish farming family who initially disapproved of his racing exploits. He first competed in rallies and other local races under the guidance of his friend Ian Scott-Watson;

later he joined a team run by Jock McBain known as the Border Reivers. In one of these races he drove a Lotus Elite against none other than Colin Chapman. Chapman was so impressed by the young Scotsman that he continued to keep an eye on him. Ironically, in 1959 the Border Reivers planned to buy a single-seater Formula Two Lotus for Clark, but after watching Graham Hill lose a wheel in a similar car Clark decided that the Lotus cars were not safe and that he would stick to sports cars for the time being.

Eventually he graduated to an Aston Martin, which brought him to the attention of Reg Parnell, the factory team manager. Aston Martin was planning to enter Formula One, and after a test Parnell signed the young Scotsman, who had also by this time signed a Formula Two contract with Chapman's Lotus team. Aston Martin's Formula One car was a disaster and the factory decided to abandon its efforts, but Clark was enjoying immediate success in Formula Two. When the Aston Martin drive failed to materialise, Clark signed on with Lotus to drive in Formula One as well.

His first race for Lotus was at the Dutch Grand Prix in 1960, where he raced instead of John Surtees who was still competing on motorcycles at the time. By all accounts it was a pretty uneventful race as he worked his way up to fifth place before retiring with a seized gearbox. The next race was at Spa in Belgium, the most dangerous course in Grand Prix racing, a nine-mile monster. In 1960 it took the lives of two drivers, including Clark's team-mate, Alan Stacey. However, in spite of this Clark managed to finish fifth in only his second Grand Prix. The next year Clark enjoyed limited success. Disaster struck at the Italian Grand Prix when Clark's Lotus came into contact with the Ferrari of Wolfgang von Trips. The Ferrari was propelled into the crowd and killed several spectators as well as the German driver, Germany's best hope in decades.

The 1962 season had to be better, and it was. In those days the calendar was sprinkled with non-championship Formula One races, and this season began with two which Clark promptly won. However, his hopes were dashed by another broken gearbox at the championship season opener in Holland. A week later at Monaco, a race Clark would never win, he was again betrayed by his machinery. This time, though, it was down to engine failure. Lotus began to struggle to find reliability. The Lotus 25 was a beautiful racing car, if only it could finish a race that counted. The answer came in Belgium at the track Clark liked the least. He stormed to victory at Spa, but after a season-long battle Clark lost the championship to Graham Hill when his car broke down as he was leading the final race.

During a break in action Lotus took their Grand Prix car to Indianapolis and tested it on the famous speedway when the track was closed. Clark soon had the car lapping at 140mph. Little did they know at the time, but the Americans who were there that day were catching a glimpse of the future.

In 1963, Clark dominated the World Championship, winning an amazing seven out of ten races and garnering seven poles in the process, and at his first race at Indianapolis he finished second to Parnelli Jones. The 1964 championship was fought out between Hill, Surtees and Clark. The final and deciding race in Mexico saw Hill bounce out because of a controversial collision with Surtees' team-mate Bandini. This left Clark leading the race until the last lap when his engine seized and the title fell to Surtees and Ferrari. The championship in 1965 was again a duel between Clark, Hill and Surtees, but a fourth British driver was now challenging the leading trio: his name was Jackie Stewart, and the fellow Scot served notice that he would be a force to reckon with in the future. However, this year it was Clark's turn again, and he recorded a win at Indianapolis for good measure. Leading the race for 190 laps out of 200, he left a lasting impression on his American rivals.

The new three-litre formula introduced in 1966 led to an unimpressive year for Lotus as the team did not have an engine that was competitive. It was not until the arrival of the Ford Cosworth DFV in 1967 that Lotus dragged themselves back to the fore. Clark won at Zandvoort in the legendary engine's first start, but it came too late in the season and he had to settle for third place in the World Championship. The next season started with a win in South Africa that allowed Clark to surpass Juan Manuel Fangio in numbers of Grand Prix victories. Sadly, it was his last win.

A shy, unassuming man, Clark's reputation as a world-class gentleman driver lives on. Without a doubt he is among the giants of the sport alongside the likes of Nuvolari, Fangio and Senna.

SIR JACKIE STEWART (1939–)

In the history of motorsport, few people have achieved quite as much as Jackie Stewart. As a Grand Prix driver between 1965 and 1973 he set new standards in professionalism, recording 27 victories from 99 starts and taking the World Championship title in 1969, 1971 and 1973 with a racing style that comprised flair, precision and courage. He took over Jim Clark's mantle as the public face of Formula One and brought with him a completely different attitude to his role as leader of the pack, helping to make Formula One safer and more fashionable and becoming the role model for a rising generation of stars in all racing formulas. If Clark hid his light under a bushel, Stewart made sure he was centre stage, increasing the sport's profile and maximising his earning potential with the same professionalism he applied to his driving.

The great man's involvement with cars started with the family business, Dumbuck Garage in Dumbarton, Scotland, where Stewart worked as an apprentice mechanic. His family were Jaguar dealers and had built up a successful practice. Stewart's older brother Jimmy was already a racing driver with a growing local reputation. He drove for Ecurie Ecosse and actually competed in the British Grand Prix of 1953 (he went off at Copse in the wet). It was only natural that Jackie would soon become involved in motor racing, but when Jimmy was injured in a crash at Le Mans their parents discouraged him from taking up the sport and instead pushed him towards target shooting. Stewart made a name for himself in that discipline, too, and almost got to the Olympics, only just missing the team for Rome in 1960.

Then he took up an offer from Barry Filer, a customer of his family business, to test in a number of his cars at Oulton Park. Stewart impressed all who were there that day. Ken Tyrrell, who was running the Formula Junior team for Cooper, heard about this young Scotsman from a track manager and called Jimmy to see if his younger brother was interested in trying out. Jackie came down for the test and took over a car Bruce McLaren was testing. McLaren at that time was already an experienced Formula One driver, and the new Cooper F3 was a very competitive car in its class. Soon Stewart was equalling, then bettering, McLaren's times, which forced Bruce to return to the track for some quick laps. Again Stewart went round faster, and Tyrrell, realising the obvious, offered Stewart a position in the team.

In 1964, Stewart drove in Formula Three for Ken Tyrrell and won his first race at Snetterton. Because Tyrrell wasn't competing in Formula One at that time, Stewart joined Graham Hill at BRM in 1965, his first contract netting him £4,000. On his debut in South Africa he scored a championship point, and by the end of the year he'd won his first race, at Monza. Stewart almost won the Indianapolis 500, too, on his first attempt in 1966, but was denied victory by a broken pump with just eight laps to go.

All the world seemed to be at his feet in that 1966 season, until Spa. A sudden downpour made the course treacherous, and cars began to slide off the track at an alarming rate. Unable to control his car, Stewart crashed into a ditch. His team-mate Graham Hill recalled, 'I spun round like a top myself. When I came to a stop at the side of the road I saw

Jackie's BRM in the ditch. He was in considerable pain, trapped by the side of the car, which had been pushed in. The petrol tanks had ruptured and he was covered with petrol. There was a big risk of fire, so I turned off the fuel pump switches and tried to lift him out. The steering wheel was jammed up against his leg and it was obvious that this would have to be removed before I could get him out.' Stewart lay trapped in the car for 25 minutes while Hill and American driver Bob Bondurant went to get some spanners from a spectator's toolkit and tried to release him. 'There were no doctors and there was nowhere to put me,' Stewart said. 'They in fact put me in the back of a van. Eventually an ambulance took me to a first-aid spot near the control tower and I was left on a stretcher, on the floor, surrounded by cigarette ends. I was put into an ambulance with a police escort, then the police escort lost the ambulance, and the ambulance didn't know how to get to Liège. At the time they thought I had a spinal injury. As it turned out, I wasn't seriously injured, but they didn't know that.' From that day on, Stewart always rode with a spanner taped to the BRM's steering wheel.

When Tyrrell moved up in class to Formula One in 1969, Stewart joined him. With a Matra-Ford, the two of them won the drivers' and constructors' championships. In 1971, the Scotsman was champion again, racing a Tyrrell-Ford. The following year saw him miss some races because of illness brought on by stomach ulcers, and 1973, his final year, was marked by triumph and tragedy, his third and final World Championship marred by the death of his friend and protégé François Cevert. Stewart followed through with a decision that he had made at the beginning of the year and retired from racing. His 27 Grand Prix wins were not equalled for two decades.

Driving achievements aside, few people have pushed the cause of safety in motorsport as hard and as far as Stewart, who lived through many of the sport's darkest days. The current generation of Formula One enthusiasts probably won't be aware that Stewart mounted a successful and at the time controversial campaign to improve track and car safety. At the time his demands for better conditions were viewed by sections of the Formula One community as wimpish, but that crash at Spa that had left him upside down and drenched in petrol among picnic debris at the trackside convinced Stewart that something had to be done. When race-track owners dragged their feet over his calls to provide circuit ambulances, Stewart employed his own doctor. In the end, though, Stewart (and other drivers) brought about long overdue changes to the lives and conditions of racing drivers. Today's racers may be grateful to Stewart for improving their pay, but they can also thank him for helping them to live long enough to spend it – a thought that might have crossed the mind of Mrs Sato at the 2002 Austrian Grand Prix when Nick Heidfeld's Sauber sliced through her son Takuma's Jordan at one of the fastest sections of the A1-Ring. It would be easy to say that Takuma Sato had a miraculous escape that day, but in recent years the teams and the Formula One authorities have worked together to improve safety standards. Particular attention has been paid to side impacts because of the dangers such accidents present. The Heidfeld–Sato shunt illustrated just how successful those safety campaigns, initiated by Stewart and his Grand Prix Drivers Association, have been.

Both Jackie and his son Paul have also been responsible for the rise of drivers such as David Coulthard and Luciano Burti on the staircase of talent Paul Stewart Racing has provided for young drivers, from the junior categories through British Formula Three and beyond.

Each of Jackie Stewart's three World Championships was won in chassis powered by the legendary Ford Cosworth DFV, and the partnership continued after Stewart hung up his racing boots in 1973. For almost three decades he has contributed to many of Ford's road-vehicle development programmes, and a new chapter in their long association began in 1996 with the creation of the Stewart-Ford team, which in only its third year netted Ford's 175th Grand Prix victory. With Jaguar Racing having picked up the baton from Ford and Stewart Grand Prix, the powerful presence and determination of Sir Jackie Stewart continues.

PIERS COURAGE (1942–1970)

A scion of the famous brewing dynasty, Piers was truly obsessed by racing. Although heir to an empire, he was bitten by the racing bug at Eton from the moment when a friend lent him a copy of *The Vanishing Litres*, a book on the Bentley team's Le Mans adventures. He turned his room into a shrine to racing, the walls hidden from view by volumes of *Autosport* magazine. A chequered flag even masked the ceiling.

Piers truly got involved in motor racing when he met Jonathan Williams – the very same Jonathan Williams who was to receive an unexpected call-up from Ferrari in 1967 – in South Kensington. On 2 July 1961, Jonathan and Piers met Frank Williams at a rainy Mallory Park and joined his circle. The following year Courage's father presented his son with a Lotus 7 kit car. Soon afterwards Piers gave up accounting to devote himself to racing full time. With the help of his chum Jonathan, and with the support of his parents, Courage had worked his way up to an international level by 1965, the pair of them driving Charles Lucas's Formula Three Brabhams.

The Englishman's first opportunity to enter Formula One came in 1968 with Tim Parnell's BRM, but it was too early in his career to shine. He did, however, get himself noticed by blitzing the opposition, including Jim Clark, in the Tasman Series in his self-entered Formula Two McLaren, which had been acquired from John Coombs. Driving Formula Two for Frank Williams brought him infinitely more pleasure than driving the obsolete BRM, and the pair were reunited in 1969 when Williams acquired a BT26 which was subsequently modified to DFV-spec by Robin Herd. After their Spanish debut went unnoticed, Piers and his Brabham truly came to the fore at the Monaco Grand Prix where the combination finished runner-up to Monaco king Graham Hill. Of course, in a season when the Grand Prix organisers were happy if entry figures exceeded fifteen it was relatively easy to finish up in the points, but Piers showed his grit on many occasions and from his mid-grid positions managed to steer the Brabham to the front more often than not. Unfortunately, retirements were a common occurrence until Courage scored another second at the US Grand Prix, picking up places as the front-runners – McLaren, Siffert, Stewart, Hulme, Beltoise, Ickx and Hill – fell by the wayside.

By 1970, Piers had received an apparently irresistible offer from Ferrari. Perhaps wiser after Jonathan Williams' unjust treatment at the hands of the *Scuderia* in 1967, Courage turned it down and chose to stick with Williams for the 1970 season. The decision might have lost us an almost certain Grand Prix winner, for he crashed fatally that year at the Dutch Grand Prix in Frank's F1 de Tomaso. It was a tragic fate for the highly motivated 28-year-old. He's still missed.

JOHN WATSON (1946–)

Competing against legends such as James Hunt, Alain Prost, Niki Lauda and Nigel Mansell between 1974 and 1983, John Watson was the winner of five Grands Prix, including the 1981 British Grand Prix at Silverstone.

Madly enthusiastic about motor racing from an early age – his father, Marshall Watson, won the first saloon car race to be held in Ireland at the wheel of a Citroën Light 15 – John's rise from club racing to international Grand Prix stardom proved to be a gruelling and at times frustrating career path. Watson's father was a successful Belfast motor trader who bankrolled his son's racing up to the level of Formula Two, in which he competed for three years (1969 to 1971) in family-owned Lotus and Brabham cars.

By 1973 he was ready for Formula One, and he made his championship debut in the British Grand Prix at Silverstone where he drove a Brabham BT37. He drove for the Hexagon Brabham F1 team, backed by prosperous Highgate motor trader Paul Michaels, throughout 1974 and scored his first championship point with a sixth place at Monaco. In 1975, he briefly drove for Team Surtees before switching to the new Formula One operation established by American millionaire Roger Penske, taking the place of Penske's original driver Mark Donohue who had died of brain injuries sustained when a tyre failure caused him to crash during the warm-up on race morning at the 1975 Austrian Grand Prix. Watson earned the team a superb victory in the following year's Austrian Grand Prix, forfeiting his beard in a wager with Penske. The Ivy League team boss disapproved of such appendages.

When Penske withdrew from Formula One at the end of the 1976 season, Watson switched to the Brabham-Alfa squad for two seasons during which he was unable to reproduce that winning form. In 1979, he moved to McLaren as team leader when the position fell vacant after Ronnie Peterson's death at Monza the previous September, but his high hopes were dashed when the new McLaren M28 proved disastrously uncompetitive. John's self-confidence was also somewhat undermined by the not-always-sympathetic strictures of team manager Teddy Mayer. Only when Ron Dennis and his colleague John Barnard became involved with McLaren did the team's fortunes pick up dramatically, and Watson proved to be the initial beneficiary of this upsurge when he won the 1981 British Grand Prix at Silverstone in the Barnard-designed carbon-fibre McLaren MP4. In 1982 and 1983, Watson found himself psychologically overshadowed by the reappearance of former Brabham team-mate Niki Lauda as his partner in the McLaren line-up. Nevertheless, John drove outstandingly to win the 1982 Belgian and Detroit Grands Prix and the 1983 Long Beach event before the suddenly available Alain Prost replaced him at McLaren for 1984.

Apart from a single guest outing for McLaren at Brands Hatch in 1985, that was the end of Watson's Formula One career. It was a shame, for although John's form could vary alarmingly – he was a perfectionist when it came to the complicated business of setting up a chassis, and if he was unhappy with his machinery he was frequently less than inspired on the track – he was a natural driver with innate skill. When he did hit top form he showed he had World Championship potential. As an individual, his personality remained unspoiled throughout his Formula One career, and he remains as congenial now as he was in the fledgling days of his single-seater apprenticeship.

Since retiring from Formula One, Watson has raced for the Jaguar and Toyota sports car teams, and can often be seen testing cars for magazines and television programmes. He's also an accomplished broadcaster with credits for Eurosport, BBC, ESPN, Fox Sports, CBC and Channel 9. 'I'm there to use my experience, knowledge and passion for racing to give viewers an understanding beyond the pictures,' he said. 'I want the audience to know what's going on in the minds of the drivers and the team personnel. Interactive television provides a fantastic insight for Formula One fanatics.'

JAMES HUNT (1947–1993)

James Simon Wallis Hunt, a Wellington-educated public schoolboy, was a flamboyant, talented Englishman, a playboy who was always out to enjoy life to the full and never made the mistake of taking himself too seriously.

As a young twenty-year-old medical student, Hunt took a drivers course at Brands Hatch and started club racing in 1967 with a self-built Mini Special. It wasn't long before he realised that a racing career would be a better bet for him, and single-seaters followed in 1968 when he acquired an Alexis Formula Ford 1600. He raced it to victory in 1968, and another win followed a year later. In 1969, Hunt also acquired a Formula Three Lotus, and in typical Hunt fashion raced it to two victories. Due to a lack of finance, as well as his propensity for crashing cars – no doubt partly due to his driving style, which made his nickname 'Hunt the Shunt' stick – he remained in Formula Three until 1972, collecting six more wins, as other Formula Three 'colleagues' such as Emerson Fittipaldi, Ronnie Peterson and Niki Lauda moved up to Formula One.

Then the young British lord Alexander Hesketh swept on to the scene, with characteristic gusto and plenty of cash. He equipped Hunt with an old Surtees to use in various events, then began to take the sport a little more seriously, and in 1973 bought Hunt a brand-new March 731. Hunt and Hesketh Racing had arrived. In only his third Grand Prix, cheered on by the British fans, Hunt recorded a fine fourth place at Silverstone; in the next race he took his first podium with a third place, and a fantastic drive at Watkins Glen in October saw him finish runner-up, less than a second behind the winner Ronnie Peterson. By the end of his debut season, Hunt had collected fourteen points and finished eighth overall.

Hesketh asked Harvey Postlethwaite to design their own car for 1974, the DFV-Hewland 731, before moving on to the 308 with which Hunt collected a number of third places – at Anderstorp, the Osterreichring and Watkins Glen – as well as a win in the BRDC International Trophy at Silverstone. Once again, Hunt finished the season eighth overall with fourteen points. The Hesketh 308 was developed further for 1975, which allowed Hunt to win that season's Dutch Grand Prix at Zandvoort by a matter of feet from Lauda's Ferrari. The team finished the season with 33 points and a fourth place in the championship.

Colourful and exciting to watch though the team was, Hesketh was funding the team with his own money rather than relying on sponsors. He obviously couldn't keep this up for ever, and during that 1975 season Hesketh left the team; the 308c and its designer Harvey Postlethwaite were sold to Walter Wolf the following year. Team manager 'Bubbles' Horsley continued to run the team for a few more years, but sadly without success.

Hunt joined McLaren for the 1976 season as Emerson Fittipaldi's successor and had a terrific year, battling back into contention for the World Championship after having a victory taken away from him at the British Grand Prix. Admittedly helped by Lauda's temporary absence from racing following his horrific Nürburgring accident, Hunt took the title race all the way to the final Grand Prix at Mount Fuji, where third place in torrential rain was sufficient to clinch the crown by just one point from the Austrian, who had pulled off the track believing conditions to be too dangerous.

That proved to be the pinnacle of Hunt's racing career. A gentle decline followed, Hunt racing a series of uncompetitive cars at a time when car design was undergoing a revolution (the future belonged to the ground-effect cars such as the new Lotus 78). He eventually retired where his Formula One career had started, in Monaco in 1979. Thereafter he carved out a career as a BBC television commentator alongside Murray Walker, only to die prematurely in 1993 from a heart attack at the tender age of 45.

NIGEL MANSELL (1953–)

There's no doubt that Nigel Mansell came up the hard way in racing, investing all his own money as he attempted to climb the greasy pole from the lower ranks. From karting, he worked his way into Formula Ford, where he enjoyed great success, but his Formula Three outings were dogged by poor engines and a lack of cash. It was not until Colin Chapman gave Mansell his break as a test driver for Lotus in 1980 that his career finally took off. As a test driver, Mansell contested three Grands Prix for Lotus that year. An engine failure forced him to retire in Austria after he'd spent most of the race in a fuel-soaked cockpit, then a spin in Holland and a failure to qualify in Italy completed Mansell's misery.

He was given a full-time seat for the following year, and his performances improved slightly. His best qualifying was in May in Monaco where he started third, and a few decent races saw him earn his first points as well as his first podium finish. In 1982, Mansell took third place in Brazil, a race that saw the two drivers in front of him ultimately disqualified for having underweight cars. A fourth place in Monaco gave him his final points for the year. A further year with Lotus in 1983 witnessed the introduction of Renault engines. Mansell's team-mate, Elio de Angelis, benefited from the new engine from the start of the season, but Mansell had to wait until the British Grand Prix to get his. He did, however, manage a sixth place in Detroit with his Ford engine before recording three more points finishes, one of which was at Brands Hatch. De Angelis, who'd had the engine advantage, finished three races, only one of which was in the points. Mansell's final season with Lotus in 1984 was very much the same. The Lotus was fragile and more often than not failed to finish the race. Nevertheless, five points finishes for the year, including two third places and one pole position in Dallas, showed that Mansell was capable of results. In the four years Mansell had spent driving for Lotus, he'd retired only eleven times.

In 1985, Mansell joined Williams. Although Frank Williams now had the powerful Honda engine on board, the team had struggled the previous year. Mansell qualified fifth in his first race for Williams in Brazil, picked up points finishes in three out of the first five races, and went on to his best finish to date, a second place in Belgium. He also beat his team-mate Keke Rosberg for the first time. His debut win came on an unusually warm October day in front of a home crowd at Brands Hatch. With that European Grand Prix victory under his belt, he arrived in Kyalami a fortnight later, started from pole position and won for a second time. Both drivers used Williams' new car well that season, and the team finished third in the constructors' championship. Mansell finished a respectable sixth in the drivers' championship with 31 points.

By 1986, Mansell had become a much more mature driver. Although his season got off to a poor start, he went on to win in Belgium, Canada, France, Britain and Portugal, results that put him in contention for the drivers' title with new team-mate Nelson Piquet and McLaren's Alain Prost. Indeed, everything rested on the last race of the season in Australia. Mansell started on pole and was placed high enough to clinch the championship when he suffered a spectacular puncture at 180mph. The image of him wrestling the car as Murray Walker described the scene with his usual gusto has become legendary. The fact that he managed to control the car under such circumstances was testament to

Nigel's skills as a driver. All those who saw it happen live were filled with awe and admiration as Mansell kept the car running in a straight line and brought it to a halt on a run-off area. Who won the title now depended on whether Prost or Piquet could win the race. Piquet went into the lead when Rosberg also suffered a puncture, but when the Brazilian pitted for new tyres, Prost went past and took the title from Mansell by two points.

In 1987, Mansell was in fine form again. He hit the front row at every race until Japan and notched up eight poles during the course of the season, but his six wins and some minor points finishes left him twelve points behind Piquet in the final standings. In 1987, only the best eleven results counted. Piquet had already finished in twelve races; unfortunately for Mansell, he crashed at Suzuka, injured his back and was unable to compete in the race, thus handing the title to his team-mate. He was gutted.

The following season, Williams found itself without an engine. A hastily conceived deal with Judd got the team back on track, and when Mansell qualified in second place for the season's first race things were looking up. Sadly, though, Mansell finished only twice that year (he came second both times).

After such a disappointing season, Ferrari beckoned. When Mansell won his first race for the team, the *tifosi* immediately took him into their hearts. He was christened *il leone*, the lion, and the season witnessed some memorable results, especially in Hungary where Mansell started twelfth on the grid and managed to win on a circuit notorious for its lack of overtaking opportunities. Further podium finishes in France, Britain, Belgium and Germany sent the *tifosi* wild.

For 1990, Mansell found that team-mate Berger had been replaced by 'The Professor', Alain Prost. Even though Mansell produced some fantastic drives, he managed only one win during the season – his sixteenth, to equal Stirling Moss's number of wins. But Mansell was becoming disenchanted with Formula One and he quit Ferrari, although an offer from a rejuvenated Williams-Renault team tempted him back in 1991.

The season didn't start well. Mansell retired in the US and Brazilian Grands Prix because of gearbox problems, and then came a collision with Martin Brundle at the San Marino Grand Prix. A second place at Monaco looked set to be followed by a win in Canada, but when Mansell rounded the corner leading the race, his car ground to a halt as he waved to the crowd. Then Williams' year picked up. A second place in Mexico was backed up with wins in France, Britain, Germany, Italy and

Spain, but by then Ayrton Senna in his McLaren was beyond Mansell's grasp and he had to settle for second place in the championship for the third time. With 21 wins to his name, Mansell was Formula One's most successful non-champion of all time.

The following year, 1992, was a totally different kettle of fish, the Williams FW14b, a quite brilliant car, boosting Mansell right from the start of the season. It was clear to all that he had the bit between his teeth and was more determined than ever before to win that championship title. He won the first five races of the season, beating Senna's record of four wins; he also started all five of those races from pole and set the fastest laps in two of them. More poles and wins followed in France, Britain and Germany, putting him well ahead of the pack. Mansell was finally crowned world champion, and finished the season a massive 52 points ahead of team-mate Riccardo Patrese in second place.

But, as ever with Nigel, there was a sting in the tail of his success. At the very hour of his World Championship triumph, he fell out with Williams in a row about money and kudos, and left for the US IndyCar circuit as negotiations with Prost were being conducted. He was at the peak of his driving form in 1993, and he won the IndyCar series at his first attempt. After Senna's death in May 1994, Renault put pressure on Frank Williams to get him back in the team, and Mansell competed four times, qualifying on pole for the season's last Grand Prix in Australia and winning the race when Michael Schumacher and Damon Hill collided.

Everyone thought Mansell was returning to Formula One full time in 1995, this time in a McLaren, but the car was too small for him and the team had to modify it. Mansell returned for the third round of the championship in Imola, where he qualified ninth and finished tenth, two laps down on the leaders. At the next race, in Spain, Mansell qualified a disappointing tenth and retired after eighteen laps, complaining that the car was handling poorly. He never sat behind the wheel of a Formula One car again.

There is absolutely no doubt that Nigel Mansell ranks as one of the greatest of the British drivers. He was also a curious mixture of contradictory emotions, which sometimes overshadowed his achievements. Still, it says everything about him as a driver that he couldn't be intimidated, even by the great Ayrton Senna himself.

DEREK WARWICK (1954–)

Blessed with an enormously gregarious and attractive personality, this son of a Hampshire agricultural-trailer manufacturer was a tough driver who was rated as a better prospect than Nigel Mansell in the early

1980s, but never had the same break as his countryman. Race wins were regarded as a certainty; some even whispered about the possibility of Warwick winning a World Championship.

Encouraged by his father and uncle, who had jointly founded the family trailer-building business, Derek was a stock-car champion on dirt ovals when little more than a child. Graduating with honours from Formula Ford, he made it into the closely fought world of Formula Three. All the while being financed by his family, he raced competitively against Nelson Piquet to win the 1978 British National Championship. His career path progressed through to Formula Two where he forged a bond with the Toleman team, spearheading their ambitious graduation into Grand Prix racing along with Brian Henton in 1981. As time passed, he and the Toleman improved, and Warwick helped to build up the momentum of the turbocharged Toleman-Harts, which by the end of 1983 had scored nine points.

Warwick gave Toleman three loyal and determined years before switching to Renault in 1984. When he was recruited, it was widely expected that he would sustain the race-winning ways established by his predecessor Alain Prost. Sadly, over the next two years the team gradually slipped further away from the form that had helped Prost challenge for the title, and Warwick never got the win that had seemed inevitable after a strong first race. Renault eventually withdrew from Formula One.

Without a drive when the 1986 season started, and having missed out at Lotus, Warwick returned to Formula One with Brabham after the death of Elio de Angelis. He then switched to Arrows from 1987 to 1989, driving with characteristic determination all the while but seldom scoring any worthwhile results. The closest he came in the drivers' championship to the heights of his seventh overall in 1984 was with Arrows in 1988 (tied seventh with the March-Judd of Ivan Capelli). A switch to Lotus-Lamborghini for 1990 was even more disastrous. The team's best days were long gone, and Formula One abandoned Derek at the age of 36 at the end of that season. He concentrated on sports car racing for 1991 and 1992, winning at Le Mans in a Peugeot in 1992 and sharing that year's sports car championship with Yannick Dalmas, but those fleeting halcyon days with Renault in early 1984, when victory seemed just round the corner, continued to call, and Warwick hammered on F1 doors with a ferocity and determination of Mansell-type proportions. Derek's universally sunny disposition had made him enormously popular in a business where ego can be a destructive force, and in 1993 he made a return to Formula One with the Footwork team.

A fourth place in Hungary, and nothing else to show for his efforts, was pretty much the end of the pleasant Englishman's front-line career, which had promised to deliver so much. Warwick was, by common consent, one of the outstanding Formula One protagonists to slip through the net without registering the success his talent so obviously deserved.

JOHNNY DUMFRIES (1958–)

John Colom Crichton-Stuart, the Earl of Dumfries, wanted to make it in his own right, so he stuck with the more basic Johnny Dumfries. With his aristocratic background, he was a colourful addition to the Formula One pack.

He started out in 1980 driving karts, and in 1981 he moved on to Formula Ford. Already 28 by 1986, Dumfries entered the sport in an age when Grand Prix racing had become synonymous with the FIA Formula One World Championship, the playground for 25 to 35 talented men, some of them hugely talented, others hugely sponsored. Dumfries arrived on merit, having already logged many miles on the race track before getting his race seat at Lotus. Back in 1984, Johnny had been crowned British Formula Three champion driving a Ralt RT3/83-Volkswagen for Dave Price Racing; he finished the season with 106 points and ten wins. The blue-blooded Scot was on his way to the double in 1984, but he eventually finished second in the European Formula Three Championship on 53 points; still, thanks to his four wins Dumfries finished ahead of Gerhard Berger, who scored 49 points. Moreover, his testing skills were already highly regarded. In 1984, he'd sampled a Lotus-Renault 95T at Donington Park. In 1985, Johnny drove an Onyx March 85B and a works Lola T950 in the inaugural F3000 International Championship. He tasted little success in that championship, but by the end of 1985 he'd logged many miles in Grand Prix cars for Brabham, McLaren, Lotus, Williams and Ferrari. So, in spite of being a rookie, he had been well prepared for his entry at the sport's highest level.

The offer had come about when Ayrton Senna told the team that he would not accept Derek Warwick as his new team-mate, after Elio de Angelis had left to go to Brabham. The Brazilian reasoned, quite possibly correctly, that Lotus was, at that stage in its illustrious history, unable to properly field two competitive cars. It might not have seemed that way to Warwick, but Senna probably felt it would be unfair for a driver of his talents to be saddled with second-rate equipment. Of course, he was also trying to make sure that efforts would not detract from his own prospects; therefore, a rookie team-mate was just what was called for, and Dumfries stepped in to accept what would definitely be the number two seat. And so it proved: by the end of the season Senna had scored 55 points with two wins, and Johnny had managed only three points.

Still, Johnny had had a promising debut for Team Lotus in Brazil with a fine eleventh on the grid and the fourth fastest lap. Some mid-race confusion in the Lotus pits meant that he was unlucky not to score points in his first Grand Prix. Dumfries' Lotus had developed a misfire halfway through the race and he arrived in the pits just when Senna was about to pit for new tyres. The pit crew promptly changed the tyres on Johnny's car and sent him out again. Next time around the pit was occupied by Senna, so Johnny had to struggle around for another lap with a misfiring engine before being able to pit again. During the third stop in as many laps the misfire was swiftly dealt with, but Johnny's chance of a point-scoring finish had vaporised.

Unfortunately, the early promise shown at Jacarepagua wasn't quite fulfilled, and Brazil remained the highlight of Dumfries' season. An early accident during qualifying at the twisty Monaco track meant that poor Johnny even had to put a DNQ on his 1986 résumé. On a track he knew well, Johnny was again inside the top ten during qualifying for his home Grand Prix at Brands Hatch, but he finished the race just outside the points in seventh place. On equal terms with all the other drivers on the grid on the new Hungaroring track, Johnny performed well all weekend: he qualified in a best for him of eighth place, and drove a solid race to come home fifth. In the penultimate race of the season in Mexico, Johnny was again plagued by problems; he qualified in seventeenth place and was out of the race by lap fourteen. In contrast, Johnny's team-mate Ayrton Senna had put his similar Lotus on pole for the seventh time that season. Johnny bowed out of Grand Prix racing by finishing a fine sixth at Adelaide.

This Australian Grand Prix was also the last time Lotuses wore the famous JPS colours. During the 1987 season the cars appeared in an unfamiliar bright Camel yellow, and more importantly Honda engines had been secured. They'd come courtesy of Japanese veteran driver Satoru Nakajima, so Johnny was elbowed out of the Lotus team. He had talks with Zakspeed for 1987 but they eventually signed Martin Brundle and Christian Danner instead.

Johnny had to look elsewhere and, as the cynical would say, chose the popular option for washed-out Grand Prix drivers – Group C racing. But he was still remembered for his testing skills and he signed a testing contract with Benetton as well. In sports cars he was entered in a Sauber

C9, which for his first Le Mans in 1987 he shared with the enigmatic Mike Thackwell and none other than CART team owner Chip Ganassi. They lasted only 37 laps. Arguably, Johnny's finest hour came during the following year's 24-hour race when he scored a popular win for the TWR Jaguar team with driving partners Jan Lammers and Andy Wallace. Johnny also returned to competitive single-seater driving that year when he replaced Wallace in the GEM Motorsport Reynard 88D for the last races of the season. But in the ultracompetitive F3000 Championship Johnny seemed lost, and did not have any strong showings.

His testing duties for Benetton continued through the 1989 and 1990 seasons. His final test was at Estoril in December 1990 with a B190. Johnny also spent these two seasons driving a Toyota for the TOM's Taka-Q team, again with not much to show in the way of results; unreliable cars and strong opposition from TWR Jaguar, Sauber-Mercedes and – no doubt much to the dissatisfaction of the Toyota top brass – the improving Nissan cars prevented it. A seventh place at Jarama and an eighth at Spa Francorchamps were Johnny's poor rewards.

His final appearance at Le Mans came in an ancient Porsche-powered Cougar C26S. It expired on lap 45, and with that the Earl of Dumfries faded away from the big scene. But for the 2000 Festival of Speed, Johnny – in the art business nowadays, and himself a talented painter – put on a new set of overalls and reacquainted himself with his Le Mans-winning Silk Cut Jaguar mount. A happy rendezvous with his erstwhile team leader Jan Lammers preceded a spectacular run up the hill – or rather towards the hill, as Johnny missed his braking point at Molecomb, the sharp left-hander turning towards the hill ascent. The Big Cat slid off straight ahead and comprehensively thumped the haystacks. Johnny climbed out and raised his hands towards his helmet in despair, but fortunately the XJR9 proved much more durable than the Maserati Birdcage that had gone off earlier and was towed away with a severely bent nose. Johnny happily returned to his painting.

MARTIN BRUNDLE (1959–)
The boy from west Norfolk started his racing career near his home in 1973, driving a Ford Anglia grass-track car he'd built himself. In the 24 years that followed, he never missed a season's racing.

He moved on to Hot Rod short oval racing in 1975. The 70mph quarter-mile tracks generated many wins and 'Star Grade' status, which prepared him for the cut and thrust of circuit racing. A few days after his seventeenth birthday he passed his driving test which meant he could get a circuit racing licence. This was the beginning of his saloon racing achievements. He got into pole position in a Toyota Celica on his first proper circuit at Oulton Park in 1977, and over the next twelve months he learned the circuits of Great Britain.

In 1979, he was offered his first opportunity to race in a single-seater, sponsored in Formula Ford 2000 by a local company, Carter Builder. One win and several placings later, Martin wrote to Tom Walkinshaw asking for the opportunity to drive one of his cars in the BMW Championship at Snetterton. Amazingly, Walkinshaw agreed, and Martin lined up on the front row against an international field, eventually finishing second after an epic race. There was more BMW in 1980, and this time Brundle won the championship and Formula Ford 2000, but a lack of sponsorship then forced him back into saloon cars, partnering the great Sir Stirling Moss in the BP/Audi team of 1981.

BP sponsorship took Brundle into Formula Three in 1982 where he recorded five pole positions and two wins and won the prestigious Grovewood Award as the most promising Commonwealth driver. The next year he joined Eddie Jordan's fledgling team to take on the mighty Ayrton Senna in Formula Three, the Brazilian taking the championship from Brundle only in the concluding laps of the final race. Both were immediately elevated to Formula One. Martin spent three seasons between 1984 and 1986 with the Tyrrell team, collecting a second at Detroit in June 1984 behind Piquet, and many World Championship points.

Broken ankles and feet sustained during a high-speed crash in Dallas in 1986 were a serious setback, and a difficult season followed in 1987 with the German Zakspeed team which produced only a fifth place, at Imola. In 1988, Brundle left Formula One for Jaguar in the US. Starting in January with a win in the famous Daytona 24 Hours, the World Championship was also his by October in Suzuka, Japan. A test schedule for the Williams Grand Prix team and driving as a stand-in for an unwell Nigel Mansell at the Spa Grand Prix completed an exhausting year. Two years with the Brabham Grand Prix team in 1989 and 1991 had limited success, divided by a further season with Jaguar, the highlight of which was winning the Le Mans 24 Hours in 1990. Martin also made history by finishing first and second in the same race at Monza in 1991, driving both of the Jaguar XJR 14s during the race.

His most successful Formula One season came in 1992 alongside Michael Schumacher in the Benetton Ford team: he scored points in eleven of the final twelve races, including five podiums. To everyone's surprise he was then replaced by Italian Riccardo Patrese. Brundle moved to the French Ligier team for 1993 and finished seventh in the World Championship, the highlight a podium finish in the San Marino Grand Prix. Early 1994 saw some brinkmanship as Brundle gambled on and claimed the Number Eight McLaren seat vacated by Senna. Second and third in Monaco and Australia were the highlights and poor reliability the very public low points, although he again finished seventh in the World Championship. Among a series of strong performances on his return to Ligier in 1995 was an excellent podium finish at the demanding Spa Francorchamps circuit in Belgium, and in his last season in Formula One Brundle drove for the Benson and Hedges Jordan Peugeot team. After a spectacular crash in Melbourne in March 1996, the season progressively improved with very competitive top-six placings in five Grands Prix.

In 1997, Brundle moved into the ITV commentary box alongside the legendary Murray Walker, but he carried on driving. Further Le Mans assaults in 1998 and 1999 for Toyota led to a stunning pole position, although mechanical problems forced him out of both races, and in 2001, Brundle led the Bentley team back to Le Mans after 71 years. Now chairman of the British Racing Drivers Club (BRDC), he continues to provide insightful commentary at Grands Prix for ITV, and is also involved with the management of David Coulthard's career.

JOHNNY HERBERT (1964–)

This happy chappy's career as a racing driver has scaled the heights and plumbed the depths. Through good times and bad, however, his chirpy personality has won him many fans and friends. Johnny was truly one of the most cheerful and bouncy characters in Formula One, but at the end of 1998, in an intriguing insight into what it takes to be a top racing driver, he told *F1 Racing* magazine that his personality had changed after the F3000 accident that nearly ended his promising career. 'Before the accident, I had got a reputation for not talking to anyone else, of being a little bit miserable and stuck-up. That was because I was super confident. I felt invincible. I could take on anybody, in any car, any time, anywhere, and beat them. After the accident, the way I dealt with the pain and discomfort was to laugh it off, to say, "Look, I'm fine." I was bubbly on the outside because it made me feel better on the inside. As time went on, I recovered, but I kept the same good attitude. If I hadn't had the shunt, I'd probably still be the way I was before. This doesn't mean I'm any less committed, but it's slightly different from the invincible feeling. The way I was is how Michael [Schumacher] is now. In the wet, in the dry, he believes he's the best. We all think we are, but

Michael knows it. That gives a driver something extra, a special feeling. There's usually only one guy on the grid at a time who feels it. I lost a bit of that mentality because of the shunt, but I'm just as focused today as I was back then.'

There's no doubt that Johnny had more than his fair share of bad luck. He gained an unenviable reputation for finishing races early, usually through no fault of his own, but he always seemed to remain even-tempered. 'I'm told I was unusually calm even when people accidentally had me off, like Eddie Irvine did at Monza in 1994, or in Melbourne in 1997. I've always looked at it that if you have a confrontation after somebody has done something stupid, it never does anyone any good. I think the last time I had anything remotely like that was when I went from junior to senior karts racing at Tilbury, and we both ended up getting banned.'

In 1994, respected motorsport writer David Tremayne summed up Johnny thus: 'It's hard to find people in F1 who don't like him, such is his bubbly personality, even though at times he has been known to launch himself playfully at somebody and bite their nose, Hannibal Lecter-style. His most endearing aspects are his naiveté and his candour. He speaks as he sees, without political subterfuge. Being honest with himself comes easy . . . He is one of the most popular racing drivers in the world. Nobody in the Formula One pit lane has a bad word for him.' When Johnny won his first Grand Prix, at Silverstone in July 1995, the other drivers on the podium, Jean Alesi and David Coulthard, spontaneously lifted him on to their shoulders in celebration. That David bore him no ill will was remarkable, given that the race could so easily have been the Scot's own first Formula One victory. Though Johnny's relationship with Alesi soured later when they were team-mates at Sauber, everyone was happy for him after that first win.

Johnny fought back from the terrible injuries he sustained in that horrendous F3000 accident at Brands Hatch in August 1988 with incredible spirit and the support of his family. Peter Collins, then with Benetton, honoured his commitment to Johnny, signing him for 1989 to partner Alessandro Nannini. But it almost didn't happen. This is how *Autosport* recounted (in April 1999) Johnny's first return to the cockpit after his accident:

It's a cold winter's day at Silverstone in 1988. Johnny Herbert's career is on the line. Tension hangs as thick as the fog which envelops the deserted airfield. Not four months have elapsed since the Formula 3000 shunt at Brands Hatch which shattered the golden boy of British racing's legs. Nobody says it out loud, but everyone is asking the same question as mechanics lower him into the Benetton: can he still do it?

He cruises round on an installation lap, then drives three more. All of them slow. Worried glances are exchanged on the pit wall. The car tours into the pit lane and is pushed back into the garage. Its occupant stays slumped inside. Team boss Peter Collins, whose neck is also on the block, leans into the cockpit.

'What's the matter?' he asks.

His blood chills with the reply.

'I don't think I can do it.'

'Will you give it another try?' implores Collins.

Subdued, his driver agrees to have another go.

Bang, bang, bang, in come the lap times. The invalid hasn't just beaten the bogey lap time, he's demolished it. The faces are brighter when the car rolls to a halt for a second time.

'Got yer!' says Herbert, with a triumphant beam.

Collins had a sense of humour – just as well. He also had faith in Johnny, and it was amply repaid during that superb debut on 26 March 1989 at the Autodromo Nelson Piquet in Rio de Janeiro, where the plucky Brit – after being carried to his Benetton because he still could not walk properly – qualified an excellent tenth, one place and 0.24 seconds ahead of his team-mate. Many regard this race as among the most stunning drives ever by a Formula One newcomer. Johnny finished in fourth place, fewer than eleven seconds behind the victorious Nigel Mansell's Ferrari, within three seconds of Alain Prost's McLaren Honda, and right on the tail of third-placed local Mauricio Gugelmin. The 1989/90 edition of *Autocourse* commented, 'Not since Reine Wisell took one of Colin Chapman's Lotus 72s to third place in the 1970 US GP at Watkins Glen has any new driver produced as good a result on his debut as Johnny Herbert achieved at Rio. It was hard to believe that Herbert had last completed a race as long ago as the Monza F3000 event the previous June. The strain of the 106-degree Brazilian heat left Johnny remarkably unflustered, his only complaint being that his neck felt rather stiff towards the end of the race.' Unfortunately, the result in Rio was deceptive. The characteristics of the Brazilian circuit did not put too much stress on Johnny's ankles and helped to hide the fact that he had not fully recovered from his injuries. By mid-season Benetton was 'resting' Johnny, and he wasn't to be seen in one of their cars again for over five years. When he did drive a Benetton again, for the 1995 season, he recorded his best ever finish in the drivers' championship, fourth place with 45 points.

At least the enforced absence gave Herbert the opportunity to make a full physical recovery. He worked hard on his fitness and took advantage of a brief return to Formula One with Tyrrell in Belgium to show that he still had the pace. Johnny received several offers for 1990, but eventually chose to combine a testing contract with Lotus with a racing programme in Japan, competing in the All Japan Sports Prototype Championship and the Japanese Formula 3000 Championship. An opportunity to return to the Formula One circus unfortunately came about because of another terrible accident: he replaced the injured Martin Donnelly at Lotus when Donnelly's career came to a premature end after a heavy crash in practice for the Spanish Grand Prix. Johnny stood in for Martin in Japan and Australia, the season's closing Grands Prix, before going on to spend most of 1991 and all of the next three seasons at Lotus.

In 1991, he was also offered the opportunity to drive for Mazda in the Le Mans 24 Hours, although the man who assembled Mazda's squad, David Kennedy, admitted that he'd encountered strong resistance when he included Johnny in his line-up. 'Mr Ohashi, the big boss, was asking me, "Are you sure he's OK?" I was saying, "Yeah, yeah, of course," but if you saw him in the morning – when it took Johnny half an hour to get out of bed, and another half an hour before he could walk – you would have thought I was crazy. But whenever he was in the car, in the tests or for the race, he flew.' After partnering Volker Weidler and Bertrand Gachot to the first win a Japanese manufacturer had achieved in the French classic, Herbert collapsed on the car out of sheer exhaustion. 'By then his eyes were sunk right back in his head and he looked as if a feather would knock him over,' Kennedy recalled. 'Mental and physical fatigue are your biggest enemies at that race. I asked the girls in the team to take Johnny away from the pits whenever he was out of the car, just to get his mind off things. He just thought he was really popular.'

In early September 1998, it was announced that after three relatively unspectacular years at Sauber Johnny was joining the Stewart-Ford team on a two-year contract; it was later confirmed that he would partner the team's existing driver, Rubens Barrichello, for the new season. Johnny was excited at the prospect. 'I've been looking at what Stewart's doing,' he said, 'and I'm very happy about it. The Ford deal with Cosworth is a good thing, and getting [ex-Jordan chief designer] Gary Anderson along is another positive step. He's done a good job at Jordan over the years, and it's a good idea to get someone who has that experience and knowledge to come to a young team like this, which needs a little bit of pulling together. I want to work hard at getting that to work, and I'm sure Jackie and Paul Stewart, and Ford, want the same. The way things are changing is very encouraging. It's a new challenge. The relationship with Jackie and Paul, and all the guys, will be good. I know the Ford people very well; I seem to have spent most of my career with the company for some reason. The whole thing is moving in a positive direction. I can't wait.'

In January 1999, Jackie Stewart explained why he had signed Johnny. 'He brings many things to the team: experience, knowledge, a great British following, great enthusiasm and motivation. In a funny sort of way, we might have needed him more last year for motivation than we do this year because there's a real buzz in the team now. I think he's going to be very competitive. He's got to a turning point in his career and he knows it. He's very keen to deliver for us this year.'

Johnny had his first run in the new SF3 that January at Silverstone. 'With this first run,' he summarised on the team's website, 'the signs look good for the feel and balance of the car. It does not have any of the bad feelings that I had in the SF2 at Barcelona before Christmas. The new engine ran with no problems during my 25 laps and it felt good for its first outing, with a very smooth power delivery. We now have a full test at Jerez to see if our expectations will turn into reality.' After the Jerez test, Johnny again drew comparisons between the SF2 and the new car. 'Things are looking very bright. The chassis is a big improvement on last year's. I feel that we have made a big jump and I'm looking forward to a competitive year. With the modifications we have to come and with further development work, we can approach Melbourne with confidence.'

The team made a promising start in practice for the Australian Grand Prix in March, with both cars well up in the free sessions. Rubens qualified the SF3 a magnificent fourth, but Johnny was still coming to terms with the car and ended up thirteenth on the grid. Was it unlucky thirteen? It was certainly a portent for the early part of the season. After all the promise of Friday and Saturday, the Stewart-Ford team endured a nightmare start to the Australian race. As the cars slotted into their positions on the grid after the parade lap, a plume of smoke appeared at the rear of Johnny's car. The wisps of smoke then turned into a white pall, and Johnny exited his car as the marshals turned their extinguishers on the SF3. Almost simultaneously, team-mate Barrichello's car went up in smoke. The race start was aborted. Rubens ran back to the pit garage, knowing the spare car was his for the weekend; Johnny ambled back more slowly, knowing his race weekend was over. 'As we came round to the grid,' he later told ITV's Louise Goodman, 'it seems that we both had a similar problem. I could smell a lot of burning from the bodywork at the back, and then, from what we can gather, it burned the wiring loom, because my throttle stopped working. It's a bit of a shame because we started so well.'

Rubens Barrichello was on great form for most of that 1999 season, his third (and last) with the Stewart-Ford team. For the first thirteen races (that unlucky number again), the Brazilian outqualified Johnny at every meeting, sometimes by as much as a second. As Johnny struggled to get to grips with a new car, engine and team, his confidence was hit by Barrichello's impressive performances. It didn't help that the team seemed incapable, for more than half of the season, to field two competitive and reliable cars. In the first seven races, Johnny recorded six DNFs.

The tide began to turn a little in June in Canada. On the weekend when Ford gave team boss Jackie Stewart a welcome 60th birthday present – they bought the team in a multi-million-dollar deal – Johnny added to the celebrations by driving an excellent race from tenth on the grid to fifth place, claiming his first ever points for Stewart-Ford. After the race, Johnny's official comments were: 'I'm delighted to finish my first Grand Prix of the year, and to come away with two points is a bonus. It's been quite a weekend for the whole team, with the announcement that Ford has acquired the team and Jackie's 60th birthday. I'm really pleased for my crew. They did another great job, but this time they have been rewarded.'

But the rumours about whether or not Herbert would stay with the team had already started in earnest. Rubens, who was at the top of his form, continued to outqualify and, generally, outrace Johnny, so much so that by mid-season the second year of Johnny's contract was the subject of much speculation. Possible replacements mentioned in *Autosport*'s news pages were Ferrari supersub Mika Salo, Ralf Schumacher, Heinz-Harald Frentzen, Alex Wurz, F3000 champion Nick Heidfeld and even Stewart Formula Three racer and Formula One test driver Luciano Burti. The on-off rumours continued for weeks, but Johnny kept his head down, dismissing them with a curt 'As far as I'm concerned I'm driving for Ford in Formula One next year. It would cost a lot to buy me out of my contract.'

Johnny held his nerve, his on-track performances continued to improve, and he was rewarded in mid-September when it was announced that the team would honour his contract. At the same time, another *Autosport* rumour, in fact the worst-kept secret in Formula One, proved correct: the team was to be renamed Jaguar. It had already been confirmed that the other Jaguar driver would be Eddie Irvine, who was to swap places with the Ferrari-bound Barrichello. The press took to calling Irvine the team's number one driver, but that was given short shrift by Jackie Stewart, retained as team boss by Jaguar, in an interview on BBC Radio 5. 'You can't afford, with the amount of money we spend in Formula One, to have a number one and number two,' he said. 'We have to give equal equipment and performance to both of our drivers and we want Johnny to step up. I think he is capable of doing this.' In the official Jaguar launch press release, Jackie said, 'Johnny is already part of the family and we are pleased to have him with us for another year. It was good to see him move closer to Rubens in the latter half of 1999 and we anticipate him running consistently closer to the front of the grid next season.'

September turned out to be a good month for Johnny. Not only was his place with the team confirmed, but at the Nürburgring he outqualified Rubens for the first time. Even better than that, he won the race. It was the Stewart team's maiden victory, a fantastic achievement for a team in only its third season. That 1999 European Grand Prix victory was probably the best of Johnny's three GP wins. In tricky conditions, with two heavy showers causing mayhem, Johnny called the strategy just right, switching to wets at exactly the right moment and back to drys again as the track shed its dampness. Barrichello finished third, and the two main title contenders, Mika Hakkinen and Eddie Irvine, were fifth and seventh. Self-effacing as ever, Johnny put the win down to two lucky stones given to him by his Jamaican mechanic Ricky, one inscribed with the word JAMAICA and the other with LUCKY. 'Before the race,' he joked, 'I got all the mechanics together and we rubbed them.' In a more serious assessment of the win, Johnny said that the real secrets of his success were hard graft and self-belief, which had brought him through what had until then been a disappointing season. 'For me it's so satisfying because of the difficulties I've had. I've stuck to my guns. I believe in myself. I've always been someone who, when it's tough, has worked at it.'

In the remaining two races of the season, Johnny maintained his newly found good form, outqualifying Rubens and beating him both times. Buoyed by this, Johnny looked forward to the new millennium and felt he was ready to show Eddie Irvine just what he was made of. He was also excited about driving for Jaguar, as he told the Jaguar

Racing website at the launch of the Jaguar-Cosworth R1 on 25 January 2000. 'We're certainly looking to recapture the glory days of Jaguar from sports cars,' he said. 'As a British driver, it's probably the most emotional job you can have. We're bringing in a name the like of which can only be compared with Ferrari. Jaguar has a great heritage, it's very popular, and it's legendary at Le Mans. I think a lot of people will want us to carry that through to Formula One. I hope that the following for Jaguar in Britain and abroad is huge.'

The new season got off to a great start for Johnny with some encouraging performances in pre-season testing in Spain; in January, he was quickest or near the top of the time sheets in Jerez and Barcelona. Then what was thought to be a temporary glitch caused by the car's oil circulation system led to a few problems, which the team thought it had remedied. Unfortunately, the problem turned out to be more serious, and it set back the development of the car. Johnny, however, was still optimistic. 'The feeling of the car has been very positive,' he insisted, 'but, like everyone else, we've got to improve it a bit more. We're OK. If we can do what we did in the first test, we'll be absolutely fine.'

But it was a disastrous start to the 2000 season in Melbourne. Mechanical problems haunted Johnny all through practice – after which he qualified a dismal twentieth – and continued into the race: he lasted less than a lap before his clutch failed. Although team-mate Irvine manfully monstered the ill-handling big cat to seventh on the grid, his race lasted little longer than Johnny's. Gearbox problems were to account for another five DNFs for Johnny, and what was almost certainly his last season as a full-time Formula One driver turned out to be one of the biggest disappointments of Johnny's career. The campaign ended with zero points against his name and only four finishes in the top ten. Irvine seemed better able to wring the recalcitrant car's neck, put in a banzai lap and qualify it higher than it deserved, but neither man had the car he needed. With inadequate aerodynamics, the car lacked rear-end stability at speed. Anyone who saw the twitchy, ill-handling big cat tackling high-speed corners had another name for it, totally lacking in feline grace: the Jaguar R1 was a dog. Gary Anderson was held responsible, and he was summarily dismissed when the team's new chief executive officer, Bobby Rahal, formally took charge after the season ended.

Johnny Herbert's season ended with a horrific crash at Sepang, Lady Luck having deserted him again. On lap 48 of his last Grand Prix, Johnny's Jaguar's rear suspension collapsed spectacularly at one of the quickest parts of the circuit, throwing him into the barriers at high speed. Fortunately the car remained upright when it could so easily have pitched into a barrel roll, but it hit the barriers hard and hearts sank as Johnny was lifted from the cockpit by the marshals. Memories of his horrific F3000 accident sprang unbidden to mind. But the damage wasn't as bad as it first appeared: he suffered only severe bruising to his legs. Of course, he recognised the irony of the situation: 'I guess it was inevitable that, because I began my career being carried to a car, I would end it being carried out of one. There's nothing like ending your career with a bang.'

On 26 July 2000, Johnny told a news conference in Frankfurt that his Formula One career was over and that he was seeking a drive in the US. 'I've decided that I will go to the American CART series next year,' he announced. 'Obviously I've got to sign a contract for a drive, but that's what I want to do next year.' When the hoped-for CART drive failed to materialise, Johnny reconsidered his options and decided to take an offer from the Arrows Formula One team to be its test and development driver, leaving him free to pursue drives in both the Indianapolis 500 and the Le Mans 24 Hours. The man is still at it, and he has plenty of racing left in him yet.

EDDIE IRVINE (1965–)

Although he never shied away from speaking his mind when perhaps he should have kept his opinions to himself, Edmund 'Eddie' Irvine, the son of a former amateur racer of the same name from Newtownards in Northern Ireland, was one of the fastest, most consistent and hard-working drivers in the sport, a fact sometimes disguised by his larger than life personality.

He started racing in 1983 at the age of seventeen in his father's Crossle Formula Ford car. He went on to compete in (and win) Formula Ford championships in his native Ireland and in mainland Britain, and in 1988 he made the move to Formula Three, driving a Ralt-Alfa for West Surrey Racing and finishing fifth in the British F3 Championship. The following year he graduated to Formula 3000 with Pacific, and then moved to Jordan in 1990, winning at Hockenheim and finishing third in the championship. In 1991, he went to Japan to compete in Formula Nippon, a series in which he figured strongly for three consecutive seasons.

Towards the end of this period in Japan, he made his Formula One debut with Jordan Grand Prix and went on to race with the team full time in 1994. In his second season with Jordan, Irvine got on to the podium in Canada and finished the championship in twelfth place. In

1996, Irvine got his big break and signed for Ferrari to partner Michael Schumacher. He proceeded to outqualify and outrace the world champion during the season opener in Australia, then diligently played his part as the number two driver for the rest of the season, finishing in tenth place. He recorded five podium finishes in 1997 and played a major role in Schumacher's assault on the title, and the following season he improved further, reaching the podium eight times on his way to fourth place in the championship.

The 1999 season turned out to be the high point of the Irishman's career to date. He chalked up his first win at the Australian Grand Prix in March, but it was assumed that the rest of the season would be business as usual, supporting another Schumacher championship bid. Then, in July at the British Grand Prix, the German crashed and broke his leg as a result of a component failure as he tried to overtake Irvine. Eddie immediately picked up the gauntlet, and a two-way title battle between Irvine and McLaren's Mika Hakkinen soon developed. Irvine won four races and ran the chase right up to the wire, but in the end he narrowly missed out, although he'd helped Ferrari to win its first constructors' title for 21 years.

Irvine was now hot property, and for 2000 he signed a lucrative three-year deal with Jaguar Racing. That year Irvine scored just six championship points, a fourth place at Monaco his best result. He did manage to get the big cat on to the podium in May 2001, again at Monaco, but after an uneventful 2002 season, throughout which he was handicapped by a poor car, Irvine failed to secure a drive for 2003 and decided to hang up his driving gloves.

Say what you want about Eddie Irvine, he was indubitably a racing-car driver to the end, a hugely competitive individual with enormous self-belief. As such he was utterly committed to doing whatever he could to get to the top. He now appears to be relishing the cut and thrust of the property world, but watch this space. Eddie won't be quiet for long.

DAVID COULTHARD (1971–)

Like most of the great racing drivers of our time, David started his racing career at a young age, in karting. At the age of twelve he became Scottish Junior Kart champion, a title he successfully defended until 1986 when he moved into the Open Championship. In 1989, David moved into Formula Ford racing. He took not only the Dunlop/Autosport Championship but also the P&O Ferries Junior Championship. This culminated in his receiving the prestigious McLaren/Autosport Young

Driver of the Year award. The following year he joined Paul Stewart Racing to race in Formula Vauxhall Lotus and the GM Lotus Euroseries, and in 1991 and 1992 he moved on to British Formula Three and Formula 3000. His last full season in F3000 was in 1993, again with Paul Stewart Racing. That year he also raced for Jaguar in the GT Class of the Le Mans 24 Hours.

In 1992, Coulthard had tested for the Camel Benetton Ford Formula One team; a year later he tested for the Canon Williams Renault Formula One team, in the FW15C car. As a result of that he became the Williams test driver for the 1994 season. He raced just once in the F3000 Championship that year, gaining a second place, because the death of Ayrton Senna elevated David into the number two driver seat for Williams, alongside Damon Hill. His first Grand Prix was in Spain at the end of May 1994. That year he also received the awards of Scottish Sports Personality of the Year and ITV Young Sports Personality of the Year. David continued with the Rothmans Williams Renault team in 1995. In the first race of the season he was disqualified from his second place due to fuel irregularities, but later reinstated.

In 1996, Williams hired US CART champion Jacques Villeneuve to partner Damon Hill, so David moved to the then somewhat ailing Marlboro McLaren-Mercedes team. He started the 1997 season with a bang, taking the chequered flag in Australia to give McLaren its first win since 1993, and backed this up with victory in the Italian Grand Prix. He was an effective partner for Mika Hakkinen during his back-to-back World Championships, is still at McLaren today racing with another 'Flying Finn', Kimi Raikkonen, is known for his sensational grid starts, and to date has won thirteen Grands Prix.

RALPH FIRMAN (1975–)

As the son of Van Diemen boss Ralph Firman senior, Ralph junior grew up in a household that lived and breathed motor racing. The Norfolk-based Van Diemen is the world's biggest maker of single-seater racing cars for British and American junior series such as Formula Ford. Back in the early 1980s they took on a young Brazilian by the name of Ayrton Senna who, as well as winning four titles for them, spent time living with the Firman family.

With all these influences, it's hardly surprising that Firman was eventually bitten by the racing bug. A successful career in karts set him off on the road to racing success, and he won the Formula Vauxhall Junior Championship on his car-racing debut back in 1993. Two years later he was unlucky not to win the Formula Three Championship at his first attempt after a close fight with Oliver Gavin, but in 1996 he went one better and saw off the likes of Juan Pablo Montoya to win the famous series. After taking victory at the unofficial Formula Three World Championship in Macau that winter he looked destined for Formula One, but the call didn't come and he began a six-year 'exile' in Japan.

There must have been many low points during this period in his racing career. A succession of poor teams and hand-to-mouth budgets stymied his challenge, but the right package did finally come along, and during the 2002 season he dominated the Nippon Championship with PIAA Nakajima. Perhaps it isn't the series it once was, but it has long been another traditional route into Formula One, one the likes of Ralf Schumacher, Eddie Irvine and Heinz-Harald Frentzen have followed.

By the standard of today's kindergarten racers, at 27 Firman was quite old to be making his debut in Formula One for Jordan. But his call-up held no fears for a principal who has been so adept at discovering great Formula One drivers in the past. 'Firman's pedigree is impressive,' said Eddie Jordan, 'despite the fact that he's been out of the limelight recently. But he will be a big, big surprise.'

JUSTIN WILSON (1978–)
One of British motorsport's hottest properties, Justin Wilson also started his racing career in karts, in 1988, before he was ten years old. At fifteen he graduated earlier than is normal to Formula A and finished fifth in the British Championship. Then, after a regulation change that allowed sixteen-year-olds to race cars, Formula Vauxhall Junior beckoned. In 1994, he made history by winning his first ever race, the first sixteen-year-old in fact to win a motor race. The following year he won the Junior Challenge Cup, took third place in the Formula Vauxhall Junior Championship, and won the BRDC Chris Bristow Trophy for the most promising driver to race at Silverstone. He was also one of the six finalists for the McLaren/Autosport BRDC Driver of the Year award.

In 1995, Justin came third in the Formula Vauxhall Winter Series and was selected by Paul Stewart Racing for a full assault on the 1996 Formula Vauxhall British Championship. Still only seventeen, Wilson won the first round on the Brands Hatch Grand Prix circuit, beating his team-mate into second place and taking the fastest lap. The next season, too, began in the best possible way at Donington Park, where Wilson set the fastest lap of the race from pole, but the rest of 1997 was a time of mixed fortunes.

The following year, after having signed up for the inaugural Formula Palmer Audi Championship, proved to be a turning point for Wilson.

After a shaky start, Wilson's experience and cool temperament shone through. He gradually climbed the points table to reach twelfth by the middle of the season, and then got to third with seven races to go. Six wins later, Wilson secured the championship, his prize a fully funded season in F3000, traditionally a feeder into Formula One.

The 1999 season proved to be a challenging one for Wilson with Team Astromega, and the next year saw him switch teams to Nordic Racing. He finished the season fifth in the championship and remained with Nordic Racing for the 2001 season, which he started and finished by spraying champagne and becoming the first British driver to win the F3000 Championship, triumphing where illustrious names such as Damon Hill, David Coulthard and Allan McNish had failed. Wilson's domination of a campaign where the winner usually has to fight to the very last race allowed him to wrap up the title with one round to go with a points tally that broke Juan Pablo Montoya's record for points in a season. He also set a new record for the number of podium finishes in a season – ten from twelve races.

Justin's path to Formula One was given a boost in October 2001 when he was invited to test with the Jordan team at Silverstone. Having proved a match for the team's star driver Jean Alesi, Wilson was invited to test again with the Silverstone-based squad. In 2002, he was asked to compete for Racing-Engineering in the inaugural Telefonica Nissan World Series, during which Wilson continued to attract the interest of Formula One team bosses. Indeed, he only narrowly missed out on a seat with Minardi in the second half of the season as the PS02 chassis was too small for his six-foot-three-inch frame. However, he did enjoy testing a PS01 at Donington in August. Team boss Paul Stoddart went on the record stating that Justin would be in contention for a ride with the team in 2003.

Sure enough, in December 2002 Stoddart officially signed Justin to Minardi, and in March 2003 the Yorkshire-born racer lined up on the grid in Melbourne with the likes of the Schumacher brothers, Montoya, Coulthard, Barrichello and Villeneuve, though at the time of writing he has yet to complete a Grand Prix.

JENSON BUTTON (1980–)

You could see that Jenson Button was a winner when he was just eight years old. His father, a distinguished rallycross driver himself in the 1970s, soon spotted his speed and talent and helped to develop it. Their joint efforts were rewarded in 1991 when Button took the British Cadet Championship with 34 wins – out of 34 races. Victories continued to flow, Jenson racing to success on the British, European and world stages. He was British Open champion twice, and in 1995 he won the Italian ICA Senior title; two years later he crowned his karting achievements by becoming the youngest ever winner of the European Super A title. A trip to Japan that year also saw Button leave with the Ayrton Senna Memorial Trophy – a fitting climax to a stunning kart career.

The talented youngster had long been the talk of the motor racing world, and seasoned observers couldn't wait to see how he would adapt to racing cars. The answer came quickly: Button dominated Formula Ford in the 1998 season. Driving for Haywood Racing, he took nine wins in the ultracompetitive British Championship on the way to claiming the title. He also secured the runner-up spot in the European Championship, and rounded off a superb first year in cars with victory in the Formula Ford Festival. Recognition of the young man from Frome's special talents came at the end of that season with the award of the prestigious McLaren/Autosport BRDC Young Driver of the Year title.

A jump straight into Formula Three for the 1999 season saw Jenson rock the established stars by placing his car on pole position for the very first race of the year. Racing against drivers with more than a season of Formula Three under their belts, and with an engine not quite on a par with the best, Jenson took three wins, claimed the Rookie of the Year title and took third place in the championship.

That November, as his prize for winning the BRDC Young Driver award, Jenson had a taste of Formula One for the first time, taking to the track in a McLaren MP4/13. A couple of weeks later a test for the Prost team saw Button outpace the experienced Jean Alesi. The Williams team immediately put Button into a high-pressure shoot-out against another young rising star, the far more experienced Brazilian Bruno Junqueira. Jenson won through. Suddenly the world had a new Formula One star, and the media went mad.

In Melbourne in March 2000, at the age of twenty years and two months, Button became one of the youngest drivers ever to sit on a Grand Prix grid, and he impressed everyone with his coolness and race pace. A point in just his second Grand Prix signalled his intentions, and by the end of the season the youngster was eighth in the drivers' championship – an amazing feat for a rookie racer. Button then moved to Benetton for the 2001 season, and it proved to be a difficult year for the young driver. The team was developing an innovative new car, a task which took up most of the year, although Button did pick up two points at Hockenheim.

The 2002 season opened with a change of fortune. Button took a fourth-place finish in both the second and third races of the season, and a fifth place at the subsequent San Marino Grand Prix; he secured further points at the European, French, Italian and Japanese Grands Prix and ended the year in seventh place in the championship as one of the most consistent points scorers.

Now that Button is driving for the up-and-coming BAR team under David Richards' leadership, alongside Jacques Villeneuve with whom he quickly developed a somewhat prickly relationship, the next few years promise to be very interesting indeed.

14. WHAT NEXT FOR THE BRITISH FORMULA ONE INDUSTRY?

'The first thing is that we have to recognise what we've got. The most important thing is for us to retain our core competencies. People are going to go for low-cost manufacturing bases wherever they next pop up. We have to make sure we retain the creative juices, the John Barnards of tomorrow, the creative, challenging, competitive, innovative young people.'

Chris Aylett, President, MIA

There is no doubt that for the last thirty-odd years, Britain's Motorsport Valley with its specialist teams, racing-car manufacturers and suppliers has dominated the global motorsport industry. This has created a highly skilled labour pool in the country, particularly in composites and aerodynamics, but in the increasingly manufacturer-driven Formula One sector, is Britain's motorsport cluster being threatened by other countries?

One of the reasons cited for Ferrari's current success is that it has the support of some major high-technology companies in Italy, while German car makers Mercedes-Benz and BMW are able to rely on the precision-engineering businesses for which Stuttgart and, to a lesser extent, Munich are famous. Germany has three major car manufacturers – Volkswagen, BMW and Mercedes (and the small-scale but impressive operator Porsche) – all of which have their own networks of specialist suppliers. For many years there was almost no involvement in international motorsport beyond the factory operations, and the local racing scene was never as developed as it was in Britain, but since German drivers and engine makers started to become more successful in Formula One the popularity of the sport in Germany has boomed, and with it has come growth at the grass-roots level. A motor racing industry has been gradually growing, and what is known as perform-ance-critical engineering has been developing. Toyota Motorsport's decision to base its team in Cologne was perhaps not as foolish as it at first appeared. Formula One motorsport is vulnerable to the world markets. In Britain, there have been a number of bankruptcies across the industry, notably with Reynard. The French have also lost all their major racing teams in recent years because of unfavourable legislation, but Germany has been quietly continuing to grow. For now, the worries are concentrated on the engine business, for Britain still rules the waves in terms of composite skill and knowledge, but how long will it be before others decide to follow Toyota and set up chassis-building businesses in Germany?

'If you're a serious player in motorsport, you've got to be here in some shape or form, even though you may have satellite offices around the world,' insisted Chris Aylett, president of the UK's motorsport lobbying organisation, the MIA. 'This is why Britain shouldn't worry if, for example, South Africa right now is a strong place for metals, for aluminium with a low-labour cost. It can't do the design, the global marketing, and it doesn't have the innovative, competitive edge we've got. Motorsport Valley still has a pool of competitive and innovative people which probably is still unique. We have a higher concentration of people who enjoy the competitive challenge of technology and engineering. This is exemplified in motorsport, but you can see the same in aerospace, or marine engineering. This pool of people has been added to by many international players. Brazilians, Australians and Italians like to come to this unusual community of competitive people. Those involved in this sector also include logistics, freight, IT, and so on, all of whom are competitive and keen to get their products to market faster and better than anyone else.'

The determination to compete, to be the best, to be a winner, is all pervasive within the valley, and 'that probably hasn't been flawed by this short-term, two-year downturn in marketing spend,' Aylett added. 'When global players started to have trouble in 2000, when the dotcoms started the rot, that's when we realised that global marketing spend was also probably the driver of this current Formula One circus. Unless we kept the market buoyant, we knew there were going to be hard times ahead. As far as Britain is concerned, you can't enjoy the up without enjoying the down. With seven of the eleven Formula One teams in Britain, clearly if Formula One hits a dry patch then these seven are going to hurt Britain first. This is where we are at the moment [2003]. Whether it will get worse before it gets better, we don't know.'

RenaultF1's executive director of engineering Pat Symonds believes that, essentially, Formula One is still reasonably healthy, though 'it can no longer afford to be as decadent as it used to be. Over the last twenty years, teams have come and gone, even strong teams like Lotus and Brabham. It's difficult to get sponsorship and to keep a team going at the levels we have been used to, but it is not difficult to keep a Formula One team just going. Audiences may be down a few per cent, but we're a long way from going into panic mode. We must recognise that these are difficult times. However, outside Formula One, into the general realm of motorsport, that's a much more serious problem. The demise of Reynard was an absolute tragedy. We're now left with just Lola and Van Diemen, and we have extremely strong competition from French teams like Dallara. We must not regard the production of racing cars as a God-given right to the British. Still, we have every reason to be very proud of what we've done and what we're doing. Current strengths lie in our work ethic. There is a good tradition of motorsport in the UK, and from generation to generation the ethic of what's required to be successful in motorsport has been passed down. This is why the valley's cluster is such an important thing. It does ensure that this expertise and work ethic is passed on because it's a local environment. It's absolutely our strength. It encompasses information, a competitive spirit and the will to work no matter how many hours it takes to do the job.'

Jaguar's Tony Purnell agrees. 'The British Formula One industry is still pretty healthy. If you want to build a Formula One car, there's no better place. You rely so much on subcontracting, and if you want specialists it's much easier to pop down the road than it is to get on a plane, say to Europe or the US. It's also a lot cheaper to work and live here for the specialists and engineers. Pi, though, has been using some of the low-cost economies for its work, simply because that's the way to remain competitive. We've turned to India and eastern Europe for much cheaper software development. You have to remain lean and efficient. The commercial world isn't romantic. This is the culture I have to preach to all three companies [Jaguar, Cosworth and Pi]. The future is in cost-effectiveness.'

Although the British Formula One industry has made a number of its professionals redundant in recent years, skills haven't been lost. The industry has merely been streamlining itself, and skills have passed to others in the motorsport chain. 'Because Britain is the home of not just Formula One but a host of other global motorsport categories as well [Le Mans, the World Rally teams, European touring cars], we probably have a wider net to take up some of these highly skilled people,' said Aylett. 'They are not leaving the industry, they are settling at another level. So, if Formula One is the Premier League, suddenly Division One becomes quite strong because some very talented people are being passed down the local supply chain, which is being strengthened. They'll maintain those skills, even improve them, and be available to move back later when the marketing spend and the global economic cycle inevitably returns. That has to be a positive. If our sport just served national rather than global markets, then it would be hard. We'd be dancing on the head of a pin. But we have a wide client base in Britain whose companies are getting more and more involved, for example, in the US motorsport scene, right across the sport, not just with open-wheelers but also with drag racing.' This pool of talent is also being continuously reinforced by the education system in the UK, which recognises that motorsport and competition can breed good engineers, not just for motorsport but for other forms of British manufacturing too. 'Delivery on time, fast prototyping, innovative solutions and thinking outside the box are all qualities many industries would die for in an employee,' Aylett added.

There have been times, though, when the sector has seemed both misunderstood and poorly represented in the public's consciousness. Although the general public focuses on just seven British Formula One teams, the UK has some 2,500 companies involved with motorsport. 'This is two and a half times more than in Germany, so we're a long way ahead of everyone else,' said Aylett. 'But we could come tumbling down. The first thing is that we have to recognise what we've got. The most important thing is for us to retain our core competencies. People are going to go for low-cost manufacturing bases wherever they next pop up. We have to make sure we retain the creative juices, the John Barnards of tomorrow, the creative, challenging, competitive, innovative young people.'

Are the traditional trades disappearing?

'Some are,' said RenaultF1's Pat Symonds. 'The prime example is in fabrication; they are disappearing rapidly. Here in the valley our prime supplier of skilled fabricators was Pressed Steel Fisher. Over the years, nearly every fabricator I've employed has served an apprenticeship there. Of course, as the motor industry has declined so have those skills, but equally, motor racing no longer requires many fabricators. We simply do not fabricate many components. In the last ten to fifteen years we've built up a huge skills base in composites, which hadn't existed before. Going back twenty years, we probably employed five fabricators; these days the percentage of fabricated parts on the car has plummeted, yet we still have six fabricators. Twenty years ago we didn't employ any composite laminators. We didn't do our own fibreglass in those days either, but now we probably have forty people in our composites department [craftsmen, not engineers]. So the skills have been replaced, and interestingly, because it's a new technology, we've had to generate those skills ourselves. We have not been able to go out to larger industry to coax these skills in, we've had to teach and develop these skills from year to year. The same is true of machine shops. We used to employ a lot of people on manually operated machines; now all of them are numerically controlled so there are fewer people operating them – on average, one person per two machines, maybe one for three. These skills are different. Although any one of our guys could get on a manual machine and do an extremely good job, I can see that in another twenty years' time they would struggle with it. But in order to get the best people on the machines, we teach them to program the NC machines, so they increase their skill base.'

Jordan also runs an apprenticeship programme and a graduate training scheme, but marketing director Mark Gallagher, as impressive as he believes modern skills are, does bemoan the passing of the traditional-skills era. 'Gary Anderson is self-taught,' he said. 'He will come down to the workshop and build a bit on the car himself. He's hands-on. That's a tremendous quality, and we're all the poorer for losing people like that.'

There is certainly not a crisis in British Formula One's skills base yet, but the industry needs to stop and have a think about the way things are developing. Making sure new talent comes into the industry is now a top priority. All the teams maintain links with academia in order to ensure that the next generation of British Formula One engineers and aerodynamicists get the necessary breaks. Through its funding arm, the Engineering and Physical Sciences Research Council (EPSRC), the UK government is also pumping money into automotive research. Bolstering these activities, not only by providing education but also by conducting advanced research into all aspects of vehicle, powertrain, component and materials engineering, are around fifty universities and other centres of excellence around the UK.

But, are we producing the right skills? Indeed, which new skills are most needed?

'So much has changed,' said Symonds. 'Moving on from the craft to the engineering level, the teams in the old days employed very few engineers, and they had to be multidisciplined. When I started in 1981, our design office was three people. We moved to six for a while. These days, the design office encompasses so many other people – vehicle dynamicists, aerodynamicists, research and development – it's up to eighty. With this number you still need only a few multidisciplined engineers, but a greater number of specialists. CFD code, finite element analysis and so on is so specialised that you need people who are using it every single day. If you have to pick it up once a month, you're just not going to be productive. It's too complex.'

The Formula One teams approach skills development in a variety of ways. BAR is involved with a range of student training programmes that offer work experience. 'Most of our recruitment is done internally, so we have a very key training programme,' explained team principal David Richards. 'We're not unique in this, but we are very progressive. As a matter of course we don't just poach the best person from another team; we'd rather develop them internally and build them within the whole culture of our organisation. This has been a key aspect of the business we've developed around.'

Some of the best engineers in the country want to work for McLaren. 'We've reached a point where the best graduates in industry don't want to be in industry, certainly not in engineering,' said McLaren International's managing director Martin Whitmarsh. 'The services sector is more sexy, more interesting, and that's where the best graduates in the land are going. An exception to that in the industrial sector is motor racing. We can draw world-class minds into our industry. Some of us are big enough to take these brilliant brains and shape them into engineers and leaders of the future who are going to innovate and lead others to innovate.'

Historically, McLaren has been associated with a number of institutions. For aerodynamics, it has enjoyed links with Imperial College; for simulation, mathematical modelling and control system development it has joined minds with Cambridge University, and for operational research, Southampton University. 'We pick fields that are strategic to us,' Whitmarsh explained. 'We also look for developing sciences. A few years ago, CFD was relevant to us. We started to develop this specialism with Imperial. However, we felt at the time that although we had some bright young engineers working in the field, we didn't have enough to make the critical mass required for advancement, so we partnered with BAe Systems, which had a CFD team.' That was seven years ago. BAe Systems engineers were seconded to the McLaren team in Woking. 'This didn't just add to our own critical mass of skills, it also gave us a conduit to work with the CFD team, which is also an important area for British Aerospace. And we got to use their supercomputing facility. We wanted to see who was leading industrially, and how that could benefit McLaren. It works fantastically. It's also a stimulus in their organisation. Just like the motor industry, these businesses recognise that it's vitally important that they reduce the cycle time for developing complex engineering products. Within the aerospace industry you have thirty-year project cycles, from initial conception to the end of the plane's life. It takes time because of the complexity of the product, its cost, the way it's developed, and so on. For them to be able to put their engineers in an environment where they can see the time to market is critical. They could design a new part, get it into the wind tunnel within days, and then have it on the product within weeks.'

B3 Technologies' John Barnard takes the question of training and nurturing Formula One talent very seriously. He even lectures to students at Cranfield about it. 'We're producing people with the skills,' he said, 'but how do you produce someone who can innovate? That's the problem. There are various branches of mechanical engineering, but fundamentally, if someone presents you with a problem or something to do that is mechanical in any shape or form, you should be able to sit down and attack that problem. You don't have to be trained in a motor racing course to be able to go and do it, you just have to apply good basic engineering knowledge, with some lateral thinking. It's this that we need to develop. But at the same time, there is only so far you can go in college. At the end of the day, there's nothing like someone sticking a piece of clean white paper in front of you and saying, "By the first of March next year we want one of those, a thing that does A, B or C on the ground." Then it's down to you. There's no subsitute for this. Racing used to provide it, but no one is prepared to take those kinds of risks now. A lot of my production staff have been with me for quite some years now. I have young design staff, one of whom I took all the way through university [aeronautical engineering at Bristol], and who worked here in his gap year. He's a racing enthusiast, but he's also working on a bike project now as well as Formula One. For him, the interest is in the fundamental design aspects. If you're a true engineer or designer, you know that the component you're creating or solution you're designing is right, and you feel it. It gives you a lot of pleasure.'

Barnard puts his finger on it. You can't 'teach' Formula One.

'What I loved about Formula One was the technology, and the flexibility to try something different,' he added. 'When things worked, that gave me a lot of pleasure. I liked to be quick, and I liked to have a car that was quick. That was the rubber stamp on what you did. You learned by doing everything, to get the overall understanding. But now we're suffering from a lack of those middle skills. Where do we get our next NC operators from, our fabricators, welders? The system is not in place to produce them. This process of "everyone" going to university has screwed the middle ranks. Those who get trained to operate the machines in the workshop are computer operators. You don't just wind a few handles any more. People used to do five-year apprenticeships. These have gone. Half the time we have to get a young guy and train him up. Certainly in composites, we bring in young guys with no knowledge of the subject and we train them up for three to four years.

But when the big Formula One teams need people in their composite shops, they pop along with 50 per cent more wages and there go our trained guys.'

Jaguar's Tony Purnell doesn't like the idea of specialised education for Formula One. 'Good engineers, managers and salespeople for good engineering companies tend to be people who have had a nice broad base of education, so they see different facets of the way the world works. Different approaches to things, rather than one recipe. Don't think anything associated with Formula One will get you a job in the industry. It won't. It is much better, say, to have a really good understanding of physics, and then begin to specialise. Rather like the US approach. If you want to be a doctor or a lawyer, you have to go and get a degree in something else first; only then do you get into medical or law school. That makes you much more rounded. A degree used to be a way of broadening the mind, not vocational. I've no problem with vocational schools, but the top people, those with fine minds, should have the broadest education possible so that they can approach problems with a bit of lateral thinking and open-mindedness. Our head of Vehicle Sciences used to be a leader in Cambridge Consultants' medical instruments division. When we made the appointment, we thought a lot of people would think we were barking mad. Absolutely no motor racing experience at all. He's going to fail. But our feeling was that he was right for the job because his approach to product development was just perfect, in the way he organised processes to create improvement. He's very inventive and innovative, rides a Harley Davidson. You'd think he was a doctor. He's very clear-minded and takes a step-by-step approach.'

Vehicle Sciences encapsulates and distils all the effort that tells the design team how to make a better car for the following year. 'It's sort of research and development, about understanding better what we have,' Purnell added. 'You can't improve something until you understand what you've got, its shortcomings, the gaps in the understanding you have when you try to predict its performance. If you look at a technology's performance and it doesn't come up to scratch, why doesn't it? Understand the gaps, create new ways of doing things, and make the hole smaller. These people have to ooze leadership. Sitting in a room with, say, ten people, they must get everyone buzzing. If there's respect for the chap in charge, a feeling is generated that you can conquer the world.'

'A few years ago, I was quite certain what we needed,' Symonds reflected. 'Going back five to six years, I could see we were expanding, but I didn't anticipate we'd expand at quite the rate we have.' It was around this time that Benetton began to sponsor students studying race-car engineering at Oxford Brookes and others at Cranfield doing automotive engineering, and latterly with the MSc. in Motorsports Engineering and Management. 'I felt we needed to go back to grass-roots level to get the engineers we needed for the future. I still think that was the right thing to do, but as these programmes have started to come to fruition we've found ourselves with a little glut of engineers due to the recession, with companies like Reynard and Arrows closing. But I do believe this is short term, providing we take the appropriate action to make sure it's not the death knell – and it isn't, because enough people are paying attention to the industry now.'

Ensuring that this kind of training continues, rather than forcing teams simply to poach staff from other teams, is important. The MIA is doing a great deal of work in this area, studying the whole career path of engineers. Work is also being done by regional development agencies, and now, with some extra support from the government in the form of the DTI's Automotive Unit, the whole subject of how the valley's motorsport cluster can be developed for the future is on the agenda.

But are the academic institutions churning out people with the right skills? 'Some always have done,' said Symonds, 'but it's a mixed bag. Imperial, Southampton [both strong on aerodynamics], Oxford Brookes, Cambridge [excellent general mechanical engineers], Cranfield [automotive and aeronautical] and Loughborough [automotive] produce good-quality students. Some of them, particularly Cranfield and Brookes, are tailoring mechanical engineering to motorsport. This is excellent. But it worries me that others are almost selling their courses as gateways into Formula One. You have to serve your apprenticeship first. I did Formula Ford, Formula Three and Formula Two before Formula One. I believe everyone needs a grounding in mechanical engineering, but the specialisations are now so intense that they have to concentrate on them. I put all my students through the design group. To me, it doesn't matter what you do, you have to understand design. It's no good an aerodynamicist coming up with this super wing that's got 5 per cent better performance than the last wing if it's only three millimetres thick supporting a kilo Newton of load. There's no material in the world you'll be able to make it from. It's not going to work. It's why I like the course at Brookes, which is essentially mechanical engineering but with a bias towards automotive. They don't neglect basic stress analysis, mechanics and properties of materials. Our mechanical design group, which does the hydraulics, suspension and fuel system, has an ex-Rolls-Royce guy as part of its team too, so we also look at industry. A sound engineer, he was used to dealing with lightweight, low-inertia structures, but he adapted to motorsport very quickly and he's an excellent designer of real quality and elegance.'

Skills and talent-nurturing aside, the real future for Formula One appears to lie in how well it is marketed as a sport. Now that qualifying has been revamped and several other rule changes have been introduced for the 2003 season, does Formula One have a show that warrants the marketing spend? It has dawned on many, John Barnard included, that it's not good for the sport to have huge wealth polarised at the Ferrari end of the grid, and a fraction of it just six places back. 'One of the big things with the racing industry in Britain is that over many years, because of the way it started, with the enthusiast virtually working out of his garage and then developing into a small business, that spun off a lot of very small subcontracting outfits which knew all about racing because most of the people had worked in it. They knew what was required, the type of constraints peculiar to the racing business, and that fitted together as one great big jigsaw puzzle. As soon as the manufacturers get involved they approach it from a very different angle. First, they have an enormous chequebook, and the capability to do a job with forty people we would have done before with ten. That's the way they think, and the way their usual road car industry operates. And they don't think anything of it. But in terms of the racing industry we know, that's a very different animal.'

'The teams have to think more strategically about their sports marketing budgets,' said the MIA's Chris Aylett. 'They have to husband their marketing dollars more carefully, and make sure clients get best value. They can run lean and mean for a period. They don't have to spend all their money. They were driven to spend because the budgets were made available. You can run a team for a lot less. You don't have to have your own corporate jet [Eddie Jordan flies economy], you don't need two wind tunnels. You can scale your operation up or down, as long as the spectacle remains worth buying into. When money is made available to one team, then the others feel as though they must have it to catch up. But if you reduce the budget, teams will still race, and very competitively. They will cut out the genuine excesses and simply do a better job for a better price.'

Perhaps the industry should produce more British drivers to boost the country's interest in Formula One?

'The nationality of a driver is irrelevant to us,' said BAR's David Richards. 'We just want to employ the best people for the job. It's very nice if they are British, and it helps from a morale point of view internally, but our priority is to find the guy who can do the best job for us. In this business, there isn't a great deal of room for sentimentality. If British drivers think British Formula One teams will prioritise them, then they've got to think again. They've got to earn their stripes. However, I don't think they do expect special treatment compared with foreign drivers. We've been fortunate that we've developed some great drivers over the last few years. We do have a flourishing Formula One industry and great opportunities, but we haven't done enough in terms of development programmes for drivers, providing the right kind of incubatory environment for them, as has been the case in France, Scandinavia and Germany. Other countries seem to take a more proactive approach to what's required to develop young drivers. The best thing we can do is make sure that British drivers are at the top of the sport as beacons and ambassadors for everyone else. However, the Damon Hills and Jackie Stewarts happened by default, not as a result of a structured programme.'

Of course, drivers from the Moss and Stewart eras are very different to modern drivers. 'If we generalise about how drivers have changed, they are like all athletes – the level of professionalism has increased immensely,' Symonds observed. 'If you compare Beckham and Geoff Hurst, I would bet that Beckham is much fitter. He might still possess the same basic skills, but he has this incredible publicity machine around him. The same is true of the drivers. They still possess the inherent skills of balance, nerve, reaction time – the physical attributes – but they have now combined it with a lot more professionalism. They're driving every week. The likes of Jackie Stewart and Jim Clark, for them Formula One was just one of the things they did. They also drove Lotus Cortinas, Can-Am cars, and so on. The Formula One driver of today is a much more dedicated individual, driving solely Formula One cars, usually, every week. He maintains a very high level of fitness and uses personal trainers. The only driver of a past generation who did anything remotely like this was Jody Scheckter. And, of course, this incredible publicity machine around them now includes managers, PR people and personal assistants. I don't exactly know how many people it takes to run a racing driver these days, but it's approaching the same number we used to have to run a Formula One car. So that's changed, from the British viewpoint. It's individual. Some are massively motivated. Nigel Mansell's a good example. He was someone who so truly believed in himself, he made it happen. Not all drivers are like that. But what we do see with British drivers over the last few years is that it has been much more difficult for them to generate local support and get to the top than it has for the Italians and South Americans, and the French.

'British Formula One is quite healthy,' Symonds concluded, 'but the same is not true of British club racing. If we in Formula One wish to perpetuate what we've had in the past, then we need to filter down and look at the lower formulas.' RenaultF1 already does this. It runs a driver development programme to sponsor a Formula 3000 team, as do most of the Formula One teams. 'But it would be nice to think that somehow it was getting right back down to the Formula Ford level, or indeed the karting level, which these days is where you need to start. McLaren does support karting, but no one else does. By that, I don't necessarily mean we should plough a percentage of our budget into club racing. It's more generic than that; it's about the whole infrastructure of racing, about generating enthusiasm. But it is important to have local racing at the highest level to generate enthusiasm right down to the lowest level so that, say, twelve-year-old karters will want to drive in Formula One some day.'

TIMELINE

1950

The first race of the World Championship is held as the British Grand Prix on the Silverstone circuit. Giuseppe Farina wins the race in an Alfa Romeo.

The first rear-engined car in a World Championship event makes its appearance at the Monaco Grand Prix. It's a Cooper-JAP driven by Harry Schell.

1951

Constructor BRM makes its World Championship debut.

1955

Stirling Moss wins his first World Championship event. It's the British Grand Prix, this time held at Aintree, and Moss is driving a Mercedes-Benz.

1956

Vanwall introduces its new car. It has a Colin Chapman-designed chassis, and bodywork by Frank Costin.

Driving a customised Maserati 250F, Stirling Moss wins the Italian Grand Prix.

1957

Tony Brooks and Stirling Moss give Britain its first win by a British constructor. Driving a Vanwall, they win the British Grand Prix at Aintree.

1958

At the season-opening Argentinian Grand Prix, Stirling Moss gives Cooper its first win in a World Championship event. It is also the first championship win for a rear-engined car – a private entrant (Rob Walker) and the Coventry Climax engine. In Monaco, using the same Cooper-Climax as Moss, Maurice Trintignant wins the second consecutive championship race for the Rob Walker team.

Peter Collins is killed during the German Grand Prix at the Nürburgring when his Ferrari crashes and hits a tree.

Stuart Lewis-Evans dies from injuries and burns received while crashing during the final championship event of the season, the Grand Prix of Morocco in Casablanca.

Mike Hawthorn wins the World Championship by a margin of one point over Stirling Moss, and retires from racing.

Vanwall wins the first constructors' championship, but withdraws from Grand Prix racing.

1959

Mike Hawthorn dies in a road accident.

Rear-engined Grand Prix cars begin to replace front-engined cars on the starting grids.

Jack Brabham wins his first championship event, the Grand Prix of Monaco.

Stirling Moss is now driving for private entrant Rob Walker.

Bruce McLaren becomes the youngest driver to win a championship event when he triumphs at the United States Grand Prix at Sebring.

Jack Brabham wins his first World Championship.

Cooper-Climax wins the constructors' championship.

1960

Stirling Moss gets home first in the Monaco Grand Prix driving Rob Walker's Lotus 18.

Jim Clark makes his Formula One debut driving a works Lotus at the Dutch Grand Prix.

A tragic accident at the Belgian Grand Prix claims the lives of two promising young British drivers, Chris Bristow and Alan Stacey. Stirling Moss breaks both legs in an accident during practice.

The Italian Grand Prix is held on the Monza banked track. British teams boycott the race on safety grounds. Ferrari scores a hollow victory. This is the last ever front-engined Formula One win.

Jack Brabham successfully defends his drivers' title driving a Cooper-Climax.

1961

Stirling Moss wins an epic Monaco Grand Prix driving the outdated Lotus 18.

Innes Ireland scores a Team Lotus win at the American Grand Prix. Unfortunately, he is sacked just weeks later.

1962

Stirling Moss suffers his career-ending crash at a pre-season Goodwood meeting, again driving Rob Walker's Lotus.

Lotus introduces its ground-breaking new model, the 25, with a monocoque chassis making the standard spaceframe designs obsolete overnight.

Jim Clark scores his first ever win at the Belgian Grand Prix.

Jack Brabham enters the German Grand Prix with his own car.

British teams commence a long period of Formula One domination. Graham Hill wins the Dutch Grand Prix for BRM and goes on to win the drivers' championship.

1963

Graham Hill notches up the first of his five Monaco victories.

John Surtees scores his first ever championship victory for Ferrari when he wins the German Grand Prix at the Nürburgring.

Jim Clark totally dominates the season. He records seven wins to secure his first drivers' championship.

1964

Jim Clark wins the first ever Grand Prix to be held at Brands Hatch.

Jochen Rindt makes his Grand Prix debut in the inaugural Austrian Grand Prix held at the Zeltweg airfield circuit. He's driving Rob Walker's Brabham-BRM.

John Surtees secures the drivers' title and becomes the first (and only) man ever to win world titles on both two and four wheels.

1965

Jackie Stewart makes his Grand Prix debut for the BRM team. He finishes sixth in his first race (South Africa) and scores his maiden win at the Italian Grand Prix at Monza.

Team Lotus misses the Monaco Grand Prix to concentrate on the Indianapolis 500. Jim Clark wins and scores his first ever rear-engined victory at the Brickyard.

Jim Clark and Team Lotus are totally dominant all year long and Clark secures his second (and last) world crown.

1966

BRM produces its H16 engine. It proves to be heavy and complicated, and scores its one and only victory at the US Grand Prix.

Jackie Stewart is trapped in his car after crashing out of the rain-affected Belgian Grand Prix. This experience would lead him to commence a safety campaign that would eventually transform the sport's attitude to all aspects of driver safety.

Jack Brabham wins the French Grand Prix at Reims to become the first driver to score a race win in a car bearing his own name. He goes on to secure his third World Championship.

Bruce McLaren debuts in Formula One with his own team. The first McLaren is powered by a Ford engine and is not successful.

1967

The ground-breaking Lotus 49 wins on its debut at the Dutch Grand Prix with Jim Clark at the wheel. The car is powered by the Ford-financed, Cosworth-built Double Four Valve (DFV) engine.

Honda scores its first ever three-litre formula win at the Italian Grand Prix. John Surtees is at the wheel.

The first ever Canadian Grand Prix is held at Mosport Park. Brabhams finish first and second.

New Zealander Denny Hulme wins the drivers' crown in a Brabham.

1968

Wings appear on Grand Prix cars for the first time to aid downforce. The DFV engine is now available to all.

Jim Clark is killed in a Formula Two race at Hockenheim in Germany. The greatest driver of his era is lost to the sport. BRM Formula One driver Mike Spence is also killed, at Indianapolis.

McLaren scores its first ever Formula One win at the Belgian Grand Prix with team founder Bruce McLaren in the cockpit.

Jackie Stewart leaves BRM to join Ken Tyrrell, a partnership that will win three drivers' titles over the next six years.

Graham Hill in a Lotus wins his second drivers' title.

1969

The DFV-powered teams dominate. The Cooper-Maserati and Eagle-Weslake teams withdraw from Formula One.

Four-wheel drive is tried by Matra, Lotus and McLaren, but it is not a success.

Piers Courage finishes second at Monaco driving a Brabham entered by Frank Williams.

Jackie Stewart wins his first drivers' title.

1970

Jack Brabham wins the South African Grand Prix. By the end of the season he has retired from Formula One.

March and Team Surtees make their debut.

Jackie Stewart wins his first Grand Prix for March at Jarama in Spain.

The wedge-shaped Lotus 72, with side-mounted radiators, makes its debut. Jochen Rindt drives the car to its first victory at the Dutch Grand Prix.

Pedro Rodriguez wins the last Belgian Grand Prix at the original Spa-Francorchamps for BRM. This is also Dunlop's last victory.

Piers Courage burns to death in the Williams-de Tomaso at the Dutch Grand Prix.

Bruce McLaren is killed at Goodwood while testing a Can-Am car.

Tyrrell makes its Formula One debut at Mont Tremblant, Canada.

1971

Jackie Stewart scores Tyrrell's first Grand Prix victory at Jarama.

Niki Lauda makes a low-key debut in a privately owned March at the Austrian Grand Prix.

Peter Gethin wins the Italian Grand Prix by 0.01 of a second from Ronnie Peterson – still the narrowest winning margin.

Emerson Fittipaldi races a gas-turbine Lotus 56B 'in disguise' as World Wide Racing.

Jackie Stewart wins the World Championship for the second time.

For the first time since 1960, Lotus fails to score a single race win.

1972

Bernie Ecclestone takes over Brabham.

Team Lotus runs for the first time in the black livery of John Player Specials, or 'JPS' as the cars will soon come to be called.

The Argentinian Grand Prix returns to the calendar; Jackie Stewart takes the win.

Fittipaldi wins the Italian Grand Prix to become the youngest ever Formula One champion, at 25. This win is also Firestone's last victory.

1973

Shadow make its Grand Prix debut.

Ex-champion Graham Hill sets up his own Embassy racing team.

McLaren introduces its classic M23 design that will race in various forms for the next six seasons.

The Ford DFV engine wins every Grand Prix of the season.

At the South African Grand Prix, Mike Hailwood saves Clay Regazzoni's life by pulling him from his burning BRM. Hailwood is later awarded the George Medal for valour.

The Belgian Grand Prix moves to Zolder, where Tyrrell grabs a one-two victory.

Denny Hulme wins at Anderstorp in the return of the Swedish Grand Prix.

As Jody Scheckter spins at the start of the British Grand Prix, a massive collision involving over a dozen cars occurs at the Woodcote Corner. Andrea de Adamich is the only casualty, but nine drivers fail to take the restart.

Roger Williamson burns to death at the Dutch Grand Prix in his March 731. David Purley attempts to save Williamson's life, for which he is awarded the George Medal.

The German Grand Prix is Stewart's 27th and last Grand Prix victory. He becomes the drivers' champion for a third time but withdraws from the US Grand Prix after François Cevert is killed during qualifying.

1974

Lord Hesketh builds his own Formula One car designed by Harvey Postlethwaite; James Hunt is the driver.

Mike Hailwood retires from racing after suffering injuries during a crash at the German Grand Prix.

Emerson Fittipaldi wins the drivers' championship for the second time with McLaren.

Denny Hulme retires from Formula One.

1975

The Brazilian Grand Prix is Graham Hill's 176th and last race. Later that year, he and Tony Brise, together with other team members, are killed when a plane Hill is piloting crashes as it attempts to land in fog.

Hunt scores the first and only win for Hesketh, at the Dutch Grand Prix.

1976

Tyrrell introduces a six-wheeled car.

John Watson scores the first and only win for Penske, at the Austrian Grand Prix.

James Hunt is declared the drivers' champion, driving for McLaren.

1977

Patrick Head joins Frank Williams' team.

The Lotus 78 ground-effect car is introduced.

Tom Pryce is killed after hitting a track marshal at the South African Grand Prix. This is also the last race for the BRM team.

At Monaco, Jody Scheckter scores the 100th Grand Prix victory for the Ford DFV engine.

Alan Jones scores his own and Shadow's first Grand Prix victory at Austria.

March withdraws from Formula One.

1978

Arrows enters Formula One and nearly wins the South African Grand Prix. Riccardo Patrese leads for most of the race, but retires because of mechanical failure.

The Williams team introduces its first car, the FW06. Alan Jones is the team's number one driver.

Mario Andretti becomes the world champion for Lotus. He wins six Grands Prix during the season.

Team Surtees leaves Formula One.

1979

The Monaco Grand Prix is James Hunt's last race.

Clay Regazzoni scores Williams' first Grand Prix victory, at Silverstone.

Jackie Ickx and the Wolf team retire from Formula One.

1980

The battle to control Grand Prix racing erupts between the Formula One Constructors Association (FOCA) and the Fédération Internationale du Sport Automobile (FISA). Its eventual resolution by an agreement known as the Concorde Agreement sees Bernie Ecclestone and FOCA win control of the commercial aspects of Formula One, a situation that continues to this day.

Alain Prost competes in his first race, in a McLaren at Argentina.

Reserve Lotus driver Nigel Mansell also makes his Grand Prix debut, at the Osterreichring in Austria.

Australia's Alan Jones wins the World Championship, a first for Williams.

1981

Ron Dennis takes over McLaren, and the team debuts a carbon-fibre chassis designed by John Barnard.

After the innovative twin-chassis Lotus 88 is banned by officials at Long Beach, Colin Chapman threatens to pull Lotus out of Formula One. He boycotts the new San Marino Grand Prix at Imola.

In his last race for Williams, Alan Jones dominates the first Las Vegas Grand Prix, held in the vast car parks of the Las Vegas casinos.

Mike Hailwood is killed in a road accident.

Brazilian Nelson Piquet wins his first World Championship for Brabham, but the constructors' title goes to Williams.

1982

Niki Lauda returns from retirement to join McLaren.

BMW debuts its turbo engine in the Brabham.

Keke Rosberg wins Williams' second drivers' title, Ferrari the constructors'.

Colin Chapman, Lotus founder and Formula One's most innovative designer, dies of a heart attack.

1983

Spirit debuts the new Honda turbo engine at the British Grand Prix.

Michele Alboreto's Tyrrell scores the 155th and last win for the Cosworth DFR/DFY engine at the United States Grand Prix in Detroit.

There is the first appearance of the TAG-Porsche turbo with McLaren at the Dutch Grand Prix.

Nelson Piquet wins Brabham's last and BMW's only World Championship. Ferrari retains the constructors' crown for the last time until 1999.

1984

Tyrrell is disqualified for the entire 1984 season after allegations of infringements with water tanks, ballast and undertray.

Niki Lauda wins his third drivers' title by half a point from McLaren team-mate Alain Prost.

1985

Nigel Mansell wins his first race, the European Grand Prix at Brands Hatch.

The first Australian Grand Prix is won by Keke Rosberg.

Benetton commences its involvement with the Toleman team, initially as a sponsor (it was sponsor before to Alfa Romeo and to Tyrrell). But in no time the clothing giant will purchase Toleman and enter the 1986 championship as Benetton Grand Prix.

Triple world champion Niki Lauda retires from Formula One.

1986

Williams team principal Frank Williams is paralysed in a road accident while driving back from a Williams test at Paul Ricard.

Elio de Angelis is killed in a private Brabham testing session at Paul Ricard.

Jacques Laffite equals Graham Hill's record for the most Grand Prix starts (176) at the British Grand Prix, but during the start he crashes, breaking his legs and pelvis. This ends his career.

Alan Jones and Keke Rosberg retire from Formula One.

Alain Prost wins the Australian Grand Prix and becomes the first back-to-back world champion since Jack Brabham in 1960. Williams wins the constructors' title.

1987

Lotus and Williams experiment with active ride suspension, while Honda extends its engine supply to Lotus.

A messy last race is held at the Osterreichring, where Nigel Mansell wins after two start-line pile-ups and a chequered flag shown a lap late. Earlier, Stefan Johansson had struck a deer in practice.

Alain Prost breaks Jackie Stewart's record for the most Grand Prix wins (27) after winning the Portuguese Grand Prix.

Adrian Newey is appointed technical director of March.

Nelson Piquet wins his third World Championship for Williams. Jonathan Palmer wins the Jim Clark Cup for naturally aspirated engined cars.

1988

Gerhard Berger takes an emotional win for Ferrari in the Italian Grand Prix at Monza – the only non-McLaren win of the season. Shortly afterwards, Enzo Ferrari dies, at the age of ninety.

Ayrton Senna's eighth win of the year at the Japanese Grand Prix at Suzuka is a new record for a driver in a single season. McLaren dominates, winning fifteen out of sixteen races.

1989

Renault returns to Formula One as engine supplier to Williams.

At the Brazilian Grand Prix, Riccardo Patrese breaks Graham Hill's and Jacques Laffite's record for the most starts.

1990

Adrian Newey joins Williams around the middle of the year as the team's aerodynamics specialist. Later he will be made chief designer, and his cars will dominate the 1990s.

Rookie Jean Alesi leads half the race in Phoenix in a Tyrrell.

Ivan Capelli and Leyton House almost win at Paul Ricard after failing to qualify in the previous round.

Nigel Mansell announces his retirement after his car fails at the British Grand Prix while he was in the lead.

Martin Donnelly miraculously escapes death in a practice crash at Jerez.

1991

Nigel Mansell un-retires and returns to Williams.

The Jordan team makes its Grand Prix debut. The Jordan 191 is powered by the Ford HB engine and the team finishes fifth with thirteen points in its debut year.

TWR boss Tom Walkinshaw becomes technical director of Benetton, following John Barnard's departure.

Michael Schumacher makes his Formula One debut at Spa in a Jordan, where he qualifies an impressive seventh only to retire right at the start of the race. At the next race, however, he appears driving for Benetton.

Nigel Mansell is disqualified in Portugal after a wheel-change fiasco.

McLaren wins its seventh title in eight years, while the Honda engine makes it five in a row.

Max Mosley is appointed head of FISA over Jean-Marie Balestre, who ends a thirteen-year tenure.

1992

Williams reintroduces active suspension. The car is often in a race of its own.

Nigel Mansell wins his first five races in a row, setting a new record.

For the first time in Formula One, the safety car is used at the British Grand Prix as a means of allowing the race to continue at a reduced pace in the event of a serious accident.

Ayrton Senna wins in Hungary, but Mansell is crowned drivers' champion, giving Renault its first title. Mansell also sets a new record of nine wins in a season, and retires again to join American CART racing.

The Hungarian Grand Prix sees the last appearance of the Brabham team.

Giovanna Amati becomes the first woman to appear on the entry list for a Formula One Grand Prix since Lella Lombardi drove for March in the mid-1970s. She fails in her attempts to qualify for the early-season races and is replaced by Damon Hill for the Spanish Grand Prix.

Former world champion Denny Hulme dies from an apparent heart attack while driving a BMW M3 in the Bathurst 1,000-kilometre touring car race.

1993

FISA is abolished. All motorsport activities now come directly under the FIA, to the presidency of which Max Mosley is elected unchallenged.

Alain Prost returns to Formula One with Williams, where he is joined by Williams test driver Damon Hill, son of Graham.

Damon Hill scores three consecutive wins after retiring from the lead in earlier races.

Ayrton Senna punches debutant Eddie Irvine in Japan after a disagreement.

McLaren passes Ferrari in numbers of Grand Prix wins.

James Hunt, 1976 world champion and BBC racing commentator, dies from a heart attack at his London home.

Innes Ireland, winner of Team Lotus's first ever Grand Prix, dies from cancer.

1994

Team Lotus is sold to a court-appointed administrator. The Australian Grand Prix is the team's last race.

Ayrton Senna joins the Williams team and is considered the safest bet for the championship.

The blackest weekend of the decade at Imola. Rubens Barrichello crashes during Friday practice; Simtek's Roland Ratzenberger is killed during Saturday practice after crashing at the Villeneuve corner; J.J. Lehto and Pedro Lamy crash during the race, sending debris into the crowd and injuring eight people; and fewer than two laps after the restart Ayrton Senna is killed after going off at Tamburello.

Damon Hill wins an emotional Spanish Grand Prix for Williams. Michael Schumacher finishes second after spending more than half the race stuck in fifth gear.

Schumacher overtakes Hill twice during the formation lap of the British Grand Prix, then ignores a black flag, and eventually receives a two-race ban.

Damon Hill wins the race of his life in a wet Japan to close up the title battle.

Going into the final race of the season, Schumacher, with a one-point lead, controversially collides with Damon Hill, taking the two out. Schumacher is the first German world champion.

1995

McLaren begins a partnership with the Mercedes-Benz-funded Ilmor engine builder.

Bernie Ecclestone makes it on to the *Sunday Times* Rich List, in 196th place.

Nigel Mansell ends his Formula One career with McLaren after 'giving up' during the Spanish Grand Prix.

Damon Hill and Michael Schumacher collide again at the British Grand Prix while fighting for the lead. This allows Johnny Herbert to take his first Grand Prix win.

Schumacher wins the Belgian Grand Prix from sixteenth on the grid in changing conditions. He's once more involved in a contact with Hill. They will collide yet again, in Monza.

Mika Hakkinen is severely injured as a result of a qualifying crash in Australia. Hill wins the race by two laps after David Coulthard crashes into the pit wall while leading.

1996

McLaren announces the end of the longest sponsorship association, with Marlboro, signing instead with West.

Reigning CART champion Jacques Villeneuve joins Williams, grabbing pole position on his Formula One debut at the new Australian Grand Prix venue in Melbourne. He later wins his first race at the Nürburgring.

Bernie Ecclestone launches his digital television service at the British Grand Prix at Silverstone. The service commences live coverage at the

German race two weeks later. Swipe cards are also introduced to control entry to the Formula One paddock.

Williams sacks Damon Hill just before Monza, despite his success.

Damon Hill wins the World Championship in Suzuka and becomes the first son of a world champion to grab the title himself.

Tom Walkinshaw buys the Arrows Formula One team.

1997

Adrian Newey leaves Williams and joins rival McLaren as its technical director.

Stewart-Ford enters Grand Prix racing under the chairmanship of three-times champion Jackie Stewart. The team vows to win a World Championship in five years' time, and promises to run a tobacco-sponsor-free car.

The Michael Schumacher–Ross Brawn–Rory Byrne combination is reunited when Brawn and Byrne join Ferrari as technical director and chief designer.

Damon Hill ends up at Arrows, and retires on the formation lap at the first race.

The Senna trial begins. Five principals from the Williams team, including Frank Williams, Adrian Newey and Patrick Head, are charged with manslaughter.

Damon Hill almost wins in Hungary, but electrical problems see Jacques Villeneuve pass him on the final lap.

Prodrive boss Dave Richards replaces the flamboyant Flavio Briatore. He's put in charge of the Benetton team from the Luxembourg Grand Prix.

Williams and McLaren are cleared of allegations that they colluded to determine the placings during the Jerez Grand Prix.

Ken Tyrrell sells his racing outfit to what will become in 1999 a new team, British American Racing, run by Craig Pollock, Jacques Villeneuve's former manager.

1998

David Coulthard lets Mika Hakkinen win in Australia, later revealing that the two had a prior agreement that whoever reached the first corner first would win the race.

McLaren's 'turning' brake is banned, but it has little effect on the car's speed.

Ford buys long-time engine partner Cosworth from German car maker Audi.

Jordan finishes one-two in Belgium to take its first win. However, controversy erupts after Michael Schumacher collides with David Coulthard while lapping him. Schumacher has to be restrained when both drivers return to the pit lane.

1999

Frank Williams is knighted in the New Year's Honours List for his success in Formula One.

Eddie Irvine scores his first win in Australia.

Long-time Formula One designer Dr Harvey Postlethwaite dies of a heart attack while observing a test session for Honda. Following his death, Honda ditches plans to return to Formula One as a team and instead signs a contract to supply BAR with engines from the 2000 season.

Michael Schumacher breaks his leg during a first-lap accident at the British Grand Prix. He misses the next seven races, leaving Eddie Irvine to mount the Ferrari title challenge, with Mika Salo as Schumacher's replacement.

Ford buys the Stewart Grand Prix team. DaimlerChrysler, Mercedes' owner, buys a stake in McLaren to further consolidate its partnership.

Eddie Irvine wins the Austrian Grand Prix after Mika Hakkinen is shunted by team-mate David Coulthard on the opening lap. Hakkinen recovers to finish third.

Herbert gives the Stewart-Ford team its first win, at the European Grand Prix.

Bernie Ecclestone sells 50 per cent of his shares in Formula One management to Deutsche Bank's Morgan Grenfell Private Equity in a deal worth $1.3 billion.

2000

Williams signs up twenty-year-old Jenson Button to partner Ralf Schumacher.

Stewart-Ford becomes Jaguar Racing, and Eddie Irvine leaves Ferrari to partner Johnny Herbert.

2001

McLaren's Mika Hakkinen retires from Formula One.

Ken Tyrrell dies at the age of 77 from cancer. The sport is poorer for his passing.

Renault returns to the Formula One arena.

David Richards replaces Craig Pollock as head of BAR.

2002

Tom Walkinshaw's Arrows team bows out of Formula One.

Tony Purnell replaces Niki Lauda at Jaguar, and David Pitchforth becomes managing director.

Michael Schumacher claims his third consecutive drivers' championship to equal Juan Manuel Fangio's haul of five.

2003

The new Formula One season gets under way, as usual, in March in Melbourne, but the teams and drivers must contend with a raft of rule changes aimed at making the weekend more of a spectacle for racing fans. They immediately make a difference: an exciting race at Albert Park is followed by Renault's Fernando Alonso claiming pole position in Sepang and Mark Webber putting his Jaguar on the second row of the grid in Brazil.

INDEX